MISperformance – essays in shifting perspectives

CIP - Kataložni zapis o publikaciji
Narodna in univerzitetna knjižnica, Ljubljana

7.038.531(082)

MISPERFORMANCE : essays in shifting
perspectives / edited by Marin Blažević and Lada
Čale Feldman. - Ljubljana : Maska, Institute for
Publishing, Production and Education, 2014

ISBN 978-961-6572-36-1
1. Blažević, Marin
274165760

MISperformance – essays in shifting perspectives

Edited by Marin Blažević and Lada Čale Feldman

Maska

Performance Studies international

Drugo more

Faculty of Humanities and Social Sciences,
University of Zagreb

Ljubljana, 2014

MISperformance is a joint publication project of Performance Studies international, Maska (Ljubljana), Drugo more (The Other Sea, Rijeka) and Faculty of Humanities and Social Sciences - Doctoral program in literature, performing arts, film and culture (University of Zagreb).

MISperformance is a pilot book that explores the model for possible future collaborations of PSi with regional and local publishers and organizations. Appropriately, this pilot book springs from the first PSi Regional Research Cluster which took place in September 2010 in the city of Rijeka.

Performance Studies international faces the challenge of representing members in very different situations, contexts and conditions, and also with different understandings of what Performance Studies is or can be. Contrary to what some think, the spread of Performance Studies is not a matter of one single set of ideas gradually conquering the world, but rather of different emergences at different places. This has resulted in a highly diverse field with different and sometimes even competing approaches where scholars are in unequal positions with regard to access to means, exposure and representation by, for example, international publishers. Being truly international requires more than the ideas or intention to be so, as it is not ideas or intentions that will make the change but how we are willing and able to take their implications for how we do a conference or conduct a research, how we teach and publish, or, in one word, how do we actually – perform. And occasionally – misperform.

The mission of Maska has been a mutual production of artistic and theoretical practice. For twenty years Maska has been publishing critical theory and producing critical performance and art always mutually challenging and crossing over the fields.

INTRODUCTION 9

Marin Blažević and Lada Čale Feldman
MISPERFORMANCE IN FOUR ACTS 11

Part I
INVERTED / REVERTED CONCEPTS AND THEORIES 29

Morana Čale
"PERFORMANCE" AS CRYPTONYMY:
THE ECONOMY OF FAILURE IN CRITICAL THEORY 31

Jon Mckenzie
POSTHUMAN MISPERFORMANCE:
BP AND THE FLIGHT OF THE WHOOPING CRANES 45

Carol Becker
THE SPACE BETWEEN WHAT IS AND WHAT WANTS TO BE:
THE ABANDONED PRACTICE OF UTOPIAN THINKING 61

Sophie Nield
PAST IMPERFECT, FUTURE TENSE
ON HISTORY AS DISCARDED PRACTICE 69

Ana Vujanović
SECOND-HAND KNOWLEDGE
(IN SLALOM THROUGH YUGOSLAV CULTURAL-ARTISTIC SPACE) 79

Part II
MIS-INCORPORATIONS, MIS-PRESENTATIONS, MIS-SPECTATORSHIPS 89

Arseli Dokumacı
MISFIRES THAT MATTER:
HABITUS OF THE DISABLED BODY 91

Lada Čale Feldman
THE LECTURE AND ITS INFELICITIES:
RECOVERING GOFFMAN'S LEGACY FOR (MIS)PERFORMANCE STUDIES 109

JOE KELLEHER:
ON MISATTENTION 127

Part III
MIS(SING)-AESTHETICS, ETHICS, POLITICS 139

Annalisa Sacchi
MI(S)MESIS, OR THE THEATRICAL WAY TO THE STARS 141

Edward Scheer
RECOMPOSING THE SOCIAL DRAMA:
MYRA'S OLYMPIC SNAFU 157

Maaike Bleeker
CHALLENGING FORTH THE TRUTH:
RABIH MROUÉ'S *ON THREE POSTERS.*
REFLECTION ON A VIDEO-PERFORMANCE 171

Nicolas Salazar Sutil
404, THE PERFORMATIVITY OF ERROR:
WITH INSIGHTS INTO CYBER-ERRORISM IN *INTERNACIONAL*
ERRORISTA AND *ELECTRONIC DISTURBANCE THEATRE* 183

Part IV
SHIFTING MISPERFORMATIVITY 201

Branislav Jakovljević
CONTINUOUS AND ENDLESS MISTAKE:
(EVERY HOUSE HAS A) DOOR ON PERPETUAL WAR 203

Laurie Beth Clark & Michael Peterson
MISTOPIAN PERFORMANCE 219

Ric Allsopp
WALKING BACKWARDS 235

P.A. Skantze
SHIFT EPISTEMOLOGIES:
GAP KNOWLEDGE 245

CONTRIBUTORS 255

INTRODUCTION

Marin Blažević and Lada Čale Feldman
MISperformance in Four Acts

Prelude

Two events marked the opening night of the fifteenth Performance Studies international conference in Zagreb (2009). Both came to be indicative for the conference theme – *MISperformance*, and its correlative conference/performance genre – the *shift*.[1] The first event was somewhat intended, only partway directed and inadvertently spectacular, the second one being inadvertent, embarrassing but – as it seemed when it happened – negligible. We were so wrong.

The PSi#15 opening plenary took place in the neo-baroque auditorium of the Croatian National Theater. Welcoming speeches by conference organizers and presidents of the University of Zagreb and PSi were interpolated in a multi-lingual staging of the postdramatic-drama by Ivana Sajko, *Europe: A monologue for mother Courage and her children*. While six performers, including the dramatist herself, were reading the play in six different languages; while the speakers were carrying out their ceremonial roles to welcome the assembly and launch the conference theme – twenty women and as many of their small children and babies took up the proscenium. Except for a lullaby, the mothers were given no other performative tasks but to live in the stage throughout the conference opening. They were looking after their kids,

---

1 Dates for the Zagreb PSi#15 conference were 24 – 28 June 2009, and its full theme was *MISperformance – MISfiring, MISfitting, MISreading*. The first PSi Regional Research Cluster, PSi#15 follow up, took place a year later in the Mediterranean Croatian city of Rijeka, September 2 – 4. The theme was *MISperformance – an inverted approach to doing Performance Studies*. The 2010 Rijeka Cluster was part of the annual ZOOM festival organized by Drugo more (The Other Sea).

playing with them, chatting, breast-feeding and offhandedly observing the theatricality around them, in the boxes and orchestra. At first a bit confused and cautious, but then more and more casual and curious, the children were turning the stage into a playground, some of them running around and dancing, other crying or just sucking; here a giggle, there a squall, a grin or a song; here jumping, there crawling or clapping... Although older among them were cautiously becoming more reactive to theatrical situation defined by the active presence of the spectators, the kids were giving, for the most part, a highly spontaneous performance ignorant of the event genre, therefore interfering with the ritualized opening ceremony and its legitimacy function. A simple juxtaposition of the contrary modes and flows of performance – on one side, children's playful or restful living and their mothers' overriding preoccupation with their well-being on the stage (safety, spirit and eating); on the other side, strict performative protocol of the welcoming speeches and recitation of postdramatic drama – brought about a complex fortuitous dramaturgy. Collisions or coincidental correspondences of semiotic patterns and performative potentials, sounds and words, eloquence and noise, of tense and relaxed bodies, generated an environment where misperformance manifested its paradoxical nature, when disharmony, inappropriateness and oddity are not perceived as deviation and failure but recognized as momentous, complex insight into and creative gesture within the dis/misorder of things.

A misperformative scene is the one where the edge plays a decisive role, the *edge of irony* on the edge of catastrophe. As it was rightfully brought to our attention when recollecting the event, those kids were playing alarmingly close to the proscenium, which is probably why their mothers were able to disregard the performance of their own theatricalized bodies and focus on their daily-life activity, keeping an eye on the dramaturges of contingency – their/our children. Such inversion of performative function on the stage of Croatian National Theater charged the overall happening with a political stance[2] and discharged the ceremonial verification of the institutional domain that openings of the conference of an international organization are expected to acknowledge and defend. Furthermore, the inverted performative, or misperformative, when interpretively correlated with Ivana Sajko's play (*Europe: A monologue for mother Courage and her children*), attributed courage to the performance that accepts the risk of deforming itself into misperformance. Such intended and partly staged misperforming puts forward a strategy of political resistance, possibly even ideological transgression. They spring from the moment of facing immediate physical danger, a stressed (sense of) reality that occurs in defiance of any representational

---

[2] Besides, most of the mothers were representatives of the local NGO: RODA – PARENTS IN ACTION (http://www.roda.hr). At the time RODA was runnning a campaign in support of breastfeeding in public spaces, thus turning the conference opening event into an occasion for social activism.

functionality and spreads all the way from a daily (in this case – motherly) routine to the disastrous crash of organizational and technological and cultural performance (therefore, from Gofmann's *everyday self* to McKenzie's *space shuttle*).

The second of the two events illustrative for the misperformance scope was more on the irony side, far less noble and by no means arranged. It is the anecdote of white plastic chairs. In many cases misperformance is nothing but – failure. Even then, however, it can be productive as a joke that later on brings people together in setting up informal and temporary micro-communities bound with a narrative and – laughter. For the show by Croatian dance company BADco. that followed the MISceremony, spectators were seated on the rostrums placed on the two opposite sides of performance space. The lucky ones, however, managed to take the first row seats where the white plastic chairs – nowadays nearly legendary – where waiting for them. When in the middle of a highbrow performance one of the chairs crashed under the local theater reviewer everybody thought it was just bad luck. The main joke was that the eager reviewer did not allow herself to get disturbed by the accident and serenely continued to take notes about the performance even though she found herself landed on the stage floor. Like that, nothing really serious had happened. But, things got more serious the following day. A presentation of the work-in-process by Every House Has a Door was already underway as part of the *shift* entitled *Abandoned Practices*,[3] when the first spectator abruptly went down to the mixed sounds of shock and breaking (white) plastic. Then, like following a scary rhythm, the second, third, fourth, fifth, sixth and seventh chair crashed creating a continuity of ambivalent performance suspense, edgy expectation of the sudden moments when the danger of a potentially tragic outcome and the effort to suspend a comic outburst would shift attention from the stage and turn wretched spectators into – misperformers. So the word got around. The PSi#15 video documentation clearly shows Paul Rae intervening during the *Long Table on Change* by Lois Weaver & Peggy Shaw and Split Britches. He is seen suggesting other participants in the *shift* to solidify the white plastics by adding one chair onto another. By the end of the evening some people were sitting on three chairs. Then, the camera also captured a moment when Joe Kelleher warned Joseph Roach to rise from the white plastic chair in the second when it started to shift dangerously and threaten the course of *Shifting Shift* curated by P.A. Skantze. Why the wicked chairs were not removed and replaced as it was advised remains a mystery of the *MISperformance* conference.

3   *Abandoned Practices* is a concept and research interest pioneered by Alan Read. Lin Hixson and Matthew Goulish (Goat Island, Every House Has a Door) adopted it when establishing "Abandoned Practices" Institute at the School of the Art Institute of Chicago (http://www.abandonedpractices.org) and when curating a *shift* that included early presentation of work-in-process on the Every House's inaugural piece (see note 14).

As evidence of the just narrated *chair trouble*, the image of the broken white plastic chair can be found on the back cover of the *Misperformance* issue of *Performance Research*,[4] also edited by Čale Feldman and Blažević as a selection of proceedings presented at the Zagreb conference. After the preliminary rationale and experiments with and contingent embodiments of (*cultural, organizational, technological*) misperformance during PSi#15, the discussion on the concept had to be moved to the next stage. In order to queer even further the auto-critical and re-figuring impulse of *misperformance studies* that approach the distinctive forces of the all-englobing *performance* through its inherent negative/missed side, as also to point to the site in which this debate emerged – a region which historically exists in a permanent state of exception, unrest and uncertainty – the PSi#15 follow up was organized a year later as a curated event bringing invited artists and scholars around five themes[5] that generated four parts of this book and some of its chapters.

Act 1

The concept of misperformance runs the risk of its own easy-going over-exploration – based on its assumed semantic flexibility – or, what is even worse, exhaustion. Nothing could be said, however, to be further removed from the latent and lasting *uncanniness* of misperforming.

Freud's famous uplifting of an old Victorian notion to the status of "a master trope" of the 20th century is evoked here not only because its resonance in many ways pertains to the crucial components of misperforming, but also because its seminal re-appearance in the discourse of humanities under the guise of a thorough etymological research and comparative lexicology marks a date in the genealogy of theoretically inspiring negative terms and could serve as a model for any attempt to come to the core of their eloquence on/for modern experience, especially when pivotal academic concepts are at stake.

Morana Čale therefore rightfully turns our attention to the "anasemic" or "cryptonimical" aspects of "performance", through which the theory and practice of performance studies define and perform the concept supposed to warrant the identity of the discipline. She diagnoses the crack in the semantic integrity of "performance" by connecting it to the relative incommensurability between two philosophical traditions upon which performance studies alternately relies, the analytical one and the "continental" one, whereby the latter prompts understandings of the term derived from its fictional aspect – performing as "staging of a theatrical representation", while the former points to empirical outcomes, accomplishments of actions. She points out that investments in various kinds of bridging the gap between two ontological lev-

---

4   *Performance Research*, 15: 2 (June 2010).
5   The five panels were: *Misfits: inverted concepts, inverted theories; Mis(sing)-aesthetics, ethics, politics; Shifting formats; Off-regions, "failed" chronotopes; Mystifications, misidentifications, mis-incorporations.*

els, the fictional and the empirical one, the realm of symbolic and the world of historic-political intersubjectivity, inevitably inscribed in performance studies a goal-oriented promise of both artistic and academic attachments to truth and social justice, which rendered it susceptible of assessment from the standpoint of (qualitative and quantitative) usefulness, effectiveness, efficiency, efficacy, profit. These notions are themselves, however, dependent upon an irreversible linear connection between cause and effect, intention and target, which means that no questioning of the concept of the limit/limits of the concept can avoid the reinstatement of the division line between felicitous and infelicitous performance acts: the requisite of the concept's "identity" is always shaped against what is considered as a misperformance – the "outcast outside" that is simultaneously the essential, integral and non-extractable "inside heterogeneous to the inside" of performance.

Nevertheless, the performativity might eventually catch-up, or catch us up in its uncalculated spreading all over the entire onto-historical formation of power and knowledge, as Jon McKenzie contends when he warns us that the contemporary technological, organizational, financial and accompanying cultural performance efficiency and effectiveness mark the post-human condition, an ontological transmutation that undermines both liberal and critical humanism. In the neo-liberal world of global performativity, misperforming entails ecological catastrophes, spectacular disasters that no human agency can actually master: the irony is that the sense of this predicament gave rise to a whole new gamut of projects of prevention, such as "blowup preventers" that McKenzie analyses in his paper as a multi-faceted institutional symptom of a new mode of corporate intervention – the assessment of "sustainability performance", designed to assure planet, people and profit – testifying to a growing complexity of modes of governance and control. While alluding to Bruno Latour's famous dictum, McKenzie wonders if we ever have been human – autonomous not only with respect to social factors that dominated the most recent identity-oriented performance practices, but also with respect to mutations in bacteria and viruses? Performance studies are thus exhorted to acknowledge that performance stratum collapses the inherited boundaries dividing humanity from both natural and technological worlds: as we inhabit complex, overlapping performances, of humans, things, soils and waters, neither the concept of free will nor social constructivism can truly answer to the current needs of critical reflection – actually, they may even be beyond any such ambition, and lead to the *perfumance* of thinking itself.

Given such a gloomy perspective we could ponder upon our very capacity of imagining a – utopia. By treating utopian thinking as one of the "abandoned practices"[6] of contemporary theory, steeped in angst and cynicism just as the less intellectually challenging, more pragmatically oriented

---

6   See notes 3 and 14.

activities of everyday living or political decision-making, Carol Becker re-introduces forgotten ideas and thinkers, from Hesiod to Gandhi, from Wilde to Bloch, from Freud to Reich, whose impact lingers on, waiting to be creatively refashioned in the light of current concerns – the ever-renewing proofs of human destructiveness. This lineage of outstanding and martyred minds is for Becker a reminder of what art as a utopian space, and its acts of creation as a purposeful negation, must still strive for: to anticipate and to illuminate, as Bloch would put it, a possibility of change in the communal way of organizing and understanding the world, against all odds: "How do we recognize such spatial and conceptual opportunities when we encounter them in life, art, and in preparation for an as-yet-to-be imagined future?" While being aware that their formulations may materially misfire, we should not, Becker insists, abandon utopian ideas, for they belong to ontogenetic, archaic, wish-fulfilling, dreaming practice that ensures the survival of the species.

Although utopia does not figure as a debated notion in Sophie Nield's chapter, it is precisely the utopian promise of transgression that comes under scrutiny, for she diagnoses the wished-for, empowering moment of performance. Such project, or rather projection is grounded in "performance's romance of itself", that is the "romance of its own disappearance" through *chronotopic* filter. Despite the sedimentation of remains, performance is still charged with a happening, event, process, excess or an instant appearance that should momentarily offer resistance to the politics and economy of re-production, -presentation, -enactment, -iteraton etc. In order to question the traditional *liminality* rationale Nield inverts the usual perspective and, instead of further deliberations on the present of, and presence in performance, turns her critique to the tendencies that pervade much of the current production in the purview of performance, whether as artistic rendition or the object of study. The troubled concept and experience now happens to be the past, but past in its perverted transposition into the – future. Nield argues that the past "understood as complex, situated, detailed and contextual" is being deprived from performance's present, therefore causing emptiness that urges compensation through affective investment in the mere "signs of 'pastness'" such as "ghosts, sites, haunting, nostalgia, absence, ephemerality, loss, and mourning". On the other hand, the "theatrical present" is subjected to the documentation "obsession" and propels a consuming interest for "its own status as a future past". Thus pinched in a paradoxical situation, in-between always already *disappearance* and yet to come *appearance*, performance – theatrical as much as any other – keeps missing the suture of history and actuality in its present at the expense of its political efficacy. To illustrate such misperformative pragmatics, Sophie Nield herself (mis)performs an ironic, perplexing, even odd rhetorical twist in the argument when evoking Albert Speer's mis-utopian concept of the "ruin value".

This book comes about as a culmination of a prolonged endeavor to grasp the multiple modalities in which misperforming can appear as both an event and a productive conceptual deviation from the main course of inherited analytical protocols, especially if seen through the *Eastern Eyes*, as one of the more promising generative instances of academic communities doomed to rely on and expand upon their own *second-hand knowledge*. Rather than seeing in the notion of "misperformance" the mere conceptual underside of the anasemic character of "performance" outlined by Morana Čale, Ana Vujanović deconstructs the political and cultural investment of the value-laden dichotomy it might also imply, when it is used to refer to "delaying productivity, amateurism and dilettantism, always being too late, collectivism, utopianism, masochism, cynicism, laziness and un-professionalism" as somehow inevitably associated to *Eastern* labor, thinking and creating practices. Not interested in making one of the notions belonging to that list – the one of "second-hand knowledge" offered by Patrick Wilson – a positive one, but in exploring the assumptions underlying the hierarchy of "first" and "second", Vujanović spiritedly evokes the economic, social and political mechanisms by which knowledge is not only produced but above all defined: her deconstructive and postcolonial move first focuses in broad, but nevertheless bold and concrete brushes, on the Serbian cultural and intellectual scene, for long the leading mediator of contemporary performing arts in the region, and therefore to a large extent emblematic of the region as a whole. But the latter turns into just an impetus to re-think how different disciplines and cultural practices conceive of cognitive authority in general, as well as value direct as opposed to mediated contact with the supposed source of knowledge, particularly having in view the current hyper-production and digital availability of information, let alone illegal sharing and pirating of various materials. While acknowledging that the dichotomy, in fact, cannot stand, Vujanović does not lose from sight the one-way stream that its deconstruction cannot shatter (from West to East), reminding us of all the invisible facets of first-hand knowledge production coming from the *lazy, unproductive, and amateurish* periphery and therefore hardly counting on its own performativity.

In the spirit of Vujanović's reflection and statement, which precisely started with the question of self-definition of the regional artistic and cultural (notably performing arts) scenes, this book suggests that sharing knowledge is not only a matter of lofty ideas, concepts and words, but touches at the very heart of embodied performances and their cultural status.

Interlude
Expressed by a term coined with reference to the crowning concept of performance studies on one side, and various discursively well-adjusted, everyday mis-prefixed notions on the other (such as mistake, misunderstanding,

misfit, misfire, misprision and the like), misperformance is a concept that summarizes but also reconsiders and challenges the already existent reflections and performative trials pointing to both disturbing and potentially creative factors of failure. Misperforming incorporates but also foils the failure without falling into the grip of binary and its promise of success – either in view of emancipatory and liberating poetics and politics, or in the realm of neoliberal economies where failure can be endowed with strategic value in the pursue and commodification of innovation, or in a depressing correlation of the two.

Since the *MISperformance* conference in Zagreb two publications appeared in the imagined field of *misperformance studies* that treat the (mis)performative power of what seems to be its leading notion – the failure. In *Theatre and the Poetics of Failure* (2011) Sara Jane Bailes provides theoretical contextualization and elaboration of failure, in life as well as in theatre,[7] but misses the paradox in pairing of the two concepts – poetics and failure. While failure pertains to the realm of *liminal* occurrences and practices that ideally resist any framework and prescription, poetics already implies a certain degree of normative thinking, tested and accepted production-reception procedures. Poetics defuses the risk of the unknown, unfinished, unwanted in the performance of failure, thus progressively reducing its counter-charge. Poetics indicates that the process of normalization (and eventual normativization) is already in progress. Failure turned into a constitutive element of a poetics presupposes a success (a *successful failure*) that conforms and confirms that very poetics. And, in due course, constructions of theory and institution are built on and within the grounds of the – once unstable – "architecture of ruin".[8] What remains is failure that failed to fail, trapped in McKenzie's *liminal-norm* paradox.

Less than two full years after the *Misperformance* issue, *Performance Research* published *On Failure (On Pedagogy)*.[9] Although the editors, Róisín O'Gorman and Margaret Werry, moved and narrowed the focus on "the scene of teaching and learning, rather than the experimental space of performance art with its privileged freedom to fail",[10] their "Editorial introduction" and concluding catalogue "The Anatomy of Failure: An inventory" actually go along the lines of the case already made for *misperformance* and its *studies*. *On Failure* issue indeed "aims to see (…) if performance might provide us with a metaphor and methodology for failure"[11] comprehended

---

7   Bailes conducts a formal analysis and hermeneutic reading of the work of Forced Entertainment, Goat Island, and Elevator Repair Service. All tree companies are regarded as instrumental in transfer and exploration of the "discourse of failure" in the domain of performance-theatre. (Sara Jane Bailes, *Performance Theatre and the Poetics of Failure*, Routledge, London 2011, p. 2).
8   Ibidem, p. 22.
9   *Performance Research*, 17: 1 (February 2012).
10   The editors failed to mention the *Misperformance* issue of *Performance Research*, despite having acknowledged the 2009 Zagreb conference.
11   Ibidem, p. 1.

as a *moment, point, mark, performative, condition, rupture, threshold, ending-beginning*[12] that might produce, as we debated in Zagreb, something other than mere error, excess, loss, damage, waste or surplus, whether in cognitive, political, social, cultural, pedagogical and ecological spheres. Yes, instead of carving around or casting a blind eye on failure, we can attempt at inciting and representing it, even turning it into a political, social and cultural counter-act. Yet, the spell of failure might induce quite a misleading idea if it would summon an enthusiasm for counting every wrong track that performance could take as symptoms of genuine human, cultural, institutional, artistic and other fallibilities. Besides, shouldn't we also take into account the inevitability of failure's failures once we end up merely miming, repeating and therefore controlling it, engulfing its creative as well as critical vitality and eventually missing its very misperformativity?

Although misperforming encompasses failure, it attempts to go further than inscribing its aesthetic, social and political counter-capacity in a relatively safeguarded framework of poetics. Furthermore, misperforming resists listing its features and suspending its dynamics in a catalogue – or *inventory* – of its *anatomy*. While the notion of failure suggests completion of a singular failed act, misperforming stands for complications due to the continuity of failing-yet-performing actions. Instead of accepting resignation, showing restraint or hoping for relief, misperforming embodies the risk of balancing on the edge, in-between disaster and deliverance and, why not – tragedy and comedy. In the aftermath of failure, a shift remains as only one of the potential reactions. For misperforming – shifting is a vital action. It can be discerned in performances as diverse as those that effect and affect our everyday (disabled) bodies, or (mis)presentations of knowledge in academic life, or phenomenal incapacity of (theatrical) spectatorship.

Act 2

As if synchronizing with the chair-misfortunes suffered by many of the attendees at the Zagreb PSi conference, Arseli Dokumaci starts her argument in "Misfires that matter: *Habitus* of the disabled body" with a miniature „genealogy" of the disciplinary power of chair, a mini-historical overview which figures in her reflection as an instructive metonymy for a whole array of spatial arrangements that dictate the daily performances of our bodies. The critical moment concerns the extent to which the "movement regime" exerts the spell of "performative magic" which is rarely reflected upon within the flow of everyday life, but which is broken once the disabled individuals misperform. As in the case of "losing" one's health, where the synchrony between the physicality of the body and physicality of its environment – a

---

[12] Cf. ibidem, pp. 105-110.

requisite for successful execution of routine activities *in silence* – becomes disrupted, awareness shifts towards the very doing of action. Drawing on her own ethnographic research, Documaci focuses on everyday task performances of mobility-impaired individuals, and considers their misuses of various daily techniques – for instance, those of rest, of greeting, of dressing, of moving in clothes, of cooking and cleaning, of preparing food – as misfires in the *habitus* (Bourdieu), disrupting what she calls "the choreography of the everyday". She therefore suggests that, rather than being an object of study, disability could in fact be approached as – methodology, in the same way in which the study of mental impairment once "served" Erving Goffman to disclose the unsubstantial fabric of the interaction order.

These instances of *mis-habitual* mishaps suddenly revealing the fictional character of a naturalized social norm are just another reminder that misperformance as a concept stems from a respectable theoretical genealogy comprising various attempts at destabilizing Western metaphysical dichotomies – from Freudian slips via Austinian misfires, the Derridean *pharmakos/pharmakon* and the Lacanian misrecognition, to Butler's failed gender constitutions, Bhabha's inappropriate signifiers and anomalous representations. Besides moving forward along the well-trodden routes, misperforming thus goes for diversion and always turns to shifting, even when the turn implies – in reference to resistant bent of Ric Allsopp's metaphor – to *walk backwards*. Following the line of Arseli Dokumaci's interest, Lada Čale Feldman urges performance scholars to reconsider Goffman's legacy, thus pointing to one of those founding theoretical figures who formed the building blocks of performance studies but were undeservedly dismissed on the grounds of the obsoleteness of their findings for the profoundly transformed, virtualized, globalized and multi-culturally sensitized world. Čale Feldman argues that Goffman's true import may have been misinterpreted precisely due to the longstanding neglect of all the mischievous and deviant concepts populating his work, especially if they concern academic rituals, such as lectures. For Goffman, the ineradicable practice of the old-fashioned, corporeally executed lecture is a (mis)performance *par excellence* whose authority, according to Čale Feldman, needs to be reconsidered not only in the light of the more technologically advanced forms of an entire "lecture-machine" (McKenzie), but also in view of current debates on the commercialization of knowledge, particularly striking in transitional countries. Misperformance can thus be said to haunt the transmission of ideas itself, including those generated by the academic institutionalization of performance studies paradigm: under its relentless invention of concepts and self-questioning, there are disquieting, and yet unexpectedly inspiring discontinuities.

Misperformance cracks the mirror of representational illusion, not in the form of Brecht's intentional revealing of the actor's work – the never-to-be seen, repressed content of bourgeois aesthetic pleasure – but rather in the form of the irruption of the awkward or the shameful, the enlightening or the shocking reminders of what is at stake when we perform, actors and spectators alike. For, whatever our best intentions with respect to the audience may be, can any performance manage what Joe Kelleher termed to be spectator's "infinite misattention"? His contribution to the discussion on the misperformed spectatorship (or *mis-spectatorship*) reflects upon the neglected facets of audience response that, far from being undesired distractions (Kelleher) from the expected efficacy of performers' intentions – whether aesthetic or political ones, the ones striving to achieve at least instantaneous sense of communion or community – actually pertain to the norm of theatre: in Kelleher's text this norm resurfaces in the seemingly atomized, individualistic or rebellious "phenomenophiliac behavior" – that is, in distracted hallucinations we feel compelled to give ourselves over during the performance, thus nevertheless attaining at least a fleeting image of our connectivity and collectivity, no matter how fractured and disjointed.

In the dramaturgy of this book Kelleher's chapter marks a transition towards performance analysis within the realm of artistic misperformative practices. Whereas the first half of the volume presents discussions that assay the conceptual viability of misperformance and the purview of misperforming in relation to diverse though often interdependent contexts, conditions and capacities (from performance theory to history to ecology; from habitus to disability to posthumanism; from utopia to cultural-artistic and knowledge market; from attention to interpretation), the second half of the volume is devoted to a series of case studies. Act 3 foregrounds distinct (mis)performances immersed in, impelled by, or confronted to aesthetic traditions and sociopolitical situations, while the Act 4 reflects on the format and formation, conceptual derivation and amplification of the *shifts*.

Act 3

The re-emergence of ethical and political ambitions of cultural criticism and performance art has come to a point in which a re-consideration of the place of aesthetics is needed, or at least a new look at the continuities and discontinuities of these three fields, of moments in which we miss one of the constituent parts of this triangle. The following chapters explore various examples of their replacement and misplacement, lack or misfire in the context of artistic performance, all the way from reconsideration of mimesis and revision of the stages of *social drama*, to the performativity and poetics of errors in digital culture.

In the opening of her chapter Annalisa Sacchi refers to correspondences between the recently published cosmo-political reflections of the Italian revolutionary Franco Piperno and Artaud's writings on the theatre of cruelty: finding in both a fascination with stellar constellations, that is, with their hieroglyphics as powerful manifestations of the trans-individual character of the human intellect, she connects the sublime feelings that writing of/in the sky engenders in individuals with the effects of human gesture in theatre. Her interpretation of Romeo Castellucci's performance *Inferno* is thus placed under the powerful auspices of the eternal repetition inscribed in the immensity of the sky that prompts the enchanted individuals to be all the more sensitive to what is radically singular, unique and labile. Castellucci's use of la *Divina commedia* becomes a gesture defying another twisted notion, this time authored by Pier Paolo Pasolini – the one of *mala mimesi* (bad mimesis, or "mis-mimesis"), a simple imitation of a model - in favor of an encounter with the plurality of superimposed art works from the Western tradition, exemplified in the performance by the ghosts of memory encountered in the circles of Hell from Dante's epic. For Sacchi, Castellucci's performance both contemplates the loss of transcendent radiance, which once defined the essence of artistry, and at the same time revisits the entire history of theatre as traversed by the desire or compulsion to return, with the double-bound figure of Andy Warhol at its thought-provoking center. Mimesis and "mis-mesis" conflate in the eternal return, and the eternal fall of the man-artist.

A similar double-bind is most (in)appropriately encapsulated in Ed Scheer's contribution on "Myra's Olympic Snafu" (the latter being an acronym, standing for "situation normal: all fucked up"), since it deals with what is conceived as the ultimate social misbehavior – the killing of four children by a woman – and yet also with its turbulent cultural mediations in art, media, politics and social life, which assured its (mis)performativity across these different registers. It is however crucial to emphasize that the story of offense caused by the exhibition of Myra Hyndley's image – a large scale monochrome entirely composed from a child's handprints that, to quote one journalist, "seem to claw at Hindley's face" – starts within the frames of what is perhaps the most prominent remnant of old communitarian rituals: the Olympic games (closing) ceremony, during which it was projected among other "quintessentially British" items. Dealing with misfires that can occur when artistic ambivalence is co-opted for purposes of identity-formation, Scheer questions the pertinence and applicability of Victor Turner's stages of "social drama" (breach, crisis, redressive action, schism) in the age of *postdramatic* paradigm and world-wide reaching media. It is his contention that the spreading of variously legitimized moral panic and the burgeoning of contradictory reactions provoked by numerous occasions on which the pernicious image was displayed requires a "recomposition of terms", a "new dramaturgy", a model relying on metaphors of metastasis (division, dispersion, re-attachment, replication), that seems much better adjusted to the current state of affairs, famously labeled by Zygmunt Bauman as "liquid modernity".

Inspired by Rabih Mroué's performance essay *Three Posters* (based on uncut video evidence of three times repeated shooting of a testimony statement in anticipation of the 1985 suicide attack by a Lebanese resistance fighter) as well as its subsequent unforeseen reception (marked by the dominant post 9/11 sensitivity and interpretive framing), Maaike Bleeker tackles performativity of media at the intersection of human and technological performance. Disputing the inveterate arguments that talk down the discourse on truth and reality as illegitimate within the cultural condition determined through *performance stratum* (as termed by McKenzie), Bleeker wonders about the moment when such categories appear as a possibility beyond the "fabrication of the truth" that still informs Mroué's piece as its main concern. The challenge leads her to misperformance. Uncut recordings of the martyr-to-become testimony just before he left for a suicide "mission" reveal moments of "hesitations, errors and stuttering" that had to be erased from the official edition of the video statement in order to prevent the "shudder" induced by Barthes' *punctum*, a flaw that might cast doubts on the act that is (still) to be performed (in Sophie Nield's *future past*). Bleeker then turns to Mieke Bal's concept of a *navel* as a "scar" marking the moment of separation from the origin (or the *mother*). It is the cut-into-betweenness of dis-connection that Bleeker associates with a misperformative detail in the image, a "noise" and a "shift" in its act/perception that incites "renegotiations" between the historical past, the present of its technological capture and the futures of its mis-mediatizations. Such is the *(t)error of becoming* in the global digital culture immersed in *performance stratum*.

Following an introductory theorisation of performativity as a system of normativisation through technologically-mediated social activity, Nicolas Salazar Sutil enters the discussion on misperformance by scrolling up and down the ludic twists of semantic, derivative and euphonic capacity comprised in the word *error*. (Erroneous) morphological alterations as well as phonetic collisions or congruence reveal amplified and transformative viability of *error* as a (mis)concept and (mis)act operative across the networks of technologically mediated communication (where it appears in the 404 or *Not Found* message, a HTTP standard response code indicating a failed "communication with the server") as also in the domain of political management and administration. To the list of *err-* notions Salazar-Sutil adds "errorist" performance and then "errorism" that echoes its ironic double – terrorism. The sequence of morphologic-metaphoric transformations brings the case to deconstruction of a language politics applied to justify "the war on (t)error" and concluding analysis of a counter-practice – the application of *error-coding* in net art and digital agit-prop, incidental or intentional misperformances that inform political activism of the Argentine-based group *Internacional Errorista* and Ricardo Dominguez's use of *error-messaging* in Electronic Disturbance Theatre's project *Stop the War in Mexico*.

Act 4

The final part of the book casts light on the concept and enactments of *shifts*, introduced at the PSi#15 conference in Zagreb (2009) and further explored during the PSi#1 Regional Research Cluster in Rijeka (2010).[13]

How to make the interaction and mutual reflection of practice and theory or criticism of (artistic) performance more creative and complex? How to stage their confrontations, collaboration and conflations? Furthermore, how to embody the conference theme through dramaturgy of the conference event: how to shift its performance towards misperformance? Those questions motivated devising of *shifts* as experiments with the intersections and combinations of functions and protocols of diverse performative genres, such as panels, presentations, discussions, seminars and lectures; forums, happenings, actions and interventions; theatre, dance, participatory and digital performances; workshops, installations, laboratories and exhibitions. *Shifts* invite artists and scholars, activists and curators, writers and performers to jointly challenge (mis)performance *in-between* conducting its research and presenting its reach. The following case studies put forward the breadth, features, theories, hybridity of *shifts* and the initial misperformative act of *shifting* – a *step (backward)* into a *gap*.

Branislav Jakovljević's analysis of *Let us think of these things always. Let us speak of them never* by Lin Hixson and Matthew Goulish demonstrates that there is still much to discuss with respect to the programmatically resisted and *abandoned* theatricality, particularly in the shifting field of *(mis)performance studies*.[14] Hixson & Goulish's performance essay is a hybrid genre akin to the *shifts* – it is not just a staging of an essay, or a performance theoretically and interpretatively framed by reading of essays. Here, theory and analysis entwine the overall performance sequence; the autoreferential research is conducted through the tissue of performance, as a performed exploration of correlations and complementarity of both expression and reflection of both affect and concept.

Let us think... contributes to "debates surrounding theatricality" even though, oddly enough, the debate unfolds by invoking philosopher Stanley Cavell (his "On Makavejev on Bergman" essay), and filmmakers Dušan Makavejev (*Sweet Movie*) and Ingmar Bergman (*Persona*). Hence, performers are not engaged in representational continuity of a fictional character but

---

13 The *shifts* were then adopted by the PSi annual conferences in Toronto (2010), Utrecht (2011) and Leeds (2012) as a regular format for irregular forms of academic conference activities, their *irregularity* being, however, more of a formal than misperformative character.

14 The *shifts* were in many ways inspired by the manifold praxis of Hixson and Goulish, at first through their (mis)performance-dance-theater company Goat Island and the on-line *Institute of Failure*, Goulish's collaborative project with Tim Etchells of Forced Entertainment, and then through their new company Every House Has a Door and "Abandoned Practices" Institute at SAIC (see note 3). Still a work-in-process, *Let us think...* was integrated in the *shift* titled *Abandoned Practices* that Hixson and Goulish curated for the PSi#15 in Zagreb (2009). The piece premiered at the opening of the PSi#1 Regional Research Cluster in Rijeka (2010) as part of the *Abandoned Practices* sequel. Branislav Jakovljević, Carol Becker (also contributor to this volume) and Alan Read participated in both parts of the *shift*.

devoted to fragmented transpositions and embodied interpretation of the filmed actions played on the laptop screens and kept out of spectator's sight through the entire performance (except during the ballade scene, analysed in Jakovljević's essay). By bringing "spectatorship onstage", by turning the performers into "spectators who are actors at the same time", Hixson and Goulish pointed to the wedge of misperformance that makes its bodies incline – and then to *shift*. To reveal the "inner split" of theatrical representation Jakovljević goes all the way back to Jean-François Marmontel's concept of "demi-illusion", a state of *"continuous and endless mistake mixed with a self-reflection that belies the error"*. It is the stage itself that "works to undermine the very illusion that it makes possible" because – according to Jakovljević following Marmontel – "the viewer cannot be abstracted from the situation in which the beholding takes place". That gap, pause, distance, or a misperformative shift caused by framing/staging incites cryptic anti-and-theatrical turn towards the spectator's self-awareness. Critical (re)flection is innate to representation, especially the one producing illusion, for already staging the illusion brings about its break and therefore betrayal.

In the final scene of *Let us think...* the two performers announce an experiment with *the end of theater* – that is the offstage distance from which calling the performer who remained on the stage would be inaudible. Spectators are left with the expectation of the final moment, the absence of voice and consequently the absence or missing of any performing body but theirs. The initial, just as the ultimate condition of theater is the *empty space*, a place where anything, just as well as nothing, could happen. To terminate then the performance itself, the spectators themselves have to leave theatrical space/stage – only to move offstage, where the disappeared *voice* of theater awaits, again, disrupting the flux of performance by the bodies flexing in inter-action, sometimes called – drama. Anti-theatricality is in the crux of theatricality (representational situation) just as misperforming is in the heart of performance (as the threats of action/drama in its flow). Hence, (mis)performance happens to be to (anti)theatricality what (anti)theatricality is to (mis)performance – a *conditio sine qua non*.

For the program of PSi#15 follow up in Rijeka[15] Laurie Beth Clark and Michael Peterson, under the company name Spatula & Barcode, arranged a *shifting* assemblage of "artistic, culinary, academic and social ingredients". Their chapter is a description and retrospective reflection on the *shift* titled *Mise en Place / Mise en Scene / Wish you Were Here* as well as a theoretical elaboration on the issues that arose in the course of the para-touristic walk across the *scenes* of the city and its finale in the "conceptual dining" that brought together present and absent conference participants, the latter nevertheless taking part in the performance via multiple Skype links. In order

---

15 See notes 1 and 5.

to identify or rather imagine a place where "hybrid amalgamations of theorizing and sociality" would gain a performative success, Clark & Peterson invented a notion *mistopian* performance as a "permutation of heterotopia". Unlike *heterotopias* that "promise spaces outside the flow of life to dramatize or critique 'reality'", *mistopias* are akin to misperforming inasmuch as they both intervene "*within* the flow of life, embracing but also interrupting the quotidian", causing disorientation and discomfort, yet resisting "absolute failure or a malign atmosphere". In *mistopian* environment de-familiarization is recognized as a familiar procedure, "estrangement, strangely enough, comes naturally" and "asymmetry" should be accepted as intrinsic to the shaping and structure of encounter and interaction. When misperforming becomes constituent rather than contingent to a social situation, be it a theatrical representation, conceptual performance, participatory community art event, tourist tour, dinner or a conference opening or after-party, then its relevance is not measured by pragmatics of success but recurring alertness of the skeptical, (self-)critical mind.

Initially referring to Bruno Beltrao's choreography *H3* and the 2001 arrest outside the Pentagon of the Catholic peace-activist Liz McAllister, then listing works of a number of other artists in historical perspective (from Duchamp to Nauman), Ric Allsopp presents *walking backwards* as an action "often associated with resistance, ridicule, reversal", therefore being a guise of misperformance. Moreover, that action "*contra naturam*" is turned into a trope of "'interruption, interference, delay and discontinuity" that informs performance as a "temporary zone" or a "project space" where "*status quo* of the present" is being confronted with "the unpredictable". Such disruptions might act on our habitual attention in a generative way. When setting forth the "new, provisional forms of interaction and participation, temporary zones that in turn might lead to innovative forms and processes of working together", Allsopp already *walks towards* the edge of misperforming that we named – a *shift*. The edge or – according to P.A. Skantze – a gap, a "space of possibilities", a "bit of sound that had before been pulsing underneath the recognizable chord." Pondering on the "shift epistemology", Skantze (inspired by Foucault and Agamben) spotlights the "gap knowledge" rooted in the core of the concept and performance of *shift(s)*. It is from such gap that the shifting potential derives, the potential of awareness of "what was just out of range of vision, of hearing, of sensing", gained through experience and response-possibility of *motion* – to move, to engage, to oscillate, to change. But could the *motion* be somehow performed through the text? The central part of Skantze's contribution is announced as a *shift*: "A performance of Appositive Strategy". Along with introducing a new facet to the conceptualization of misperformance – that is the *appositiveness*, derived from both the *apposition* and *a-positive* position – Skantze experiments with the possibility to embody a performative *shift*, or at least its dynamics, rhythm and tone, through the flux of a written text. It is an attempt to transform a *shifting* event into a textual sensation, to transfer its form *from stage to page*. In the final moment of reading her text at the PSi#15 follow up in Rijeka, Skantze asked the audience to stand up, close their eyes and "make an appositive move", hence an epitomic *shift*. One such move would be to *walk backwards*, to perform the first step towards misperformance.

In his introduction to *Misperformance* issue of *Performance Research* Marin Blažević reconsidered and discursively re-staged the *shifts* and the dramaturgy of their invention, interrelation and (mis)performance.[16] The *shifts* program of the 2009 PSi#15 conference in Zagreb was devised as a dynamic dramaturgical installation for experiments with exuberant simultaneity of manifold events; experiments with lost and gained time, inaccessible and found spaces, missed and discovered traces, aleatoric sequences and harmonized relations, impossible, temporary and broken connections, conflict and disintegrated situations, shifting expectations, attention, choices, directions and interventions. Confronted with such an eventfulness and spatiotemporal multiplicity, recurringly finding herself on the intersections of different *shifts*, a conference participant-performer-actor was constantly given the possibility to make her own decisions about her distinct dramaturgy of attending and experiencing the performance-conference. It is the abundance, the loose structure, the heterogeneous spatial arrangements and parallel temporal flows that generated the idea and actuality of *shifting dramaturgy*.

Shifting dramaturgy is venturing upon an action that would not be lead by the need or demand for rightful (and eventually normative) reaction, direction and relation. Relations, directions and reactions, failure included, are recurrently exposed to critical reflection and contingencies of dis-, mis- and re-placements. *Shifting dramaturgy* embraces every shift, and in particular those shifts that run the risk of misperformance.

If the PSi#15 conference theme could be distinguished as an inversion of the performance studies' object of study, misperformance being a continuous and constituent threat to the unfolding of every performance, then the *shifts* might be understood as an extension of Conquergood's *crossroad*. In the formative stages of performance studies, and in concert with Schechner and Kirschenblatt-Gimblett, Dwight Conquergood foregrounded the "collaborative agenda" that should "refuse and supersede" the "difference between thinking and doing, interpreting and making, conceptualization and creativity", hence the "division of labor between theory and practice, abstraction and embodiment": "Our radical move is to turn, and return, insistently, to the crossroads".[17]

---

16   In the introduction to *Performance Research*, 15: 2 (June 2010), "Dramaturgy of shift(s)(ing)", a special attention is given to the curatorial policy and process of the *shifts* program, its rambling growth, crisscrossed schedule and broken rhythm.
17   Dwight Conquergood, "Performance Studies at Northwestern", "The Five Areas of Performance Studies" in Richard Schechner, *Performance Studies: An Introduction*, Routledge, London and New York 2002, p.18.

Shifting dramaturgy is a kind of perverted *rite of passage*, which – by *turning, and returning, insistently, to the crossroad* – should miss to pass, thus keeping its participants in persistent *liminality, betwixt and between* art/act and (self)reflection/criticism, transition without imposed direction/directive/directing, since every such action would lead to the end of *shifting* in the interest of normative – even if failing – performance. But why all this relentless *shifting*?

Coda

Misperformance lurks in the wings of every performance as its defining, therefore constitutive in-/di-/sub-/per-version.

MIS- marks the minute of performance when it finds itself beyond the already normative staging as well as just *liminal* state; when its course is obstructed and evident pragmatics – at least in the MIS-moment – is missed. However, once it approached the *end(s)* of performance, misperforming resists the ontological retreat of the conceptual or factual demise, unless it wants to or has to betray its fallibility.

Misperformance attempts to go beyond the *promise* of ultimate *disappearance* as well as the debris of performance *archive*. Misperformance sabotages the *perform or else* ultimatum. Instead, it enacts the vital and liberating challenge of humor and puzzle: *what else* – to fail and to fool? Surely, Lear's Fool embodies misperformative action, its (his? her?) missed (dis)appearance being a genuine misperformance, the one which thwarts the comfort of both normativity and liminality.

Misperformance employs *shifting dramaturgy* as a constantly self-reflecting-reviving strategy that further complicates (and possibly overcomes) paradoxical coupling of *liminality* and normativity (noted by McKenzie) in the domain of cultural performance. It is not just *embracing failure*, enhancing the irony of the negative efficacy or intensifying resistant and potentially transgressive social and political force of the *liminal* act/action/acting/activism. It means/does all that, but also this: instead of maintaining the canon of once alternative and even avant-garde performance, it will not hesitate turning normative (already *abandoned*?) practices – for instance theatrical illusion, dramatic acting, even operatic singing, or a lecture as/or an aesthetic gesture – into (now) liminal experiences, and then shift the corporeal/discursive performances forward or again backward; it will opt for mis-fail when failure misses to fool and foil its (MIS)performative pragmatics (or *happiness*); it will keep *shifting shifts* – relentlessly rethinking, reinventing and rehearsing the critical *gestus*.

Part I
INVERTED / REVERTED CONCEPTS AND THEORIES

PART I
INVESTOR REVISITED
CONCEPTS AND THEORIES

Morana Čale
"Performance" as Cryptonymy: the Economy of Failure in Critical Theory

Since the appearance of the discipline, considerable self-refexive discussion has been dedicated by PS scholars to attempts at circumscribing its axial notion of performance, "a fundamentally contested term" which "is also an extraordinarily opportunistic one",[1] in all its "suppleness" and "boldness"[2] that regularly exceeds any possibility of univocal definition. This "slippery" nature of the founding idea has raised as much satisfaction as despair among performance theorists.

It substantiated, on one hand, the programmatic hybridity and border-crossing strain ("challenging" or "liminal-norm"),[3] generally reputed to be the distinctive mark of the field in both its practice and theory, and notably of the mutual delimitation *between* its practice and theory. If the object, tools, and framework of PS tended to evaporate into a "mist",[4] this conceptual indeterminacy imposed on the apollonian drive of theory a joyful wisdom of espousing the dissolution of performance into "perfumance",[5] i.e. a humorous acceptance of the "strange loop" – the weird ability of a system to "violate [its own] system boundaries"[6]– that PS performs on itself. Thus, the awareness of "a lacuna or aporia at the heart of performance research"

---

[1] Joseph Roach, "Theatre Studies / Cultural Studies / Performance Studies", in eds Nathan Stucky and Cynthia Wimmer, *Teaching Performance Studies*, Southern Illinois University Press, Carbondale & Edwardsville 2002, pp. 33-40, p. 33.
[2] Ibidem.
[3] Jon McKenzie, *Perform or Else: From Discipline to Performance*, Routledge, London and New York 2001, p. 32, 49ff.
[4] Ibidem, p. 3, 17, 201, 203.
[5] Ibidem, p. 203, 229.
[6] Ibidem, p. 135.

has given occasion for building "a paradoxology of performance [studies]," resolving the oxymora of "boundless specificity", "antibinary theology" and "remediated immediacy" by means of "a Derridean double-supplement" as a peculiar way of "completing [...] insufficiency", which permitted to perceive the discipline's major lacks – among which its resistance to coherent explanatory narratives – also as its "greatest strenghts".[7]

On the other hand, the dispersiveness of constitutive qualifications pointed to the "semantic problem of metaphorical sliding" ("tropological drift") which induces "increasing instability in one's working definition" to the point of revealing the latter to be "a semantic impossibility".[8] Far from rejoicing at the comprehensiveness of "performance", celebrated by McKenzie and traceable back to Schechner, some other scholars continue to believe that "to say that everything is performance is ultimately to say very little" and eventually amounts to the "old habit of writing grand narratives".[9] The master cure to the renewed anxiety over that impossibility – not only to gain firm ground under the discipline's feet, but even to map its essence or "identity"[10] by establishing its "limits", "develop[ing] a term counter to performance"[11] and thereby finally, or for a start, ascertaining "what isn't performance",[12] i.e. accomplishing an exclusionary gesture in order to ultimately isolate a mysterious essence of mis-performance – would seem to be forcing upon PS the "protocols of falsifiability in the natural or social sciences".[13]

The contrast of attitudes that we have sketched above depends, of course, on the relative incommensurability between the two philosophical traditions upon which PS alternately relies, the analytical one and the "continental" one,[14] the former concerned with projects of conferring PS the dignifiying exactitude of "the good science",[15] the latter more comfortable with the acknowledgement of the uncontrollable iterability of all signifiers and the consequent undecidability of concepts. Yet, the performance theorists affected by "poststructuralism" often do not refrain from display-

---

7   Baz Kershaw, "Performance as research: live events and documents," in ed. Tracy C. Davis, *The Cambridge Companion to Performance Studies*, Cambridge University Press, Cambridge 2008, pp. 23-45, pp. 25-39.
8   Bert O. States, "Performance as metaphor," in ed. Philip Auslander, *Performance: Critical Concept in Literary and Performance Studies*, vol. I, Routledge, London and New York 2003, pp. 108-137, pp. 108-110.
9   Simon Shepherd and Mick Wallis, *Drama / Theatre / Performance*, Routledge, London and New York 2004, p. 115.
10 Martin Puchner, "Kenneth Burke: Theater, Philosophy, and the Limits of Performance" in eds David Krasner and David Z. Saltz, *Staging Philosophy: Intersections of Theater, Performance, and Philosophy*, The University of Michigan Press, Ann Arbor 2006, pp. 41-56, p. 50.
11 Ibidem, p. 55.
12 Bert O. States, "Performance as metaphor", pp. 111, 119.
13 Bruce A. McConachie, "Falsifiable Theories for Theatre and Performance Studies," *Theatre Journal*, 59: 4 (2007), pp. 553-577, p. 576.
14 Janelle Reinelt, "The politics of discourse: performativity meets theatricality", in ed. Philip Auslander, *Performance: Critical Concept in Literary and Performance Studies*, vol. 1, Routledge, London and New York 2003, pp. 153-167, p. 155; *Staging Philosophy: Intersections of Theater, Performance, and Philosophy*, eds David Krasner and David Z. Saltz, The University of Michigan Press, Ann Arbor 2006, p. 4.
15 Bruce A. McConachie, "Falsifiable Theories for Theatre and Performance Studies", p. 576.

ing taxonomies and diagrams, while the partisans of analytical delimitation, on their part, presumably contaminated by "deconstructive" habits, are sometimes tempted by hypotheses – such as the question, inspired by Kenneth Burke"s idea of a "nondramatistic" limit of the universal dramatism, whether "the radically nonperformative" should not be inscribed "at the center of performance"[16] – which sabotage their own polarities. Such unorthodox reciprocal "borrowings"[17] have, above all, to do with the fact that PS is rooted in the aporia of the "Two Fundamentals".[18] First of all, for PS "there is no fixed canon of works, ideas, practices, or anything else that defines or limits the field", because it "happens at always-changing intersections of particulars";[19] secondly, it "enthusiastically borrows from other disciplines".[20] In a word, PS has fundamentals which forbid it to have fundamentals.

One of the most interesting, if not "fundamental", side effects of this premise compelling an integration of the disparate, which is the charm and the curse of the discipline at the same time, involves a troubled relationship with "poststructuralism" and especially "deconstruction". The distinctive PS assumption of ontological transcendence, aspiring to cross boundaries between the realm of the symbolic and that of the world of historico-political intersubjectivity, renders the discipline particularly responsive to the suggestions of the so-called poststructuralist thought, among which the questioning of the foundations of metaphysical dualism proved to be one of the most inspiring ideas adopted: the presumed political, ideological, and cognitive potential attributed to the project of undermining hierarchies and subverting binary oppositions between categories which turn out to be the repressed of each other became an almost obligatory appointment of the recent PS scholarship. However, the sometimes simplistic reception of Derrida's deconstruction gave place to a most curious contradiction in the understanding of the concept of "boundary" by PS scholars, which led PS struggle against dualism to reiterate dualism: a certain pathos of overturning the "traditional metaphysical" polarity-engendering limits – such as those between symbolic representation and the world of human activity, theory and practice, art and political or social reality, fiction and actuality – entailed, on one hand, the construction of a huge quantity of new boundaries;[21] on the other, the tendency to use the rhetoric of liminality in

---

16 Martin Puchner, "Kenneth Burke: Theater, Philosophy, and the Limits of Performance", p. 54.
17 Richard Schechner, "Fundamentals of Performance Studies," in *Teaching Performance Studies*, eds Nathan Stucky and Cynthia Wimmer, Southern Illinois University Press, Carbondale & Edwardsville 2002, pp. ix-xii, p. x.
18 Ibidem.
19 Ibidem.
20 "[P]erformance studies draws on and synthesizes approaches from the social sciences, feminist studies, gender studies, history, psychoanalysis, queer theory, semiotics, ethology, cybernetics, area studies, media and popular culture theory, and cultural studies" (Schechner, "Fundamentals of Performance Studies", p. x). Nevertheless, all the enumerated disciplines, including PS itself, can be considered as subsumed by the last of the quoted list, the all-encompassing cultural studies.
21 Such as the boundaries between, alternately, performance and theatre (in so far as based on the allegedly theological

cancelling limits between binary oppositions and yearning to homogenize what appeared to be traditionally constituted distinct identities, by reinventing fictions of unity, coherence, "authenticity", "truth", "knowledge", communion of individuals and groups, merging art and politics, stage craft and cognition, etc. It would be exaggerated, or even wrong, to qualify these twists as a making up of a "new" theo- / teleology, a new dualistic "logocentrism", in which the "logos" would declare itself to be the ever moving, infinite processuality, a Heraclitean flux of "eventness" opposed to objecthood, but would still obey the imperative of a measurable norm. Rather, this is the way in which PS exemplifies the generally "aporetic project of the humanities [...] of *imparting the particular*";[22] and more specifically, it betrays the contradiction underlying the mission of cultural studies – the broader discipline in which PS is embedded, and also "the humanities' simulacrum of the social sciences"[23]– which is "its syncresis of its differences".[24] The claim of ("postmodern") novelty – which is an old procedure of instituting a limit toward what is "old", or obsoletely modern – does not protect the "performance paradigm" from enduring the performativity of what it declaratively leaves behind.

Consequently, a dissonance arises between two irreconcilable epistemological conceptions of the link between "words" and "things", or "two interpretations of interpretation":[25] the position of those who deplore the inadequacy of language to account for, represent, or mimick, the alleged truth of things,[26] and the recognition, how ever formulated with playful vagueness,[27] of the precarious fictionality of all coherent narratives de-

authority of a dramatic text and its author), the "real presence" and deceptive illusion, human embodiment and text (in so far as allegedly fixed in its meaning and ideology), performance process and the presumed petrification of the aesthetic product, "essential" processuality and "essentialism", active audience participation in performance and the "passivity" of contemplative spectatorship, performance eventness and the static self-sufficiency or completeness of the aesthetic work of art, the progressive and radical activism and the presumed conservatism of Kantian "purposiveness without purpose", instantaneous immediacy and delayed technical mediation, physical presence and reproduction, performance "presentation" and theatrical or narrative "representation", animate and inanimate, actual materiality and the abstract normative structure, postmodernism and modernism, and so on.

22   Samuel Weber, *Institution and Interpretation*, University of Minnesota Press, Minneapolis 1987, p. 144.
23   Tilottama Rajan, "In the Wake of Cultural Studies: Globalization, Theory, and the University", *Diacritics*, 32: 3 (Fall 2001), pp. 67-88, p. 72.
24   Ibidem, p. 75.
25   Jacques Derrida, *Writing and Difference*, trans. Alan Bass, Routledge, London and New York 2001, pp. 369-370; cf. Philip Auslander, *Theory for Performance Studies: A Student's Guide*, Routledge, London and New York 2008, p. 94.
26   "Words, alas, aren't things. Things, especially complex things like performance, don't obey our words for them: they are subject to continual mutation and intermixture – which is another way of saying that they are continually open to metaphorical extension" (Bert O. States, "Performance as metaphor", pp. 109-110). It is remarkable how in the regret stated by States "things" first seem to assume an ontological primacy that "words" fail to match, but then are attributed a transformational feature of a rhetorical kind, i.e. logically applicable to words only: in other words, words, in their infinite divisibility, perform infinite divisions, i.e. multiplications, upon "things".
27   "Let us name it—**Perfumance**: the citational mist of any and all performances. **Perfumance**: the incessant (dis)embodying-(mis)naming of performance. **Perfumance**: passing through the liminautics of Performance Studies, Performance Management, and Techno-Performance. **Perfumance**: the (dis)integration of the performance stratum. **Perfumance**: the becoming-mutational of normative forces, the becoming-normative of mutant forces. **Perfumance**: the odor of things and words, the sweat of bodies, the perfume of discourse. **Perfumance**: the ruse of a general theory" (Jon McKenzie, *Perform or Else*, p. 203, emphasis in the original).

signed to produce mirages of fixed meanings tying up words to things in discrete representational equivalences, constantly undone by dissemination (*différance*, iterability, divisibility of the signifier, *destinerrance*, or, in McKenzie's version, "perfumance"). Despite the axiomatic warning about the normative resistance to conceptual closure ("It goes without saying that defining performance studies once and for all is impossible"),[28] given the equally axiomatic (but also contradictory) norm of "precision and rigor" ("rigorous indeterminacy and openness"),[29] it still remains of the utmost importance to find out – be it through an excess of seriousness or through a misnaming joke – what is proper to performance, "what's in [that] name" for PS, and why "performance" is the proper name of PS. In either case – and apart from the general "double bind" for which any referent is "doomed to death [...] by the double law of the name", "the law of disidentification, the implacable necessity, the machine of the proper name that obliges me to live through precisely [...] my name, of which I am dying"[30] – the name and the "thing" named "performance" by performance studies have, perhaps more than any other name or thing, the astonishing tendency to encompass all of the human activity and coincide with "culture",[31] "social world", or simply "the world". Therefore, it (the "thing" performed by the "name") must hide, *and* display, an essential duplicity, a doubleness of "essence," an essential inessentiality, a particular sort of deceitful dividedness which precludes any (re)construction of its semantic "integrity"; a dividedness almost synonymous of divisibility, endowed, that is, with a performative power to divide itself, to perform divisions at the very point of performing its essential division-surpassing quality; the ability to perform one semantic role while temporarily holding in disguise another, equally "proper" to it. It is this hide-and-seek structure of the concept supposed to warrant the identity

---

28 Richard Schechner, "Fundamentals of Performance Studies", p. x.
29 Ibidem.
30 Jacques Derrida, *Psyche: Inventions of the Other*, Vol. II, eds Peggy Kamuf and Elizabeth Rottenberg, Stanford University Press, Stanford, California, 2008, pp. 139-140. As Bert O. States remarked with reference to Umberto Eco, this is the destiny of "any word", and all the more "any multi-featured concept" (Bert O. States, "Performance as metaphor," pp. 111 and 109); that is why "performance", a notion implying constant transformation and overcoming, is not an exception to what deconstructive practices must face, "the necessity, today, of working out at every turn, with redoubled effort, the question of the preservation of names: of *paleonymy*. Why should an old name, for a determinate time, be retained? Why should the effects of a new meaning, concept, or object, be damped by memory?" (Jacques Derrida, *Dissemination*, trans. Barbara Johnson, The Athlone Press, London 1981, p. 3). Redoubling forces, i.e. reading attentively to "a double reading and a double writing. And [...] a *double science*" (ibidem, p. 4), is dictated by the doubleness of the mark, at once identifying and dis-identifying, that concept receives within the binary oppositions in which it is founded: "one of the terms retains its old name so as to destroy the opposition to which it no longer quite belongs, to which in *any* event it has *never* quite yielded" (ibidem). It is noteworthy that this structure of "repetition without identity" (ibidem) is exemplified in Derrida's text by "literature", one of the ghostly terms in relation to which "performance" often both appropriates for itself, and is expropriated by, the opposite pole, and to which thus it could easily be substituted in the following context: "why should 'literature' still designate that which already breaks away from literature – away from what has always been conceived and signified under that name – or that which, not merely escaping literature, implacably destroys it? (Posed in these terms, the question would already be caught in the assurance of a certain fore-knowledge: can 'what has always been conceived and signified under that name' be considered fundamentally homogenous, univocal, or non-conflictual?)" (ibidem, p. 3-4).
31 Bert O. States "Performance as metaphor", p. 110 ff.

of the discipline, i.e. the "anasemic" or "cryptonymical" feature of the ways in which PS performs, and is performed by, "performance" that I will try to outline.

The term "cryptonymy" was first coined by Nicolas Abraham and Maria Torok to indicate the mechanism through which, within the analytic process, discursive traces both translate and obfuscate the paradoxical structure of the selfhood encapsulating an ambivalent attitude toward a doubly coded trauma, as "a parasitic inclusion, an inside heterogenous to the inside of the Self, an outcast outside inside the inside".[32] In Derrida's reelaboration of the notion, the presumed pathological origin of verbal opacity in a psychoanalysand's discourse, as a challenge to diagnostic reading, is converted into "the law of [...] semantic conversion"[33] encrypted in all concepts, the uncanny principle by virtue of which the word, whose meaning seems determined through the exclusion of other meanings, includes the excluded as an incorporated foreign double, an internal fissure at the core of the apparent conceptual unity. The fact that "performance" partakes of the contradictory duplicity that informs synonymical blendings between mutually unassimilable allosemic elements[34] while repressing their irreducibility to each other, or of a secret lack of "propriety" proper to all conceptual disjunctions, is by no coincidence proper exclusively to the English language, which is the birth place of the concept and the realm of cultural encryption of its very anasemic divide; nor is a mere serendipity the investment of the same concept in one of the crucial epistemological "turns", where it functions as an extended metaphor of culture, itself both the source of extreme "discontents" and the sole remedy against its own predicament.

Both the two-folded, oppositional structuration of the notion, and the idea of continuous boundary trespassing – although not always defining the two sides of a boundary to be trespassed in the same way, that is, somehow prioritizing structure over content – as its main feature figure in and are stressed by some of the seminal writings to which PS owes its institution. For various reasons, "performance" in Goffmann, Turner, Schechner, and "performative" in Austin, already result from a proficuous merging between two semantic areas: "to perform" as in "engaging in a symbolic behaviour, staging a theatrical / fictional representation before an audience," and "to perform" as "accomplishing, fulfilling a task, carrying to completion, producing a result".[35] It could be said that the link between the two allosemes,

---

[32] Jacques Derrida, "Fors: The Anglish Words of Nicolas Abraham and Maria Torok," in Nicolas Abraham and Maria Torok, *The Wolf Man's Magic Word. A Cryptonymy*, trans. Nicholas Rand, University of Minnesota Press, Minneapolis 1986 [1976]), pp. xi-xlviii, p. xvi.
[33] Ibidem, p. xxxi.
[34] Cf. ibidem, p. xli ff.
[35] An equivalent allosemy characterizes, as pointed out by Weber, the lexeme "act", analogously divided between "acting" and "action / actuality", Samuel Weber, *Theatricality as Medium*, Fordham University Press, New York 2004, pp. 46, 188 ff,

translatable with the synonym of "performance", is epitomized by Turner's pivotal term of "liminality", implying a "transformation" (for Schechner[36] in relation to performance, but also for Fischer-Lichte[37] in reference to theatre) capable of bringing about a change through bridging – making a *persuasive*, *perlocutionary*, *performative* leap across – a gap between two ontological levels, the fictional or quasi-fictional one (the one of "putting on an act"), and the empirical one, pertaining to (some kind of) social reality (consisting of accomplishing an action, whose nature is yet to be determined), or "actuality" in Schechner. The two cohabitating allosemes may give the impression that, in the works of the first theoreticians of performativity, each of them possesses not only a certain self-evident consistency, but also a share of pertinence equal to that of the other: however, although the "theatrical paradigm"[38] employed to interpret human interaction furnishes the basic conceptual tool for the endeavours made by Goffman and Turner (and, partly and implicitly, by Austin), in the respective sociological, anthropological, and linguistic-philosophical frameworks it tends, at least at a certain point of discussion, to be repressed or subordinated, precisely as a "mere" tool, to the particular issues of interest specific to each discipline, that regularly corresponds to the "productive" or "actualizational" aspect of "performing". What is more, this conceptual instrumentalization of the theatrical alloseme is bound to entail paradoxical consequences – comparable, in a way, to the Platonic "antitheatrical prejudice" – precisely in the area of PS dedicated to artistic, or "aesthetic", performance: through endorsing "a functionalist sociological approach" with a consequent "disengagement from analysis of the formal art of the artwork",[39] the discipline which proclaimed itself devoted to unsettling limits of all sorts, and especially its internal divisions, opened "a large gap between approaches which addressed society and those which formally analysed artworks".[40] This "gap", however, is frequently obscured by the intricated genealogies of PS.

Both in performance and performative, the "hystrionic," or symbolic, or theatrical-representational component – much like in Saussurian comparison of language to a single sheet of paper with "sound" and "thought" forming its two sides[41] – is supposed to *simultaneously* perform the other

---

340. When referring to theatricality, Weber eloquently avoids the ambivalent use of "performance", reserving "performance" and "performativity" for goal-oriented activity only ("teleological processes of fulfillment", ibidem, p. 117). Weber's antiperformative argument draws on his close readings of the texts on theatricality by authors usually reputed as the eminent precursors of theatrical efficacy by PS, such as Brecht and Artaud, from whom Weber quotes the following definition: "'Theater, which is to say, the immediate gratuitousness that imposes acts that are useless and without profit for actuality'", ibidem, p. 290.
36   Richard Schechner, *Performance Theory*, Routledge, London and New York, 2003, p. 191.
37   Erika Fischer-Lichte, *The Transformative Power of Performance: A New Aesthetics*, trans. Saskya Iris Jain, Routledge, London and New York 2008.
38   Richard Schechner, *Performance Theory*, p. 186.
39   Simon Shepherd and Mick Wallis, *Drama / Theatre / Performance*, p. 46.
40   Ibidem, p. 47.
41   Ferdinand de Saussure, *Course in General Linguistics*, ed. Charles Bally and Albert Sechahaye, in collaboration with Albert Reidlinger, trans. Wade Baskin, The Philosophical Library, New York 1959, p. 113.

component's function, its result coinciding with the act that produces it. This is undoubtfully the case of Austin's performative, a kind of "uttering of a sentence" which "is, or is a part of, doing of an action":[42] just as a performing actor, performative utterance belongs to the "class" of "masqueraders"[43] and it is precisely through the theatricality of this "'disguise'"[44]– through grammatically pretending to be a constative – that it performs its effect; perhaps necessarily for the context of Austin's study, not only the latter prevails as the criterion of performative's "felicity" ("the doctrine of the *Infelicities*"),[45] but the "masquerading" part is repressed (not particularly "felicitously", it is true, as far as its legacy for the humanities is concerned) by the notorious exclusion of *"peculiar", "parasitic"* theatrical or otherwise citational masquerades,[46] whose "parasitism" still remains the cryptonymical condition[47] of the contaminating inside in the midst of the "ordinary", "serious" performative. Goffman delineates his study of social interaction performance in "dramaturgical" terms of metaphorical "stage craft and stage management"[48] characterizing the individual's self-presentational strategy which "implicitly or explicitly signifies"[49]– that is, conveys the impression of certain attributes – and "automatically"[50] lays claim to social acceptance of its consequences; as Goffman underscores it, the object of his research should be the formal "techniques" employed by social (inter) actors and not "the specific content"[51]– or ideology, or aim – of their acts. In defiance of his unquestionable merit of introducing theatricality into the sociological research on everyday life, Goffman feels obliged to justify what he qualifies as "trivial"[52] in his model by claiming its ubiquity in social life, and finally makes a Wittgensteinian recourse to a *rhetorical* rejection of his own tool by denouncing it as "in part a rhetoric and a maneuver", a "mask" to "be dropped", "scaffolds" to be dispensed of once they would have permitted to "build other things".[53] Just as in Austin's exclusion, the theatricality of "performance" is (rhetorically) contrived to leave room for "other things", more "serious", presumably more "real" "things"; but it never *really* leaves the room, albeit as haunting it as a ghost.

The same coincidence of symbolic (dramatic) and pragmatic (social) activity constituting the performative event occurs in the "redressive phase" which is ritual performance in Turner's "social drama", the former both tak-

---

42   John L. Austin, *How to Do Things with Words*, Clarendon Press, Oxford 1962, p. 5.
43   Ibidem, p. 4.
44   Ibidem, p. 4.
45   Ibidem, p. 14.
46   Ibidem, p. 22.
47   Jacques Derrida, "Fors: The Anglish Words of Nicolas Abraham and Maria Torok", p. xvi.
48   Erving Goffman, *The Presentation of Self in Everyday Life*, Doubleday, New York, 1959, p. 15.
49   Ibidem, p. 13.
50   Ibidem, p. 13.
51   Ibidem, p. 13.
52   Ibidem, p. 15.
53   Ibidem, p.254.

ing meaning from and giving meaning to the latter. The very formula of "social drama" is for Turner an attempt at reconciling the primacy of social structures as required by the structural functionalism dominating his basic discipline, social and cultural anthropology, and his own conviction that ritual performance was not just an auxiliary mimetic expression derived from processes of social transformation, but their dialectical counterpart and site of production – not an "epiphenomenon", but a mechanism with an "ontological" status of its own, resisting the actual normative structures.[54] Turner's critique of structural functionalism in anthropology does not abolish its proliferation in performance theory as research on broadly social and cultural, and thus also a more specifically artistic ("aesthetic") performance, quite on the contrary. The creativity Turner emphasizes as the peculiar trait of ritual performance shows all its ambiguity when transferred to aesthetic performance by Schechner. In fact, while the redressive part that ritual takes in social reintegration or recognition of change is necessarily political and historically reflective in kind, since it is *identical* to the eminently social reality it performs (in the way Austin's performative "is, or is a part of, doing of an action")[55], the creativity of aesthetic performance does not, for Schechner, refer to the same self-accomplishing effect. Schechner acknowledges a difference between ritual and artistic performance, but ties them up in a unique "efficacy-entertainment braid"[56] forming a "binary continuum efficacy/ritual–entertainment/theater";[57] although "what efficacy refers to changes over time",[58] it is clear that Schechner values those cases of convergence in recent performance art where efficacy – be it political, psychotherapeutic, or moral-cognitive – structually dominates over entertainment. It is particularly striking that the theatrical alloseme of "performance" is now transformed into "entertainment", whose one of the most distinctive features is "fun" – so close to "nonserious", "parasitic", or "trivial" marks by which Austin and Goffman labelled theater. This equation between the theatrical "pole" and "fun" may not sound demeaning, but it imperceptibly annuls the dialectical opposition inside the performance "braid" by narrowing both of its terms to the same matter of effect. Schechner's reduction of the theatrical to a phenomenon ultimately measurable in terms of its counterpart ("efficacy") makes relevant the series of questions posed by a critic

---

54   Victor Turner, *Dramas, Fields, and Metaphors: Symbolic Action in Human Society*, Cornell University Press, Ithaca, NY 1975, p. 57. The issue of bridging or blurring boundaries, particularly as an instance of ontological transitivity characteristically implied by the conceptual discourses of PS, maintains its disturbing charge for the critics eager to establish neat terminological rubrics when referring to performance, but also theater or theatricality; not even "the notion of 'social drama'" is exempted from the objection that it "reflects a fundamental fallacy: it blurs the ontological gap between life and representation of life, between social life and thinking about it", Eli Rozik, *The Roots of Theater: Rethinking Ritual and Other Theories of Origin*, The University of Iowa Press, Iowa City 2002, p. 12.
55   John L. Austin, *How to Do Things with Words*, p. 5.
56   Richard Schechner, *Performance Theory*, p. 112ff.
57   Ibidem, p. 156.
58   Ibidem, p. 135.

whose conservative representational prejudice (according to which theater is a secondary "description of world" or "representation of life")[59] otherwise would not seem the best qualification for judging performance art theorists:

> "fun" (a synonym of „entertainment") vs. „results" (a synonym of „efficacy") [...] is not a valid antinomy [...], because „fun" is a kind of audience response (or effect) [...]. „Effect" can thus apply to both ritual and theatre only if attributed different meanings. This braided relationship could be understood as supporting Schechner's theory, since these elements are not mutually exclusive and can coexist. The questions, however, multiply. For example, is „fun" an elementary notion? Does fun exhaust the theatrical pole? Is it a category that applies to all aesthetic theatre? How should we then categorize the frustrating experience of a subversive play: under „fun" or „results"?[60]

Both ends of the binary in the braid end up meeting in the same place: efficacy. Unlike the "felicity" of Austin's performative (a quality of the performative utterance itself in relation to the circumstances in which it is pronounced), the objectives of Schechner"s "efficacy" lie elsewhere, in "other things" – in nothing less than "transformation of consciousness",[61] in an efficacious action upon an "actuality" – ethical, cognitive, possibly historical, social, political actuality – more actual, or in any case more righteous, than performance itself.

A small step separates Schechner's transitive-projectional efficacy of performance from the inclusion of economic, operational and technological performance into the study area of PS by McKenzie, who also reckons, and resigns to, the risk of explosion or implosion of the discipline. This step is in itself just a symptom of performance's cryptonymy, a not so candid testimony of how deeply performance research is permeated by the ideals of social justice, freedom and "progress", and simultaneously (and unvolontarily) subject to the rules of the masters' game of efficacy, itself "efficaciously" channelled into the schemes of profit maximization – as becomes evident from the inversion of priority between the "two contrasting challenges" to which McKenzie's book aims to respond:

> one that calls us to perform organizationally, to help improve the efficiency of companies and other institutions; the other calls us to perform culturally, to foreground and resist dominant norms of social control.[62]

---

59   Eli Rozik, *The Roots of Theatre*, pp. 204, 212.
60   Ibidem, p. 174-175.
61   Richard Schechner, *Performance Theory*, p. 193.
62   Jon McKenzie, *Perform or Else*, p. 9

"To perform culturally" (including "to perform aesthetically", which seems not to concern "us" sufficiently) would be anyway to serve a more important purpose beyond itself. Oblivious of the particularity and concreteness once emphasized by performance theorists, but pursuing their interest in social efficiency, in this ambitious theoretical enterprise performance research aligns itself with the cultural studies' "ideology of economistic thinking and technological domination",[63] "embrac[ing] technology so as to ally itself with science, progress, and membership of the global scene"[64] and promoting "economics and technology [into] metadisciplines".[65] McKenzie's "general theory of performance" absorbs indiscriminately Marcuse"s "performance principle" or Lyotard"s "performativity" into performance studies, not only disregarding the critical weight of socio-cultural polemic that these notions were supposed to have in their primary contexts, but even, and notwithstanding his claims of undecidability ("perfumance"), assigning them *the* meaning of performance as nothing less than the cypher of the epochal *"onto-historical formation of power and knowledge"*.[66] While "[p]olitics and political economy, to be sure, are implicated in every discourse on art and on the beautiful" and forming with the latter the parergonal knot of "economimesis",[67] in McKenzie's discourse on performance they seem to appropriate for themselves a domain from which they could be altered and expropriated,[68] the domain of their – cryptonymical and "parasitic" – aesthetic other, the "divisible space of a spectral theatricality"[69] that "will never be reducible to 'performance' in the sense of the accomplishing of an action or an intention".[70]

In a note to his *Postmodern Condition*, Lyotard made a significant remark (due, of course, to the univocity of the French anglicism "performance") relating Austin's notion of performative speech act to the advanced capitalism's utilitarian tenets of industrial achievement, business success, human resources management, labour optimization, economic growth,[71] in other words, to a notion of "progress", "positive change" and "knowledge" apparently very distant from the views cultivated by the PS paradigm of "liminality"; very distant, but not incompatible. Namely, the allosemic component of Austin's performative stressed by Lyotard, with its criterion

---

63   Tilottama Rajan, "In the Wake of Cultural Studies: Globalization, Theory, and the University", p. 72
64   Ibidem, p. 71.
65   Ibidem, p. 75.
66   Jon McKenzie, *Perform or Else*, p. 18.
67   Jacques Derrida, "Economimesis" [1975], trans. Richard Klein, *Diacritics*, 11: 2 (1981), pp. 2-25, p. 3.
68   Cf. Samuel Weber, *Theatricality as a Medium*, p. 292.
69   Ibidem, p. 185.
70   Ibidem, p. 188.
71   "The term *performative* has taken on a precise meaning in language theory since Austin. Later in [my] book, the concept will reappear in association with the term *performativity* (in particular, of a system) in a new current sense of efficiency measured according to an input/output ratio. The two meanings are not far apart. Austin's performative realizes the optimal performance" (Jean François Lyotard, *The Postmodern Condition: A Report on Knowledge*, Manchester University Press, Manchester 1984 [1979], p. 88).

of (in)felicity, supplanting the truth/lie alternative valid for the constative speech acts, undoubtedly inhabits the "crypt" – the secret reserve of strange contradiction, alien to the program of, and yet built in the very core – of PS. Along with the impulse of promoting new dimensions of aesthetic experimentation, the urge of reconnecting artistic action to truth and social justice, the thrust to rethink the relevance and recover the mission of intellectual intervention in the world, in a word, the aim to deploy the potential of performance art and scholarship as a critique of the current state of (social and political) affairs, PS cultivates, with equal insistence, a goal-oriented notion of performance susceptible of assessment from the standpoint of (qualitative or quantitative) usefulness, effectiveness, efficiency, efficacy, profit, and thus depending on an irreversible linear connection between cause and effect, intention and target. Whereas the concept of perfomance questions from the outset the concept of limit, and hence the concept of itself as a concept, it also strives at reinstating, in the spirit of the analytic drive, a division line, separating a good and a bad performance of performance, a felicitous one from the infelicitous one, an acceptable one from the inacceptable one. What precisely should constitute the successful achievement of a performance remains opened to an ongoing theoretical debate; but the requisite of the concept's "identity" is, as paradoxically as necessarily, always shaped against what is considered as a failure, i.e. a misperformance – the "outcast outside", simultaneously the essential, integral and unextractable "inside heterogenous to the inside", or to the crypt, of performance. Whether the normative framework rule out as misperformance some sort of inauthenticity, technical reproduction, non-human or inanimate elements, disembodiment, conventionality, the traditional theater, textual script, authorial authority, or simply an aestheticist lack of moral, political or cognitive effectiveness, it regularly proceeds by excluding – or, in Peggy Phelan's case,[72] at once melancholically identifying performance with – the error that impedes its program of arriving at a destination, i.e. the failure to attain "reality" (alternately, the "outside" reality of the social world, the "inner" reality of the individual body, the referent as "the thing", Lacanian "real"). At any rate, the error, or the impossibility of reaching a preprogrammed destination (termed by Derrida "destinerrance"),[73] does not lie "outside" performance; perhaps because there is no outside-performance.

---

[72] Phelan's hostility to "the mythos of success" (Peggy Phelan, *Unmarked: The Politics of Performance*, Routledge, London 1993, p. 106.) inspires her utopian idealization of performance, i.e. the repression of its cryptonymical, econommimetical aspects: "Performance resists the balanced circulations of finance. [...] Performance refuses this system of exchange and resists the circulatory economy fundamental to it. [...] Performance's independence from mass reproduction, technologically, economically, and linguistically, is its greatest strength" (ibidem, pp. 148-149). However, her views succumb to a literal understanding of deconstruction's (and "poststructuralist") "rhetoric of failure" (Ewa Płonowska Ziarek, *The Rhetoric of Failure: Deconstruction of Skepticism, Reinvention of Modernism*, State University of New York Press, Albany 1996), which reinscribes them, though via negativa, into the economic discourse on performance.

[73] Cf. Jacques Derrida, *Psyche: Inventions of the Other*, Vol. I, eds Peggy Kamuf and Elizabeth Rottenberg, Stanford University Press, Stanford, California, 2008, pp. 236, 351, 360, 404, 405.

The endeavour at "rehearsing" (i.e., performing tentatively) "a general theory of performance", made by Jon McKenzie's book, bearing a significantly cryptonymical title – *Perform or Else*[74], takes into account both allosemic components contained in the impossible synonym which is "performance": aware of, but all the same determined to – both cynically and parodically – censure, the irreducible tension between the (at least) two contradictory but interwined ways of understanding the object of the PS research, which makes the latter improbable to coincide with itself within a theoretical melting pot,[75] McKenzie chooses to maintain an almost poetic distance toward his own idea of amalgamating the two irreconcilable insights by quoting Nietzsche's scorn of the (European) people thoroughly identified with their social and professional roles, as actors who are victims of their own "good performance".[76] Nietzsche's cryptonym, referring both to the actor's art of illusion as the *necessary* error and illusion, and to the illusion of efficiency not perceived to be an illusion, might have served here to champion the illusionary nature of performance in both senses, as well as the joyful acceptance of its "general theory" as illusion; it might have endorsed the doubleness, the dividedness of the theatricality of performance, instead of enhancing a theoretical mythology of reintegration under the auspices of power.

---

74   One may object that my "cryptonimical" understanding of McKenzie's title results from a deliberate misreading; but intended meanings have no guardians, because iterability compels repetition to miss the identity to what it repeats, and McKenzie's own appropriations are the best illustration of this law ("there's no insurance policy against the posthumous workings of citational networks", Jon McKenzie, *Perform or Else*, p. 259). In fact, he explains "perform – or else" to be his way of paraphrasing Lyotard's description of the "terror" of performativity (in Lyotard's words: "be operational (that is, commensurable) or disappear") in the sense of "legitimation defined as the maximization of a system's output and the minimization of its input" (McKenzie, p. 163), and – hardly respecting the paraphrased author's spirit – merges it together with PS into a single "performativity condition" (ibidem) "general theory", which can also be read as a parody.

75   "Ulmer suggests that one needn't "choose between the different meanings of key terms, but compose by using all the meanings (write the paradigm [of meanings])" [Gregory L. Ulmer, *Heuretics: The Logic of Invention*, The Johns Hopkins University Press, Baltimore, MD 1994, p. 48]. Similarly: create a perfumance using all the paradigms of performance research" (McKenzie, p. 235). In a note to this programmatic sentence, McKenzie adds: "As some readers might have already surmised, this is one of the *crypto*-missions launched at the initiation of this text" (ibidem, p. 287, my emphasis).

76   Ibidem, p. 256.

Jon McKenzie
Posthuman Misperformance: BP and the Flight of the Whooping Cranes

Hacking BP

In the wake of the BP disaster in the Gulf of Mexico, which began in April, 2010, artists Mark Skwarek and Joseph Hocking created an augmented reality app for the iPhone called *The Leak is in Your Home Town*. Augmented reality refers to the virtual overlaying of information over physical reality, usually in real-time. *The Leak is in Your Home Town* overlays an animation of a spewing oil pipe on BP's Helios logo, thus allowing iPhone users to hack the logos found in their everyday life and install a gushing plume of oil into one's own home town.

BP performances

We can use the BP disaster to theorize *posthuman misperformance*. The concept of posthuman misperformance brings together two complex concepts, and it's worth spending some time introducing and unpacking them. To begin unpacking "misperformance," it helps to define "performance". My research may seem to focus far from theatrical performance – and it does – but theater itself not only involves cultural performance but also technological performance (from *deus ex machina* to computerized light systems) and organizational performance (there's a reason theatre companies are called "theatre companies" – theater requires organization). Further, theater provides an alternative to Romantic creativity and its models of the poet and painter, which stress individual genius, originality, monomedium, and expertise, whereas theatre entails collaborative effort, reworking of existing materials, multiple media, and a more open, "let's put on a show" sensibility. With this open and recombinant perspective, let's see what types of performance make up the BP disaster.

First and foremost, the BP disaster foregrounds *organizational performance*. I am not using the term "performance" metaphorically, as if its proper, literal meaning resided in theatre, in contrast to figurative uses by business managers. Rather, managers have developed specific discourses and practices of performance, every bit as real and proper as cultural performance. Organizational performance stretches from individual workers to work groups and divisions, all the up to performance of the entire organization and its top management. Traditionally, organizational performance has meant *efficiency*, in contrast to the social efficacy valorized by scholars studying cultural performance. In the wake of the Gulf disaster, much attention fell on BP's organizational performance, especially the alleged cutting of safety measures on the Deepwater Horizon rig in face of corporate pressures to quickly finish and move on to the next site. In July, 2010, BP CEO Tony Hayward was forced to announce his retirement.

Attention has also fallen on BP's technological performance; specifically, the performance of the "blowout preventers". According to the web site Technology Review, published by MIT, the gulf disaster "reveals an over-reliance on one piece of equipment that academic and industry experts have warned of for close to a decade: The blowout preventers, or BOPs, [...] are the industry's primary line of defense against deep water oil spills".[1] In other words, at issue is not only the performance of the specific blowout preventer on the Deepwater Horizon, but the technology itself. Technological performance can be generally understood in terms of technical *effectiveness*, and technologies from missiles to household appliances have "performance specs" detailing their performance.

And cultural performance is also at work in the BP disaster. While one can study organizations with charts and spreadsheets, institutions generate more than numbers and efficiencies; they also have a qualitative, social dimension that is commonly called cultural. Indeed, since its name change from "British Petroleum" to "BP Amoco" after a merger with a US oil firm, and then simply to the initials "BP," the firm has carefully crafted a public, cultural image of itself as a responsible corporate citizen, and its Helios logo – the green and yellow sunflower – was designed to convey BP's commitment to alternative energies and environmentalism. It even looks suspiciously similar to the logo of Canada's Green Party.

---

[1] Peter Fairley, "How Technology Failed in the Gulf Spill", *Technology Review*, 4 May 2010, http://www.technologyreview.com/energy/25238/ [accessed 1 May 2014].

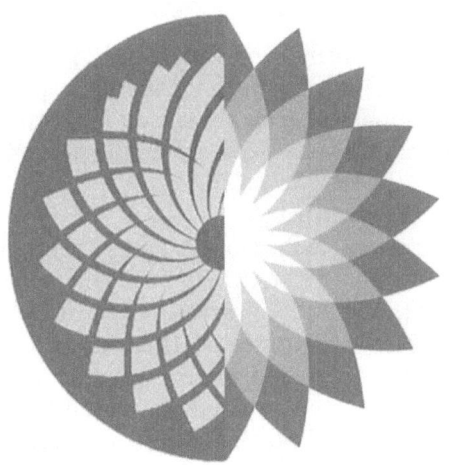

Designed by Jon McKenzie

Just as important as this external cultural performance, however, is BP's internal culture. Here we find a jarring contrast: according to numerous sources in the US and UK, the avoidance of safety measures in the Gulf disaster was not an isolated event. Rather, it reflects what the *Times Online of London* cited in 2007 as BP's "terrifying safety culture," citing an investigation by the US Chemical Safety Board following a Texas accident that killed 15 people and wounded 180.[2] The US Occupational Safety and Health Administration reports that BP has had some 690 violations between 2007 and 2010.

The exposure of this contrast between BP's sunny, responsible cultural image and its "terrifying safety culture" proved financially disastrous for the firm. This leads us to yet another of its BP's performances. As depicted in the graph of BP's stock's financial performance from July, 2009 to July, 2010, its stock value plunged beginning in April, when the disaster started. At one point, BP had lost more than half its market capitalization, a loss of some $95 billion. Again, financial performance is not a metaphorical term: stocks literally perform, as do index funds and entire markets. Indeed, the standard legal disclaimer used by financial firms worldwide reads: "past performance is no guarantee of future results". Given this dismal financial performance and the damage done to its brand, some at the time wondered whether BP might *change its name*, taking up "Amoco," the name it phased out only in 2008 (the America oil company Amoco having merged with BP in 1998).

Cultural performance, organizational performance, technological performance, and financial performance all constitute what I call performance paradigms, specific regimes of knowledge in which discourses and practices

2   See http://business.timesonline.co.uk/tol/business/industry_sectors/natural_resources/article1538641.ece.

of performance have been formalized and institutionalized. Other performance paradigms include medical performance (e.g., performance-enhancing drugs) and educational performance (the first IQ tests were called "performance tests"). All of these have emerged in the past half-century or so.

The Performance stratum

That cultures, organizations, technologies, and markets all *perform* suggests that performance may be a – if not, *the* – defining element of the contemporary world. Indeed, at the center of my research is the following proposition: *performance will have been to the 20th and 21st centuries what discipline was to the 18th and 19th, namely, an onto-historical formation of power and knowledge.* That is, underlying the performance paradigms at work in the BP Gulf disaster is a more fundamental performance, a *performance stratum* of onto-historical forces that is rein scribing and displacing the disciplinary stratum analyzed by Foucault. Whereas global disciplinarity produced liberal, industrial capitalism, colonialism, and the rise of the nation-state, global performativity entails neoliberal, information capitalism, postcolonialism, and the rise of multinational institutions, not only corporations but also the UN and NGOs.

Moreover, over the past decade, institutions around the world have begun adopting performance management practices focused not only on organizational efficiency and financial profitability but also adopting multivalent performance criteria for assessing their global citizenship and thus helping to generate a better future. Briefly put: processes of performance auditing and evaluation originally developed to improve organizational efficiency and economic profitability have been transformed into tools for activists fighting for labor and human rights, the environment, and transparent corporate governance.

One worldwide effort started in the year 2000 with the United Nation's Global Compact initiative, a project to promote global sustainability by encouraging corporations around the world to self- assess three types of performance: social (human rights), environmental (compliance with laws and standards), and economic (revenues, costs, etc.). The premise is that corporations can begin to trade off or "satisfice" between competing performative values. Collectively, these are known as the "triple bottom line", or "people, planet, and profits", a phrase coined by the Royal Dutch/Shell Group in an influential series of annual reports. The UN's Global Compact provides a highly public forum for corporations to voluntarily report their triple bottom line performance. By trying to shape corporate decision-making and policies, the Compact effectively created satisficial rituals to generate a more sustainable future.

Indeed, "sustainability performance" has emerged as an umbrella term to encompass environmental performance, social performance, and safety performance. Check page 6 from BP's 2009 Sustainability Review (http://www.bp.com/content/dam/bp/pdf/sustainability/group-reports/bp_sustainability_review_2009.pdf).

On the performance stratum – or "P stratum" for short – we thus not only see the emergence of multiple performance paradigms but also their convergence into ever more complex models of governance and control, some of which purport to build a better future.

While the disciplinary stratum institutionalized Western humanism, the P-stratum portends the emergence of posthumanism, an event that is not only historical but also ontological, as it entails a transmutation of being, not only "our understanding" of it but *what the world is*.

Posthumanism I: Which One?

What is the posthuman? A better question is *"which one?"* for there are several types, which I will also quickly outline, prefacing my remarks by stressing that we should understand the prefix "post-" not only in the sense of following or coming after, but also in the sense of *posting* or sending a letter. I will thus sketch several types of posthumanism, posing each as if it involved someone or *something* that *posts the human*.

First, the *anthropological* posting. Here what posts the human are other, non-Western cultures. In a 2008 symposium on the posthuman at the University of Wisconsin, my late colleague anthropologist Neil Whitehead stressed that different cultures have not only produced alternative concepts and histories of "the human", but also different ontologies – different types of *being human*. From a Western perspective, what does being human mean if one regularly talks with spirits, or can turn into an animal, or walk on a thin string up to sky? It is all too easy to exoticize or, alternatively, domesticate these alternative "being humans" as ideological or mythic conceptions. What posthumanism offers here is a way of relativizing the humanist ontology of Western modernity, reinscribing it in relation to other ontologies.

Second: the *philosophical* posting. I'm tempted to say that the "poster" here is Nietzsche, who might also be hailed as the grandfather – or even the grandmother – of this posthuman, though the familial metaphor is strained and staticky. I'll go with the static and mash together Derrida, Foucault, and Deleuze: with this posthuman, we face not the end of human, but its closure, its reinscription and displacement within a nonlinear space-time of onto-historical forces. As Deleuze puts it: this "death of Man" is much less the disappearance of humans and much more than a change of concept. Channeling Foucault, Man is but "an invention of recent date", "like a face drawn in the sand at the edge of the sea", about to be erased. At issue here is the philosophical status of the human as subject of knowledge, agent of history, and master of the world. In addition to Nietzsche, who or what posts the human here might be the trace, the Outside, difference and repetition.

I should note here that Nietzsche famously said "man is a bridge", and his theory of the "superman" stands as a problematic figure of the posthuman, given its sinister appropriation by the Nazis.

A third, closely related, posting is the *technological* displacement of the human, articulated most forcibly by Donna Haraway, Katherine Hayles, and Avital Ronell. What posts the human here would be *the cyborg, informatics, or technology understood as radical alterity*. Though this is not Haraway's main concern, many readings of the cyborg emphasize prosthetic devices that undermine the human body as privileged site of agency and volition. With informatics, we have a more systemic displacement, for it situates humans within broader flows of information and capital. Finally, the notion of technology as radical alterity *frontloads* technology within human history, making it co-terminus with human development and *not* some recent arrival. As Ronell famously puts it: "There is no off switch to the technological", thus suggesting that it's always been on, pushing our buttons, or – more radically – that it is what turned us humans "on" in the first place.

The *fourth* posting of the human comes from recent work on *animal rights and the distinction of human and animal*. Significantly, several of the writers already mentioned have theorized the "animal": including Haraway with her work on animal sociology, Deleuze and Guattari and "becoming-animal", and Derrida's *"l'animot"*. Here I will single out the work of Cary Wolfe, whose 2003 book *Animal Rites* and his *Zoontologies* collection from the same year have come to mark the initiation of a robust, posthumanist field of animal theory. While animal rights theorists such as Adams, Regan, and Singer have contributed to this emerging field, they have also been criticized for their *residual humanism*. By contrast, Wolfe draws upon Derrida, in particular, in attempting to move beyond the anthropocentric "speciesism" that informs most thinking about animals. Rather than extending human rights to a selection of "human-like" animals, this project involves a reinscription of the very distinction of human and animal. The interest is thus *less* about "how *human* some animals are", and *more* about "how *animal* humans are". In some sense, here *animality* posts the human.

A *fifth* posting might be called the *"ecological posthuman"*, for it situates the human within even larger, environmental processes, not only global but also cosmic. Though one could cite the work of Latour here, or that of radical ecologists, I am thinking of a lineage that connects Bateson's *Steps to an Ecology of Mind* to Guattari's late work, namely *Chaosmosis* and *The Three Ecologies*. Bateson and Guattari shared an interest in how the human mind links up with material and symbolic processes found in both organic and inorganic "life". Guattari wrote of the "machinic phylum" and the "geology of morals". While Bateson theorized the ecology of mind in terms of the positive and negative feedback loops characteristic of early cybernetic theory, Guattari relied on the autopoetic, recursive loops that became crucial to chaos theory. For both theorists, the unit of life is no longer the individual or species, but "organism plus environment". Here, *the world or the cosmos posts the human.*

The last posting is the religious, for contemporary religious fundamentalisms can be understood as offering a type of posthumanism. Here, *God, Allah, or Jehovah does the posting*. Now one might be tempted to see fundamentalist attacks on secular humanism as pre-modern or pre-humanistic, but the very terms and media through which such attacks now occur are themselves informed by modernity and humanism. This fundamentalist strain is arguably the most powerful posthumanism operating today: none of the other theories of the posthuman can approach it in terms of institutions, finances, or number of adherents. Thus, while exploring or promoting the posthuman, posthumanism, and even the posthumanities, one should also be wary of becoming unwitting *accomplices* of this fundamentalist posthumanism.

Posthumanism II: The End of Humanism and the Undoable
In light of the BP oil well dug deep in the Gulf of Mexico, we might recall here Conan Doyle's sci-fi story, "The Day the Earth Screamed", in which a certain Professor Challenger proves that the world is a living organism by drilling down through its crust and violently puncturing its skin, at which point the Earth responds by spewing foul, stinking material back up the hole and covering everything around it. While some may balk at the idea of the Earth "living", we can and do conceive of it as a dynamic system, one composed of complex processes that interact and evolve over time: indeed, anything that constitutes or can be described as a system can also be said to perform, for that is precisely what systems do: they perform. Thus, even the world performs.

If the P-stratum indeed helps produce the posthuman, that means it challenges both the liberal humanism of John Stuart Mill, based on individual freedom, and the critical humanism of much cultural theory, which relies on such human social categories as class, gender, and race. Within performance studies, these two humanisms have a long, intimate relationship. Historically, the study of ritual and theatre has long been used to support performance scholars' critiques of liberal humanist individualism and their accompanying valorization of the social, a critique and valorization that I am here calling "critical humanism" due to its stress on critical social forces.

Even with the emergence of solo performance art as a key analytical site in the 1990s, this critical humanist perspective has focused on identity's social construction, rather than the creative genius of the individual performer. However, more recent work in animal performance, digital performance, and environmental performance all test the limits of critical humanism in profound ways and connect us to the posthuman. To put it bluntly: reducing everything to social construction is itself an all-too-human gesture. Just as individualism was critically resituated in terms of the social, the social is itself being reinscribed within larger performative systems, whether these be animality, technology, the environment, etc.

At the same time, avian and swine flus, shuttle disasters and computer glitches, volcano clouds and oil disasters all bring attention to the fact that both performances and performative misfirings may be irreducible to human agency or human error, giving new and urgent impetus to the study of posthuman misperformance. Significantly, Richard Schechner effectively gestured toward something like posthuman misperformance way back in 1982, in his book *The End of Humanism*. He writes:

> I define stability as accepting limits to human action – limits that are not the outermost boundaries of knowledge or ability but a frame consciously set around what is "acceptable," defining anything outside that frame as "un-doable."
> Accepting such a frame means the end of humanism.[3]

Though Schechner does not use the term "posthuman misperformance", I find his alignment of "the end of humanism" and the "un-doable" to be a premonition of it. Like Schechner, I am skeptical that one can *know* the outermost boundaries of knowledge and ability, but I am also skeptical that one can *consciously* frame the limits of the acceptable and the undoable, the line where the human ends and its others begin.

The bacteria living in our stomach; the imprint of branches and tools on the shape of our thumbs; the role of salt water in the firing of our neurons – all suggest that we can relaunch Bruno Latour's famous dictum that "we've never been modern" into another orbit: "we've never been human". Or at least, we've never been and never will be fully, 100%, totally human, and all those frames we have tried to build and maintain – all those limits between human/divine, human/animal, human/plant, human/machine, human/inorganic – all of them are porous and leaky and escape our conscious ability to delimit the doable and undoable, the living and the dead. As the marine lover Nietzsche provokes us to ponder: life is but a rare form of death, the inorganic.

Posthumanism III: ANT and garden performance

The emergence of posthumanism, I contend, coincides with that of the performance stratum. However awash our thoughts might be with salt water, these posthumanisms help us think performance as an onto-historical for-

---

3   Richard Schechner, *The End of Humanism: Writings on Performance*, PAJ Publications, New York 1982, p. 96.

mation. At the same time, performance can help us think the posthuman as the reformatting of human agency within larger performative systems. The work of Latour and other proponents of Actor-Network Theory (ANT) articulate this reinscription. For many years now, Latour and other ANT researchers in Science and Technology Studies have been theorizing the performance of laboratories and inanimate objects.

The relation of ANT and Performance Studies can be posed in a number of ways. In a study of Latour titled *Prince of Networks*, philosopher Graham Harman describes the performative dimension of Latour's ANT (actor-network theory), while also hurling a critical stone at those who understand performativity solely in terms of subject formation. Harman writes that, for Latour:

> the essence of a thing results only from its public performance in the world, and in this respect he does agree with certain postmodernist currents. Yet one can hardly imagine the Judith Butlers acknowledging the "performativity" of *inanimate* objects as well as of human actors. In this way, Latour strikes a tacit [blow] against every version of speech-act theory: what he gives us is not speech-act theory but *actor-act* theory.[4]

Harman's engagement here with the "Judith Butlers" of the world amounts to drive-by critique, as he hurls this critical missive and then speeds away to other arguments. I should note that in a 2010 talk in Berlin titled "From Performativity to Precarity", Butler spoke of the precarity that "implicates us in a non-human world of life". But she also did so at high speed, and in the end remained concerned with the life-and-death political situations of human subjects. My interest here is not to choose between Harman's object-oriented ontology and Butler's subject-oriented political theory. As I have been attempting for some time, one can theorize the performativity of *both* subjects and objects – and beyond. Indeed, since the disciplinary formation institutionalized Descartes' subject/object opposition throughout our lifeworld, we can expect the P-stratum to produce something else. Indeed, since disciplinarity democratized modern critical thinking, we can expect perfumative thought to be something else, as well.

Another ANT perspective on posthuman mis/performance comes via the performance concepts introduced by Donald MacKenzie (no relation), a sociologist who has lately been working in the sociology of economics. MacKenzie's interest in performativity informs the title of his recent book, *An Engine, not a Camera: How Financial Models Shape Markets*, by which he indicates that economic models should be seen not as pictures or reports on

---

4   Graham Harman, *Prince of Networks: Bruno Latour and Metaphysics*, re.press, Melbourne 2009, p. 66.

the world but as engines capable of acting in and on it – in short, as performative processes. MacKenzie may appear to be importing Austin's concept of performative utterance into the field of Science and Technology Studies. But two things counter this appearance. First, as earlier noted, ANT performance concepts have long been deployed in STS by researchers such as Latour, Michel Callon and Andrew Pickering. Second, MacKenzie explicitly distinguishes his concept of performativity from Austin's performative, arguing that he does not limit his notion of model to cognitive models, linguistic utterances, or beliefs "in the head." Indeed, MacKenzie addresses the ways in which scientific models also become incorporated in *nonhuman* bodies and materials, such as algorithms, procedures, and technical devices.[5]

Let us note here that Austin's original formulation of performative misfiring was itself all-too-human, as all four conditions of success focus on human agents: namely, a social convention must be properly executed; the appropriate persons must carry it out; the utterance must be completely executed; and those involved must be sincere. These conditions do not suffice when the performativity of technologies, materials, and algorithms enter the picture – the point forcefully made by Harman and MacKenzie. While Butler has focused much attention on the paradox that subjectivity is itself performatively constructed, the ANT folks are on to something else – the performative agency of nonhuman actors.

Beyond this deeper incorporation of models into both people and things, it is MacKenzie's classification of different types or *degrees* of performativity that may be most relevant to Performance Studies and to theories of misperformance, in particular. In the book's opening chapter, he offers this diagram outlining the relation of four different concepts of performativity. [FIG. 1]

Though MacKenzie does not call these degrees of performativity, I think this is the best way to begin understanding them. At the outer, most general level is "'generic' performativity," the empirical use of an academic theory or model by economic participants, either in business or government. This use – which could be descriptive or hypothetical – has little or no impact on the economy. Next, for "'effective' performativity." MacKenzie writes that a model must *"make a difference,"* perhaps by making an economic process possible or by altering an outcome.

He contends, however, that the most interesting concepts reside in the innermost subsets. On the left is "Barnesian performativity," in which a model or theory impacts economic phenomenon to such a degree that these *conform to the model in question*. In earlier work, MacKenzie called this performativity "Austinian" but later renamed it after the sociologist Barry

---

5   Donald MacKenzie, *An Engine, not a Camera: How Financial Models Shape Markets*, MIT Press, Cambridge MA 2008, p. 19.

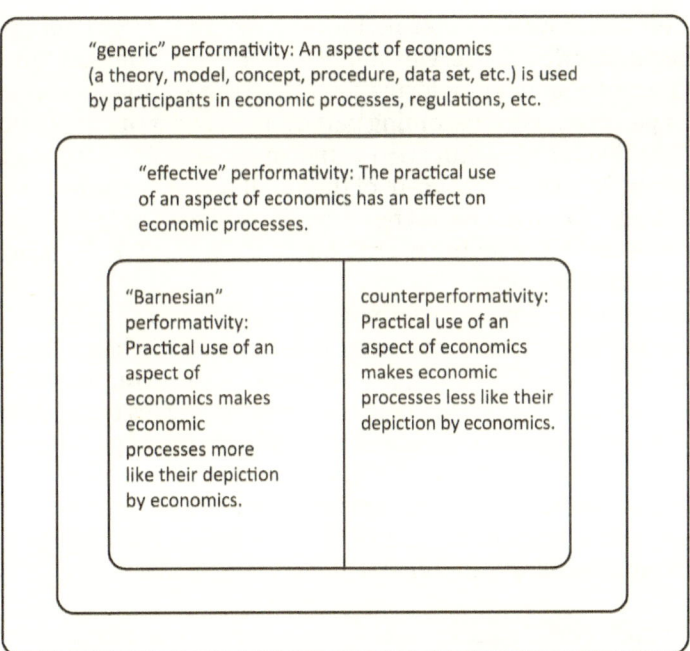

[FIG. 1] The performativity of economics: a possible classification. Drawn from Donald MacKenzie, *An Engine, Not a Camera*. Page 17, Figure 1.1

Barnes, who studied the role of self-validating feedback loops in social life. With Barnesian performativity, the model or concept becomes almost invisible, as subject and object appear to confirm one another and expectation and reality converge. This performativity is not just ideological, but also material, as it becomes built into tools, infrastructure, even the way phenomena become visible and situated in the world.

On the right of MacKenzie's chart, we find "counterperformativity," whereby a model's impact has the opposite effect: economic processes tend not to conform but rather to *diverge* from that very model. Reality appears to turn on the model using the very evidence generated by it, only now that evidence calls into question the assumptions and biases. [i] Counterperformativity would thus appear to be a version of "misfiring" or "misperformance," though following Derrida, we might want to consider its constitutive effects, essentially installing counter-performativity within generic performativity.

MacKenzie analyzes the performativity of a single economic algorithm known as Black-Scholes – one that, by the way, was once described as seeking to abolish risk by complex hedging of bets. However, the categories of performativity he provides could be applied to *any* theory or model, and my interest here lies in how counter-performativity can help us understand posthuman misperformance. One might, for instance, consider whether Butler's concept of gender performativity has itself attained the level of Barnesian performativity, becoming part of the world it once theorized. I would argue that it has within LGBT activism. Alternatively, we might consider whether Schechner's concept of the ritualization of theater ever "counter-performed, " for instance, in the early 1980s, since *The End of Humanism* deals precisely with the failure of environmental theatre in the face of actor President Ronald Reagan.

A third way to connect Performance Studies and Actor-Network Theory can be seen in the work of British geographer Russell Hitchens. [FIG. 2]

In his essay "People, Plants, Performance," – a title reminiscent of Shell's "People, Planet, and Profits" – Hitchens researches eight gardens in North London to analyze the entwined performance of gardeners and plants. He argues that each "enrolls" the other into performing. Hitchens even provides this diagram of the "chains of enrolment" that emerge as gardener and garden perform together. While the person enrolls plants within the garden and becomes a designer, Hitchens writes that:

> The plants performed themselves into existence as discrete entities such that they became almost considered as similar to people. And this was something that the gardeners enjoyed. They enjoyed their enrolment as happy stagehands, not lead actors, waiting for and coaxing out different beautiful plant performances. So it was equally through the active enrolment by plants themselves that the status of the gardener should be understood.[6]

What Actor-Network Theory offers Performance Studies is another way of researching multi-valent posthuman performances, performances composed of people, plants, animals, technologies, etc. In terms of the BP Gulf disaster, we might ask: what has been its impact on seabed performance, or the performance of air, water, and soil?

Posthuman misperformance I

As we've seen, the BP gulf disaster entails a wide variety of performance paradigms: technological, organizational, cultural, and financial. Each paradigm entails self-validating feedback loops and patterns of iterability that allow one to identify performances and their mis-firings. While the four performance paradigms seen in the BP disaster all involve both human and non-human actors, we usually attribute agency primarily to the people

---

[6] Russell Hitchens, "People, Plants, Performance: on actor network theory and the material pleasures of the private garden", *Social & Cultural Geography*, 4: 1(2003), p. 107.

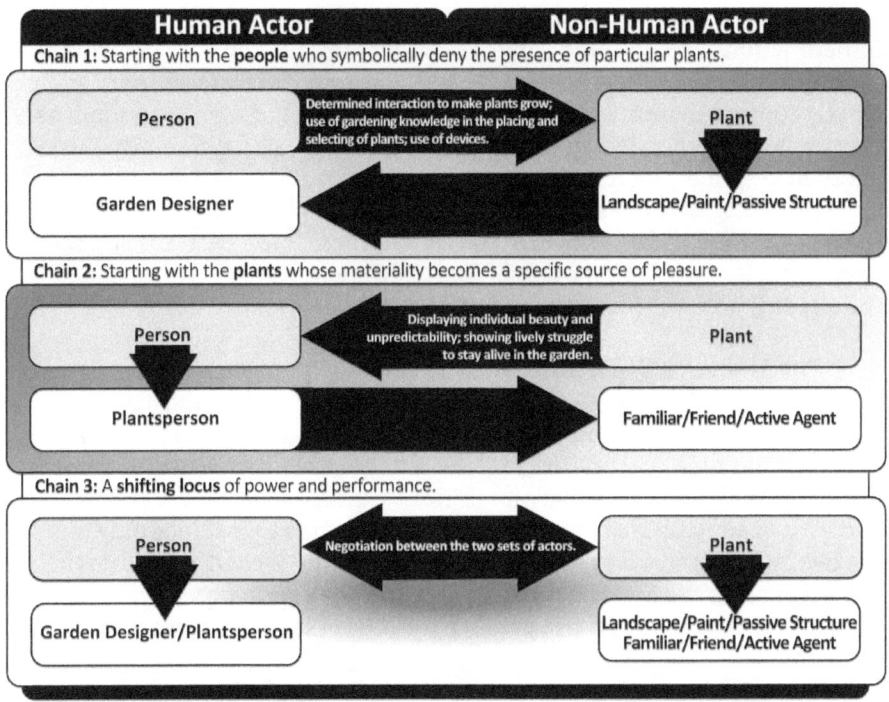

[FIG 2.] Diagram based on Figure 1 "Chains of enrolment in the garden" from Rusell Hitchens "People, Plants, Performance"

using the machinery, running a meeting, designing logos, or buying and selling stocks. What Latour, Harman, MacKenzie and Hitchens stress is that machines, buildings, materials, and financial instruments also perform, producing events not only between things and humans, but also between things and things.

Beyond the four performance paradigms, the BP disaster reveals other performances. For instance, *geologic performance* or the performance of the rock formation affected by drilling, things like geologic stability, evolution, and ability to absorb injection of fluids. There are also *water performance, soil performance, and atmospheric performance* – all are on-going, sustained performances affected in the short- and long-term by the massive release of oil and chemical dispersants in the sea water, along its winding coasts and beaches, and up in the air surrounding them. Again, I am not coining these terms or using them as metaphors: the performances of water, soil, and atmosphere are already formalized and used in mining, water management, drilling, and environmental industries. I am merely attempting to connect all these performances in the salt water of our thought.

We inhabit complex, overlapping performances in which humans initiate actions and undergo passions. We territorialize and are deterritorialized, as wave upon wave of events cascade through diverse systems, some closely connected, some not. One system's performance may trigger misperformance in another, which then gets iterated – repeated differently – in yet another. One does not navigate these massive systems as much one passes through, along, away. Disastronauts all, we are agents one moment, patients the next; at times subjects who act, at other times, objects acted up by both people and things – friends, family, and colleagues; the sea, the sand, and the air; drill holes, explosions, and contaminants.

Posthuman Misperformance II
The flight of the Whooping Crane is another example of posthuman performance – and misperformance. Whooping cranes have been an endangered species for a century. In 1941, only fifteen made the migration from Canada to their winter habitat on the Texas Gulf coast. In 1967, Canadian and American naturalists began rescuing the crane's eggs. Since only one of the two laid eggs survives, they decided to move the second eggs from their Canadian nests to a Maryland incubation lab. The eggs hatch and the babies are raised, but without proper parents, they never learned to live in the wild or reproduce.

In the past decade, a second migration plan was hatched and a more complex performance initiated. To prevent species from being wiped out by a single Gulf disaster, naturalists decided to create a second migration path parallel to first, going from Wisconsin to Florida. To keep the chicks from imprinting upon humans, caretakers always use special costumes and puppets around the birds, beginning when they hatch. Young birds are later introduced to ultra-light airplanes that will guide their migration. The project is called Operation Migration, and it has successfully flown numerous batches of cranes some 800 miles down to Florida, where they winter and then fly back on their own.

The flight of the Whooping Cranes involves animals and people, technologies and food, geography and the weather. The flights are posthuman performances and, as such, they are exposed to the travails of misperformance. In 2007, the cranes made it to Florida, but were killed in tornados near the Gulf coast.

Posthuman Misperformance III
One final thing: I began with *The Leak is in your Home Town*, and I will end with my current hometown, Madison, WI. Near it is the International Crane Foundation, which seems a thousand miles away from the BP disaster. It is, and it isn't.

The International Crane Foundation is home to some 15 species of cranes, most of which you see while walking down its curved paths. A guided tour features avian science and bird lore, and it ends at a special exhibit devoted to the whooping crane. Imagine my surprise when I discovered that the exhibit's name is the Amoco Whooping Crane Exhibit. The leak really is in my hometown.

Carol Becker
The Space Between What Is and What Wants to Be: The Abandoned Practice of Utopian Thinking[1]

"The essential function of Utopia," says Ernst Bloch to Theodor Adorno, "is a critique of what is present."[2]

I. Abandoned Practices

Why are practices abandoned? "Abandoned" connotes something that has been left behind and whose use is over. But "abandon" has another meaning, that of indulging in some uninhibited action, giving oneself over completely to something, perhaps only to find later that one has lost interest or that the practice is no longer respected or understood. However enamored we may be with an action, at some point, in response to fashion or utility, we and the species move on. To what degree this shift occurs consciously or deliberately is a matter for discussion, one that concerns the dubious term "progress" and the extent to which we are in control of the evolution of our own species – or even want to be.

In the arena of science, often one "discovery" supersedes an earlier one, which causes a way of seeing or understanding to be abandoned. Hard science attempts to "prove" the correctness of one theorem over another. "Mistaken" ideas are replaced, and then everyone's understanding should also be transformed. But even in science the acceptance of so-called objective proof can take a while to shift consciousness. Copernicus, as we know,

---

1   This essay was given at PSi No. 15 in Zagreb, Croatia, 24–28 June, 2009 in an earlier form as part of the "shift" "Abandoned Practices" in collaboration with Alan Read and Every House Has A Door. It is indebted to Ernst Bloch's magnificent study of utopia, *The Utopian Function of Art and Literature: Selected Essays*, trans. Jack Zipes and Frank Mecklenburg, MIT Press, Cambridge, Mass. 1988.
2   This epigram is taken from Bloch and from the iconic "Something's Missing: A Discussion between Ernst Bloch and Theodor W. Adorno on the Contradictions of Utopian Longing," Ernst Bloch, *The Utopian Function of Art and Literature: Selected Essays*, p. 12.

advanced a heliocentric cosmology that the earth revolves around the sun, which transformed the entire understanding of the world and our position in it. But it took one hundred years for this thinking to take hold. The earth either revolves around the sun, or the sun revolves around the earth. Both concepts cannot coexist and be understood as "truth" for very long. Eventually, observation, aided by prosthetics, proves one theorem over another, and the matter is settled, at least for rational thinkers.

In the cultural arena, the evolution of ideas and practices is much less decisive. Hand-drawn animation continues even though computer-generated animation is now available. There is even computer-generated animation that simulates hand-drawn animation – an electronic facsimile of the "real thing." Sometimes, when new practices come into use, nostalgia for the past arises. Embroidery, needlepoint, and knitting, perceived as less-than-serious endeavors for some time, have returned as "extreme craft" and have gained a niche in the visual art world, albeit one more akin to kitsch. Forms may be absent from us individually, but they may not be absent from the species altogether. For example, landscape painting, portraiture, and traditional theater have not been replaced by computer-generated imagery and performance art. The more classical forms are now merely accompanied by the contemporary remixes and re-imaginings of the older practices.

II. Utopian Thinking

When Barack Obama launched his presidential campaign with the concept of "Hope" several years ago, it seemed a strangely old-fashioned word and an even more outdated idea, yet it caught on. Hope, like faith and charity (words and even names from another time), had been long lost to the coolness of contemporary angst and cynicism. The unexpected title of Obama's book, *The Audacity of Hope: Thoughts on Reclaiming the American Dream*,[3] recognized the attitude of thinking such a revival implied. But the word did not seep into the collective consciousness until his national campaign began. Soon many people could be seen wearing campaign buttons with an image of Obama and the word "Hope" printed large underneath.

Hope is both a positive expectation and a propelling anxiety that attempts to move people into the future. It is also an emotion that can cause ambivalence and is somewhat daring because built into its aspiration is the very clear sense that the hoped-for something may or may not materialize. To *not* hope, however, is to close down possibility. For many, hope is a religious concept – hope because there is a God that will help you. The opposite of hope – despair, or the "complete absence of hope"[4] – is often called a sin

---

3   Barack Obama, *The Audacity of Hope: Thoughts on Reclaiming the American Dream*, Three Rivers Press, New York 2006.
4   *Concise Oxford English Dictionary: Eleventh Edition*, Oxford University Press, Oxford 1964, p. 388.

because it implies that one does not believe in God or that one doubts God's ability to save us from death or from ourselves.

Hope is also a spatial concept connected to the future. To hope for what does not yet exist – or, as Ernst Bloch calls it, the "not-yet-conscious"[5] – one must use one's imagination. To hope for "change," another key concept that Obama evoked, one must imagine a transformation of the present that can affect the projection of the future. Hercules wrote, "Whoever does not hope for the unhoped for will not find it".[6] An enormous retro-chic clothing billboard at the New York intersection of Houston and Broadway cleverly announced, "The Future is Back." In response we need to ask, where did it go before it returned?

III. The Unfashionable Project of Imagining the Future

For some time in the West, it has been generally understood that all hopes for a Marxist, socialist, or other alternative economic and political future have been obliterated. Even intellectuals no longer try to envision new organizations of society that are anything other than variations on known forms of capitalism. Societies that once imagined a more egalitarian state are now enamored with advanced capitalism and accept its inherent inequities, including its proffered illusion of infinite choice available to all through commodities. And those countries, like China, that had once professed commitment to such egalitarian values have long since shown their tolerance for inequity and the abuse of civil liberties. But because China is the great emerging economy, everyone is anxious to gain access to its markets, despite its prevailing political ideology. In addition, since the events of September 11 and the results of the Bush Administration's alarming policies to strengthen "national security," many people around the world no longer project an image of a welcoming democratic society onto the U.S. To them, the U.S. has become too distrustful of foreigners and too exclusionary. For many, hope – and its companion concept, utopia – have lost a geopolitical location.

These conditions have made it very unfashionable even to try to imagine a different future. And so the practice of what we might call "utopian thinking" – what Ernst Bloch calls "anticipatory illumination" – seems to have been abandoned.[7]

The word "utopia" is derived from two Greek words: *utopos*, which means "good place," and *outopos*, which means no place – a nonexistent space that is imaged into consciousness by an expectation of what the fu-

---

5. Jack Zipes, "Introduction: Toward a Realization of Anticipatory Illumination," in Ernst Bloch, *The Utopian Function of Art and Literature: Selected Essays*, p. xxxii.
6 Ibidem, p. xxv. I am also indebted to the ingenious interpretation of Bloch's theories in the introduction by Jack Zipes, pp. xi–xli.
7 Ibidem, p. xxv.

ture could be. Utopian thinking can be nostalgic, a looking back in order to move forward; a sense that in order to hypothesize the idealized future, one has to imagine an ideal past, the lost Eden or Atlantis, an imaginary conflation of time and place when the species cohabitated in an idyllic condition. That Golden Age, projected by Hesiod and others, was based on a bucolic representation of enough for all and a subsequent absence of greed, vying for power, and corruption.

Many of the great thinkers and leaders of the twentieth century also believed in the potential for humans to coexist in an ideal state. Marx was convinced that there would be progress towards equality as the inequitable system of capitalism, and the state that supported it, would inevitably collapse. Gandhi believed that within consciousness humans could achieve a personal balance, an equilibrium that would positively affect the social sphere. For his part, Oscar Wilde wrote, "Progress is the realization of utopias".[8]

Throughout the eighteenth and nineteenth centuries, there was a great deal of utopian writing – positive speculation that, in the twentieth century, became dystopian writing, like that of H. G. Wells, George Orwell, and others. Many would agree that it is much easier, and perhaps even more fun, to write about evil than to write about good; more dramatic to write about darkness than light; more compelling to read Milton's *Paradise Lost* than *Paradise Regained* or Dante's *Inferno*, rather than his *Paradiso*; to create images of hell rather than of heaven; or, for that matter, to relish the imagined evil of Satan rather than the goodness of Christ. In a similar way, perhaps it is much more engaging to talk about and re-present war and its tragedies than the equilibrium of peace. So maybe it is not too surprising that one truly compelling historic dialogue focused on the subject of peace, a conversation between Einstein and Freud called *Warum Krieg? (Why War?)*, has been all but forgotten.

Einstein's participation in the League of Nations and in its International Committee of Intellectual Cooperation offered him the possibility of inviting a person of his choice to "a frank exchange of views on any problem that [he] might select..."[9] Given world events in the years 1931–1932 and the rise of Hitler, Einstein's topic of choice should come as no surprise. Einstein posited this problem: "Is there any way of delivering mankind from the menace of war?"[10] Because he felt his understanding of the world through physics was limited, and because he knew the motivations for war were complex, he invited Freud, the recognized master of the "dark places

---

8   Oscar Wilde, *The Soul of Man Under Socialism and Selected Critical Prose*, ed. Linda Dowling, Penguin Books, New York 2001, p. 141.
9   Sigmund Freud, *New Introductory Lectures on Psycho-Analysis and Other Works, The Standard Edition of the Complete Psychological Works of Sigmund Freud, Volume XXII*, ed. and trans. James Strachey, Vintage Books, London 1932, pp. 197–215.
10 Ibidem, p. 199.

of human will and feeling," to respond. He asked Freud this question: "Is it possible to control man's mental evolution so as to make him proof against the psychosis of hate and destructiveness?" Einstein continues, "Here I am thinking by no means only of the so-called uncultured masses. Experience proves that it is rather the so called 'intelligentzia' (sic) that is more apt to yield to these disastrous collective suggestions".[11]

The result was a profound exchange that received little attention. By the time the German edition was published in 1933, Hitler, who was to drive both men into exile, was in power, and the inevitability of war and the imminent need for these Jewish intellectuals to flee their homelands were already on the horizon. Only 2,000 copies of *Warum Krieg?* were printed in German and English. So an exchange that might have received a grand reception and generated further dialogue was lost to the precipitous historical moment.

Freud ended his contribution by encouraging more discussions in the future, expressing both his fear of war's inevitability and his certainty that all that "fosters the growth of civilization" works against war. It is an interesting statement, given the extraordinary level of cultural development of Germany in the 1930s and the shocking fascination with the Third Reich of many exceedingly well-educated Europeans, such as Heidegger. But Freud believed in the potential evolution of the species, recognizing that the desire for war results from a primitive, i.e., developmentally early, and collectively shared destructive impulse that can only be sublimated by civilization. But he did not believe in false utopias. He wrote:

> The Russian Communists, too, hope to be able to cause human aggressiveness to disappear by guaranteeing the satisfaction of all material needs and by establishing equality in other respects among all the members of the community. That, in my opinion, is an illusion. They themselves are armed to-day (sic) with the most scrupulous care and not the least important of the methods by which they keep their supporters together is hatred of everyone beyond their frontiers.[12]

But he did believe that most humans despise war, and for good reasons:

> ...because everyone has a right to his own life, because war puts an end to human lives that are full of hope, because it brings individual men into humiliating situations, because it compels them against their will to murder other men, and because it destroys precious material objects which have been produced by the labours of humanity.[13]

11 Ibidem, p. 201.
12 Ibidem, pp. 211–212.
13 Ibidem, p. 213.

Recognizing that it persists and is often perceived as the only solution to national conflict, he added:

> The ideal condition of things would of course be a community of men who had subordinated their instinctual life, to the dictatorship of reason...But in all probability that is a Utopian expectation.[14]

If one were even to broach the subject of peace at this time, it would *still* be considered naïve, idealistic, foolish, or, dare we say, a hopelessly "utopian expectation" – a topic for dreamers who insist on believing that the species *is* capable of consciously determining its own future.

IV. Wilhelm Reich

Wilhelm Reich, a former student of Freud's, was a utopian thinker of an entirely different order. While Freud and others attempted to appease the Nazis by choosing a non-Jew to head the Psychoanalytic Association (fearful they would be dissolved if they did not), Reich spoke out against Hitler and was thrown out of Freud's inner circle as a result. In books such as *The Mass Psychology of Fascism*[15] and *The Murder of Christ*,[16] he made a direct connection between individual repression, group repression, group response to repression, war, and fascism. Here he attempted the psychoanalysis of civilization itself, a practice that Freud began in *Civilization and its Discontents*,[17] as if group psychology mirrored individual psychology and understanding society's collective motivations might allow us to hope *for* a happier future. He believed that humanity could be transformed through the use of orgone energy. But "orgonomy," the study of such energy, got him into trouble.

Through the creation of Orgone Accumulators – best represented by the famous orgone box – Reich hoped to harness the energy that he believed existed in the universe and use it to liberate energy blocked in the body. He perfected his understanding of the relationship of this energy to the orgasm. But by locating his theories in the body and imagining sexual energy as a key to such liberation, Reich was an easy target for his colleagues and ultimately for the U.S. Food and Drug Administration.

For Reich, as for Freud, repression was the source of individual and collective unhappiness. But he took the notion of the energy of repression and its obverse, the instinct of the libido, quite literally, believing blockages in the body thwarted the free flow of energy and thereby caused illness or at least inhibited the ability to heal. Libidinal energy and orgone energy could

---

14　Ibidem.
15　Wilhelm Reich, *The Mass Psychology of Fascism*, trans. Vincent R. Carfagno, Farrar, Strauss & Giroux, New York 1970.
16　Wilhelm Reich, *The Murder of Christ: The Emotional Plague of Mankind*, Farrar, Strauss & Giroux, New York 1953.
17　Sigmund Freud: *Civilization and its Discontents*, the Standard Edition, trans. James Strachey, W.W. Norton & Co., New York 1961.

remove these obstructions, he believed. Although engaged in extensive and durational cancer research, he never claimed that his devices could cure serious illnesses. But he did work with very ill patients in unorthodox ways, which led him to be hounded by the authorities and ultimately imprisoned.

Reich went farther and wider than his contemporaries, even inventing a machine that appeared to cause rain – a wild device called a Cloudbuster that seemed able to do for the inhibited skies what the orgone box could do for the individual body. It is reported that rain did fall on drought-ridden Arizona after Reich hooked up his machine. Inspired by this elaborate contraption, British singer Kate Bush wrote a song called "Cloudbusting." The MTV video shows the Cloudbuster inexplicably being pushed up a hill by Kate Bush and Donald Sutherland, not unlike the steamship in *Fitzcarraldo*.

So confident was Reich in his understanding of orgone energy that he even enlisted Einstein to test the ability of the orgone box to generate heat. But Einstein could find no measurable results. Reich's harassment and martyrdom in prison were also related to the prudish 1950s cultural environment and its fear of sexuality. These were the conditions that demonized the Austrian-Jewish exile who, mistakenly believed that the experimentation of new ideas would be welcomed in the United States. His assumptions, of course, proved naïve and even utopian. Literally tons of his own books were incinerated in New York in 1956, an occurrence not unlike the raiding and burning of Freud's books in Vienna in 1933. Reich died in prison in 1957.

V. The Practice of Thinking Peace and The Practice of Making Art

The use of the Orgone Accumulator became both a banned and an abandoned practice; not one of Reich's intellectual peers stood behind him when his work was condemned and he was imprisoned. Yet now it is clear how much of what we call New Age – an attempt to understand the relationship between mind and body energies – is constructed on similar notions. Many medical practitioners, especially those who incorporate Eastern philosophy into Western medical practice, would agree that there is a relationship between holding emotions in the body – i.e., repression and sublimation – and what Reich called blockages and the illnesses that can result from them.

Perhaps the practice of imagining the evolution of the species – not only in its biological sense but, in its emotional, psychological, spiritual sense – is the key to creating a world without war. As impossibly idealistic as it seems, the truth about utopian thinking is that it only exists if one is capable of aligning "one's beliefs about what is desirable with their [sic] perceptions of what is possible".[18] If one thinks that what exists is inevitable, then

---

18   Erik Olin Wright, *Envisioning Real Utopias*, Verso, London 2010, p. 285.

there *is* no space to create the imaginary, no place for utopian thought. And, it must be said, no place for art.

Art creates utopian space – an "interpretation of that which is – in terms of that-which-is-not," as Rousseau might say.[19] Every act of creation is a purposeful negation, an engagement in an organization of the world as the artist or artists would want it to be. Even if the content is somehow horrific, the fact that it could be imagined and given coordinates – a latitude and longitude externalized by the imagination – means that the particularity of this seeing has been brought into being by an individual or collective vision and given form to communicate that vision to a public. This simple act of making, or even believing that a unique interpretation of the world can occur through the act of externalizing an interior vision, is utopian. And this desire to give form to what Ernst Bloch might call "the not-yet-conscious" reveals a key imperative of utopian thought, to always "anticipate" and "illuminate"[20] what might become possible within a societal situation.

Utopia always implies a change in the communal way of organizing and understanding the world. It is never just a re-presentation of a personal desire. Art allows for an individual vision to become communal by giving it narrative, shape, color, texture, complexity, sound, movement, or whatever elements are needed to translate its intention to others. Such a belief assumes the utility of art making to demonstrate that the material world begins in the incorporeal, in ideas. We must generate new organizations of ideas, so the world will continue to progress and there will be a future.

This notion of dreaming the world into being is an ontogenic, archaic, wish-fulfilling practice, and it's also a revolutionary one. The desire to present an individual transformation of the material world that also posits a collective vision of reality, while standing in juxtaposition to the dominant collective will, is an undisputedly naïve, utopian practice. But it is one that we must refuse to abandon if the species is to survive.

---

19 Alain Martineau, *Herbert Marcuse's Utopia*, Harvest House, Montreal 1986, p. 35.
20 Bloch, xvii–xxix.

Sophie Nield
Past Imperfect, Future Tense: On History as Discarded Practice

This essay will think through some of the "mis-performances" current in our discipline, in its relationship to the past. It will outline two related problems: what we might begin to see, perhaps, as some "mis-practices" of performance history. Firstly, we will explore the increasing absence, in the present, of the past (understood as complex, situated, detailed and contextual), and its replacement with signs of "pastness": ghosts, sites, haunting, nostalgia, absence, ephemerality, loss, and mourning. Secondly, we will unpick some of the potentially interesting resonances around the apparent obsession the theatrical present currently has with its own status as a future past. This manifests, the essay proposes, in the current drive to document absolutely everything; for makers to produce and determine the legacy of the work in its very manifestation; for practitioners to resist, almost to the extent of compromising its own immanence, the possible disappearance of that work. By addressing these issues, which revolve currently in the UK academy at least, around an increasingly entrenched pedagogy of theatre history, the essay makes a case for the re-finding of the potential political efficacy of a historicised performance analysis. We begin in Berlin, with the historical encounter experienced as an encounter with the missing.

In 1988, I went to Berlin, and went through the Wall. This was my first encounter with a real and potentially dangerous border: not like crossing from England into Scotland, or even Austria into Germany, whose borders comprise painted lines on the road which the car bumps over; the passengers barely noticing. This border had checkpoints and men with guns. On that trip, we walked along lengths of the Wall, as it intersected city blocks and streets, and interrupted any kind of flow of space in that strange and interrupted city. On the Western side, there were platforms – elevations which you could climb in order to better see over the Wall into the East; often looking straight into a stretch of cleared land dotted with barbed wire and strolling pairs of East German border guards. I did not realise how much I had internalised this imposition of the Wall onto the city until I went back – around ten years later, at the time of the great regeneration of Potsdamer Platz and the centre of the city. I remember taking the 100 bus from Zoo to Alexanderplatz. It doesn't now, but in 1999 it went straight under the Brandenburg Gate. I remember the sense of shock as it drove right through the now invisible Wall. I had such a strong sense of transgression, of a superimposition of the Berlin of 1988 and the one of 1999 – the remembered space, if not as palpable as the inhabited space, at least still resonating within it.

This sense of superimposition or palimpsest of one moment of spatial production onto another is an increasingly familiar one to performance analysis, especially in relation to urban, site-specific performances. These very often take place in post-industrial, discarded spaces, or city spaces treated as the very markers of historical resonance. When site-specific performance companies such as Sans Walk,[1] Forster and Heighes,[2] Shunt,[3] or Punchdrunk[4] insert their work into environments which carry existing sets of resonances and connections, those environments produce particular sets of meanings. This is not to say of course that a conventional theatre building has no resonance – the pretence of neutrality on the part of the theatre environment has been very much exploded by the space-based analysis of Gay McAuley,[5] Una Chaudhuri,[6] and others. But where theatre architectures make claims, if not for neutrality, then at least for the production of a space which aligns with the intended meanings of the work, I would argue that there is a more complicated negotiation going on with a found space. It is not only that the space has been chosen because it has atmosphere and affect of its own to bring to the work. It is that its historical content cannot help but be deployed as a shorthand for historical meaning. It cannot help but signify "past"ness. It enacts the erasure of that which inhabited it before the performance came along. It signals the evacuation of persons, events, habits, customs, and industries. It speaks of the transition from whatever was happening before to whatever is happening now. It incorporates those

---

1 http://www.sanswalkproject.co.uk/
2 http://www.forster-heighes.org.uk/
3 http://www.shunt.co.uk/
4 http://www.punchdrunk.org.uk/
5 See Gay McAuley, *Space in performance: making meaning in the theatre*, University of Michigan Press, Ann Arbor 2000.
6 See Una Chaudhuri, *Staging place : the geography of modern drama*, University of Michigan Press, Ann Arbor 1997.

meanings, that distance, and interpolates them into the affect of the performance experience.

In disused railway tunnels behind Southwark station in 2007, watching Goat and Monkey's[7] Abélard and Heloise slop through puddles in the brick floor, shunting filthy plastic sheeting out of the way as they traverse from lecture theatre to boudoir to charnel house, the spectator cannot help but read the twin histories of the space – its function in the story of the characters, and its function as a place of brick and steam; its disguise as eleventh century France, its actual past as a piece of nineteenth century industrial London, and its present as a post-industrial signifier of absence. The impact is, paradoxically, a spatial rather than a temporal one: instead of describing, or even staging, temporal distance, the performance simply inhabits the evacuated space which historical events have left behind. That there is a profound dramaturgical and affective force to this kind of spatially dyschronous/temporally displaced experience is not in question. Yet just because it is good – perhaps even more so because it is good – it is not by default unproblematic. It still needs to be made subject to question and interrogation.

For me, what this kind of contemporary work seems to produce – and not accidentally – is an affective absence. It seems to work towards an encounter with, or staging of, the 'missing-ness' of various pasts, which the performance does not retrieve, but rather invokes through replacement, by filling the space with representation; or at the very least, the representation of absence. As I mentioned above, this is perhaps most apparent in connection to (though not exclusive to the practice of) what has come to be called site-specific theatre or performance.[8] This category, distinguishing a set of performances, interventions, stagings and events which draw particular resonance from the places in which they are produced, does not of course have the monopoly on moods of absence and nostalgia. Nevertheless, a broad range of evocatively distressed places has, over the past thirty years, housed performance work: run-down urban streets, disused hotels, decayed factories and shipyards, art galleries, trucks, warehouses. A particular point of interest here is the insistence on the transience of the performance: what Cathy Turner has termed "footprints in the sand".[9] Mike Pearson and Cliff McLucas have offered the most explicit metaphor of this relation in their proposal of the "host" and the "ghost". McLucas notes: "The host site is haunted for a time by a ghost that the theatre-makers create. Like all ghosts it is transparent and the host can be seen through the ghost." Mike Pearson

---

7 http://www.goatandmonkey.co.uk/
8 See Nick Kaye, *Site-specific Art: Performance, Place and Documentation*, Routledge, London 2000; Fiona Wilkie, "The Production of 'Site': Site-Specific theatre" in *Concise Companion to Contemporary British and Irish Drama*, eds Nadine Holdsworth & Mary Luckhurst, Blackwell, 2007, pp. 87-106.
9 Cited in Wilkie, "The Production of 'Site': Site-Specific theatre", p. 100.

elaborates, differentiating between "those (narratives and architectures) which pre-exist the work – of the host – and those which are OF the work – the ghost".[10] The sense here is of a material place, an aspect of whose "history", in the form of a performance, will come and haunt it. The peeling plaster and crumbling window frames remain as something solid that will still be seen through the air of the spectral illusion, through the fleeting and transient presence of the theatre. I have written elsewhere of the theatre's affinity for claiming the "ghost" as its natural inhabitant,[11] and, overall, I find myself still troubled by the sense of melancholy, of haunting, and of loss which permeates a lot of these spaces and works – especially where a post-industrial set of references is in play. Does a mood of reflective sorrow not create a somewhat strange set of meanings around the loss of what is, after all, everyday experience? Might we not wish to take issue with this sense of an uncontested and somehow inevitable loss and erasure? Does a tone of melancholy not work to disinvest a complex and often hard-won labour and class-based history of any political depth?

I'm not suggesting this is always the case – I saw Brith Gof's[12] HAEARN in the early 90s, which engaged explicitly and dialectically with the forging, through labour, of the industrial working class, in a site evacuated by the end of that moment of capitalist production. The issue is, however, precisely to do with performance's insistence on the moment – the moment of presence, the moment of liveness, the moment of "now". This is a consistent claim for performance, after all - one thinks of Pirandello's characters, perpetually inhabiting the moment of their crisis, or of Freddie Rokem's invocation of the actor standing in, in the present, for the witness who can no longer represent themselves.[13] So the foregrounding of this particular facet of performance's romance of itself - the romance of its own disappearance - remains troubling. Theatre history can occasionally seem to insist on its own more-ephemeral-than-thou credentials. Performance is fleeting, we say. The theatre is already fugitive, already gone, already missing in action. Of course this is so; but you can't exactly visit the French Revolution either. Pasts are all provisional – the theatre's no more or less than any other. For if the past is only empty, only loss, only absence, then where is the political; where is the potential for political interpretation, understanding, and action? Performance pasts, and performances of the past, must be construed as more than simply nostalgia and melancholy. The fantasy of theatre's ephemerality must not be projected onto all possible forms of labour, as shipbuilders and railwaymen; nurses, soldiers and vaudeville performers all

10   Cited in Kaye, *Site-specific Art: Performance, Place and Documentation*, p. 128.
11   See my: "Galileo's Finger and the Perspiring Waxwork: on Death, Appearance and the Promise of Flesh", *Performance Research*, 15:2 (2010).
12   http://www.brithgof.org/
13   See Freddie Rokem, *Performing history: theatrical representations of the past in contemporary theatre*, University of Iowa Press, Iowa City 2000.

ghost for us; appear through impossible doors, relive the long-gone bright moments of warmth and laughter and then disperse again. It is, after all, the theatre itself which has provided means to interrogate the mutability of pasts as they are exercised in any politicised present: one thinks irrepressibly here of Brecht, resisting the overtones of eternity manifest in the drive of linear, evacuated and closed narrative pasts. This illusion of inevitability must not overlay the provisionality, in the present, of the past.

And here we reach the second anxiety of this essay: the concern of the theatrical present with its own status as a future past. Much of our knowledge of theatrical history derives from the inadvertent, accidental, and random contents of the archive, which we experience in most of the great historical theatre collections. We build our versions of the past out of the material which happens to have accumulated there, through interest, inheritance, mischance and omission. There have been historical struggles great and small to identify and repair the lacunae that result from partial, and partisan, collection practices, and from the inscription of histories by particular dominant interest groups. The impetus, as well as the capacity, for performance makers to assist the future historical record by documenting both processes and outcomes is yielding an enormous amount of material. However, it is not possible to evade all of the disciplines of evidentiary selection, even by doing it in advance. As a practice, too, it begs the question: what might the impact be on the practices of the present, when a future spectator is being imagined *as the work is being made*? Is the present already being imagined as a future past? And if so, does it disappear, in and of itself, with all of its provisionality and potential? Here I introduce the second metaphor from the history of Berlin which I want to use here to expand these points: Albert Speer's identification of the conception of "ruin value". As architectural space designed to decay magnificently, this offers a model, perhaps, for a present which already contains its future past. This is not, of course, to suggest that performance documentation is a suspect practice – rather, it is to seek a historical sighting-off point for a particular kind of scopic drive: the drive, one might suggest, to see the present as the already-past.

That an architecture of totality, of magnificence and huge scale should be selected by German fascism to materialise itself is no surprise. One of the strongest trajectories within Nazi ideology was the construction of a magnificent past which would be reflected upon in a magnificent future. The present was to be organised in service of both. When, in the 1920s and early 1930s Adolf Hitler drew up plans for a monumental centre in Berlin, the plan was to build "the word in stone": monumental edifices which would be, in Hitler's words, "the shrines and symbols of a new noble culture"[14] Albert

---

14 Adolf Hitler, cited in Rainer Stollmann, "Fascist Politics as a Total Work of Art: Tendencies of the Aestheticization of Political Life in National Socialism", New German Critique, 14 (Spring 1978), pp. 41-60, p. 46.

Speer was the chosen architect: he is today most remembered in this role, but he was also Reich armaments minister, in which capacity he was tried at Nuremberg after the war, and sentenced to twenty years for the war crime of using slave labour.

The whole of the centre of Berlin was to be redrawn along monumental lines, and on a simply enormous scale. The key part of the plan was a north-south and an east-west axis. The north-south axis was a new build, and was to be a three-mile avenue, the "climactic spectacle" and "aesthetic embodiment" of the Nazi state.[15] It was planned to demolish 25,000 existing dwellings, businesses and other buildings to make way for it: the evictions were to be incorporated into the forced removal of Jewish citizens, along with others, to the camps. The boulevard was to be lined with state buildings, memorials, monuments and businesses. Scheduled for completion by the time of the planned World Fair in 1950, this moment was also to be marked by the renaming of the new, ethnically cleansed, Berlin as "Germania". The work was to be financed by wars of foreign conquest. Visitors would arrive at one of two railway termini: at the southern terminus, into a plaza 800 by 300 metres, bounded by "Avenue of Captured Weapons".

While the north-south axis itself was to be gigantic, all of its architectural proportion was to be shattered by two enormous edifices. The first was a domed Hall, "into which St Peter's Cathedral would have fitted several times over".[16] 825 feet in diameter, with an area of 410,000 square feet, it was intended that 150,000 people would be able to stand inside it. Modelled on the Pantheon in Rome, this Hall would have an opening for light in its roof larger than the entire dome of the Pantheon. It was to be fronted by a huge artificial lake, doubling its presence in reflection. The interior appointments were to be modest: seats, pillars, and a golden eagle. Like the Pantheon of the French Revolution, it was to be the utilisation of classical socio-religious space in the service of the state. Essentially, says Speer, this was to be a place of worship. Beneath the golden eagle, "the very fountainhead of the grand boulevard", would be the podium from which Hitler would speak, although Speer himself noted the pitfalls of this kind of architecture: "I tried to give this spot suitable emphasis, but here the fatal flaw of architecture that has lost all sense of proportion was revealed. Under that vast dome, Hitler dwindled to an optical zero".[17] The other monument was to be an Arch of Triumph, 400 feet in height. The model for this, the Arc de Triomphe, stands a mere 160 feet high. This Arch was envisaged as a "wor-

---

15   Wolfgang Schache, "From Berlin to 'Germania': Architecture and Urban Planning" in, *Art and Power: Europe Under the Dictators 1930-1945*, eds Dawn Ades, Tim Benton, David Elliot and Iain Boyd Whyte, The South Bank Centre/ Council of Europe, 1995, p. 327.
16   Albert Speer, *Inside the Third Reich*, Phoenix, London 1995, p. 119.
17   Ibid, p. 222.

thy monument to our dead of the world war". Chillingly, the names of projected war dead, all 1,800,000 of them, were to be chiselled in the granite. The whole project spoke of pre-imagined glory and a monstrous hubris: the triumphal arch and dome had been designed by Hitler as early as 1925.

This space was intended to invent the past, and police the present. Demonstrating the tendency of Nazi historians to simply omit the 'liberal' period, from the late eighteenth century to post-World War One, the Nazi historian Wilhelm Hausenstein wrote in 1932 of Berlin "It is as if it were grounded on nothing, but a nothing that is the nothing. Berlin has no provenance...no rootedness or history".[18] Obviously Berlin had provenance and history as an urban space. It had, however, nothing that was useful to fascism, except the memory, and continuing presence, of street violence.

The plan was also, crucially, intended to make the future secure. Deliberate strategies were generated to ensure that the space of German fascism decayed in grandeur, like the ruins of ancient Rome. Speer developed this explicitly as the "theory of ruin value," noting: "By using special materials and by applying certain principles of statics, we should be able to build structures which even in a state of decay, after hundreds or thousands of years would, more or less, resemble Roman models".[19] Hitler added: "In periods of weakness, the architecture of former glory will speak." Of course, the ruin legacies of German fascism were not decayed imperial grandeur, but the Trummelfilms made in the ruins of Berlin and other cities, as the population carted away bricks and stone from the ruined landscape.

As Julia Hell has noted, for all imperial projects, the traumatic site is Rome.[20] Ruins, according to Georg Simmel, are "places where the past with its destinies and transformations has been gathered into this instant of an aesthetically perceptible present".[21] The ruin obliterates time and gathers the past, with all its meanings, into a single present experienced moment. As Andre Bazin observed, however, in another context, the creation of any image objectifies pastness against the flow of time – creates of it, simultaneously, a present form of the past, and an anticipation of a future spectatorship. What is particularly interesting, I think, in this context, is the frequent interpolation of the spectator into the experience of the ruin: the scopic regime incorporates, often explicitly, the person of the ruin gazer into the scenario. In her sustained examination of the Nazi fascination with the classical ruin, Hell observes that many Romantic paintings of classical ruins deliberately feature a figure in the foreground, interposed between the spectator and the scene and interpreting for them/ us the "message" of the space.

18   See *Art and Power: Europe Under the Dictators 1930-1945*, eds Dawn Ades, Tim Benton, David Elliot and Iain Boyd Whyte, The South Bank Centre/ Council of Europe, 1995, p. 258.
19   Speer, *Inside the Third Reich*, p. 97.
20   See *Ruins of Modernity*, eds Julia Hell and Andreas Schönle, Duke University Press, Durham and London 2010.
21   Cited in Stephen Kern, *The Culture of Time and Space, 1880-1918*, Harvard University Press, Cambridge, Mass. 1983, p. 40.

"Scenarios of imperial ruin gazing," she notes, are often figured in such a way that "the imperial subject contemplates the metropole of a mighty empire in ruins while thinking about the future of his own empire".[22] From Scipio, weeping over the destruction of Carthage as he realises that all civilisations must, eventually, become dust, to Hitler's own tours of the Roman ruins in 1938, the "imperial melancholy" which pervades the representation of these scenes fantasises its own future, in the form of a spectator who will come and read the remains.

It would be somewhat redundant to point out that most creators of works of art of any kind have, presumably, some kind of eye on a future spectator. However, this has been, perhaps, underplayed, by a theatre and performance field which emphasises so much the moment of its presence, and explicitly figures any documentation and recording as necessarily flawed and partial – almost a supplemental piece of creative activity. It may of course seem wilfully provocative to suggest that the performance document is a ruin – or worse, that the document seeks to live forever, in some 1000 year Reich of the accompanying DVD. I think what I am trying to propose is more that the drive to document, to sustain, and to never lose anything, works to drag the event and its historicity again and again into a present, and, more explicitly, produces that present as the already past. So we wait, ahead of ourselves, already looking back – ghosting ourselves, appearing both live and in future memory; these spectres of our future selves haunting the experience of the present moment. The compressing of historical time into the "moment" of the projected ruin also smoothes out any contradictions within historical process, making a dramaturgically legible account of where we were, and where we are now, and, crucially, *where we will be* – inevitable, unalterable, incontestable. As Johannes von Moltke has observed, "At their most static, ruins suggest historicised closure... the ruin is an index of past wholeness as opposed to the open-endedness of the fragment. At their most challenging, ruins confront us with the foreclosed futures of an earlier era, reintroduce contingency into history and offer 'memory traces of an abandoned set of futures".[23] Is the past, then, to become nothing more than the symptom of the present, as the present is perhaps already symptom of the future? Marie-Jose Mondzain has pointed out that spectatorial distance is already a historical distance. In her treatment of the cave paintings of Chauvet, she notes the moment in which the hand is withdrawn from the wall, leaving its own image in pigment: this, she argues, is the moment in which the human being enters historical time.[24] It

---

22   Julia Hell, "Imperial Ruin Gazers, or Why Did Scipio Weep?" in *Ruins of Modernity*, eds Julia Hell and Andreas Schönle, Duke University Press, Durham and London 2010, pp. 169-192, p. 170.
23   Johannes Von Moltke, "Ruin Cinema", in *Ruins of Modernity*, eds Julia Hell and Andreas Schönle, Duke University Press, Durham and London 2010, pp. 395 – 417, p. 401.
24   See Marie Jose Mondzain, *Homo Spectator*, Bayard, Paris 2007.

is in the recognition of the literal, spatial, distance between the maker and the made that the spectator is born – whether there and then in that moment of withdrawing the hand, or years, even centuries later. I proposed at the beginning of this essay that the historical can be treated as a relation of space - it seems appropriate to close by proposing that the present should remain a relation of time. For it is time, and the possibility of contradiction, choice, action, and struggle which should properly inhere to it, that offers us political choice and determination. It seems to me that somewhere in the intersection of theatre histories, with their invocation of absence, presence, representation and time, and performance studies, with its paradigms of space, becoming and loss, there should be a possible fission, creating enough energy to address these questions, and strategise our recovery of these discarded practices. There must be something more for us here than ruin, melancholy and nostalgia. There must be something more to for us to see here, to be here, than ghosts.

Ana Vujanović
Second-hand Knowledge (in slalom through Yugoslav cultural-artistic space)

Initially, I elaborated the concept of second-hand knowledge in order to contribute to a rereading of history of performing arts in former Yugoslavia since the 1960s.[1] That venture, envisaged to result in a lexicon of poetic terms *Parallel Slalom*, aimed to respond to the need for conceiving new and existing terms and notions employed in self-definition of the regional artistic and cultural (notably performing arts) scenes. Therefore what I try to do in my writing on the term – following the method of the lexicon itself – is a deconstruction of the binary pairs that discursively, that is materially, frame East and West, former East and former West, the centre and the periphery, etc.

It might come as a surprise that I chose to focus on a "mis-performance", a weak and rather negative notion even when it comes to the (fairly rare) opportunity of self-definition. First of all, I would like to clarify that I am not interested in the self-victimizing glorification of the mis-performance whatsoever. But second of all, I agree that the notion belongs with those that have conceptually outlined the regional cultural-artistic scene, both in poetic terms and in terms of an outside view.[2] Therefore I find it a

---

[1] The text was initially commissioned for The East Dance Academy's *Parallel Slalom, A Lexicon of Non-aligned Poetics*, ed. by Bojana Cvejić and Goran Sergej Pristaš, Walking theory, Belgrade, Centre for drama art, Zagreb 2013, and published there under the title "Second-hand Knowledge", pp. 120-129. The version that you are reading was firstly prepared as a paper to be presented at the Performance Studies international #15 follow-up in Rijeka (Croatia) in 2010, and then reworked again in 2012 for the current publication.

[2] In fact many of the self-determinative terms included in the lexicon are usually used in a negative sense. Those are, for instance: delaying productivity, second-hand knowledge, amateurism and dilettantism, always being too late, etc. Similar

real challenge, whose deconstruction, if conducted correctly, can reveal how notions are put in binary pairs and what the political implications of their mutual defining as oppositions might be. Therefore in my revisiting the term "second-hand knowledge", I won't try to enact the inversion of the binary pair it belongs to (first-hand knowledge / second-hand knowledge), which will eventually make it positive.[3] Instead, I will rather employ Derrida's method of deconstruction in the strict theoretical terms: as a critical analysis of the very conceptual platforms on which the concepts and binary pairs are based, and which consequently render them negative, or positive as well. So the method of revisiting focuses on the questions: Why do we consider the concept of second-hand knowledge negative, why do we see it in the pair with the first-hand knowledge, how do we define their specificities and differences, and according to what (conceptual and social) criteria do we put them in hierarchical relations? Such a gesture of breaking the commonsense can create unexpected and annoying results: It can contest the natural weakness and negativity of the concepts, and face the readers with social, political, and economic mechanisms of regulation of knowledge and identities production and circulation at the art and cultural scenes (both of the past and of today).

• • •

It is a common place or even a commonsense that the largest bulk of knowledge reaching the peripheries is second-hand knowledge. And these peripheries – it is us: Serbia, South-Eastern Europe, Yugoslavia, the Balkans. There is no irony or offence here, for these are the peripheral regions, provinces, and margins with respect to the centres of the First World, Europe, the European Union, the Austro-Hungarian Empire, or the Ottoman Empire.

Let us for instance consider briefly some prominent examples from the 20th-century art in Serbia. Dadaism reached us through the studies of Dragan Aleksić in Prague and his connections with Dadaists circles. Eurythmics and Laban's method arrived directly through the gymnastic dance workout and dance practice of Maga Magazinović, who studied with Max Reinhardt and Rudolf Steiner. Early conceptual art arrived mostly with Hungarian magazines through Hungarian minority in Vojvodina, the north

---

approach one can find at the more cynical exhibition 7 Sins: Ljubljana – Moscow (2004/05). These sins, supposedly typical for Eastern Europe, are: collectivism, utopianism, masochism, cynicism, laziness, un-professionalism, and love of the West; see 7 Sins – Ljubljana-Moscow, http://www.kunstaspekte.de/index.php?tid=8731&action=termin [accessed 30 August 2011].
3   Which was an aspect of the 7 Sins exhibition's curatorial tactic: "They [7 sins] can be – from an outside, presumably Western point of view – understood as weaknesses and imperfections, but they are also 'virtues', qualities that Eastern, Slavic countries can contribute to European culture to make it richer and more diverse. For example, utopianism is an antidote to pragmatism, stressing the dimension of hope and future perspectives. Laziness gives artists time to concentrate on themselves and the questions that obsess them. Since artists from the East are often not 'real professionals', they can really love what they do, etc.", 7 Sins – Ljubljana-Moscow, "Concept of the Exhibition" http://www.kunstaspekte.de/index.php?tid=8731&action=termin [accessed 30 August 2011].

province of Serbia. Afterwards, the *Tanztheater* reached us through the modern ballet of Sonja Vukićević, and theatre anthropology of the 1990s through few local students of Eugenio Barba in Odin teatret. And today we also have our versions of new British drama and conceptual dance as predominant practices at the contemporary performing arts scene...[4]

Let me go step by step.

During the socialist period, the Yugoslav art scene of the 1950s and 60s was regulated through a system of official (state) mediators between the Eastern and Western scenes. After the period of the "programs of cultural exchange" planned by the state –which included touring of big, representative productions by the national theatre houses – several curatorial international festivals appeared in the late 1960s and 70s – such as the BITEF (Belgrade international theatre festival: New tendencies).[5] These mediators made it possible to have occasional flashes of first-hand knowledge about the international art scene. At BITEF, local audience could see Jerzy Grotowski, Robert Wilson, Performance Group, Living Theater, Pina Bausch, La Mamma, Tadeusz Kantor, Susanne Linke, Peter Brook, Wim Vandekeybus, René Pollesch, Anne Teresa de Keersmaeker, and many others. But was it really so? I will mention some additional details, such as the fact that Anne Teresa de Keersmaeker came to BITEF only in 2005, while the Wooster Group, or Jérôme Bel, Xavier Le Roy, Boris Charmatz and other authors of so-called "conceptual dance" never did. However, this sort of limitation is indispensable, since the role of the mediator does not even entail neutral facilitation of direct insights, but rather planning, selection, and representation. Therefore, even that apparent first-hand knowledge was, strictly speaking, knowledge at second-hand: it was a sort of knowledge where someone else was making decisions about its occurrence, context, and even availability.

During the 1990s the second-hand knowledge achieved an especial status in our social context. The civil wars in SFRYugoslavia, along with the impoverishment, border closing, and international sanctions against the FRYugoslavia resulted in the second-hand knowledge becoming almost the only possible option in the region. Entire generations of theatre directors, theoreticians, performers, and choreographers were acquiring their knowledge about the contemporary international scene from illegally photocopied foreign books, pirated video recordings, and even by imaginary

---

4 See the historicization and conceptualization of all practiced mentioned in Ana Vujanović, "Historical Avant-garde and Performing Arts", "Performance Art: From Neo-avant-garde to Conceptual Art", "Alternative Theatre in the 1990s", "New – Post-Political – Drama", and "The Contemporary Dance Scene" in: *Art in Serbia in the 20th Century, vol. 1.*, ed. Miško Šuvaković, Orion Art, Belgrade 2010.

5 See: http://www.bitef.rs; *BITEF: 40 godina novih pozorišnih tendencija*, ed. Branka Prpa, Istorijski arhiv Beograda, Belgrade 2008; Georg Schöllhammer, "An Ontologist Observes", *Springerin* no. 1: „Other Modernities", Vienna 2007, http://www.springerin.at/dyn/heft_text.php?textid=1900&lang=en [accessed 30 August 2012]; Ana Vujanović, "New Theatre Tendencies: Bitef festival", in *Art in Serbia in the 20th Century (Umetnost u Srbiji u 20. veku), vol. 1*, ed. Miško Šuvaković, Orion art, Belgrade 2010.

updating art books that had been published in the 1970s and 1980s. We call it "paper reality".

And today when I, and many of us educated basically in that way, take part in the international artistic and theoretical context is good moment to reconsider this term. Is it so bad? Does it make me and us weak? Late? Unreliable? Or not? Or what?

Epistemologically speaking, second-hand knowledge is a mediated, unempirical type of knowledge, gained without a direct insight into the subject. And while researching on a topic is a way of gaining first-hand knowledge, someone's account of the same topic (lecture, report, or presentation) is a way of acquiring second-hand knowledge. First-hand knowledge we gain through perception and experience; second-hand knowledge by believing what someone else is telling us.

In art, we often obtain second-hand knowledge from acknowledged authorities, regardless of whether their authorization is official, such as in theoreticians, critics, recognized artists, and professors, or we simply trust them, since they are our peers, well-informed persons, etc. In many cases, moreover traditionally, artistic knowledge is transferred as a set of *techné* through the disciples or followers of a particular school, master, or initiator of a paradigm. Besides, perhaps the most common form of second-hand knowledge on art is "knowledge from books", today including electronic formats and web sources as well. It is a non-empirical knowledge acquired from written sources depicting, describing, or explaining certain artistic phenomena, works, or events (scholarly literature, catalogues, booklets, reviews). Second-hand knowledge is not restricted to art, and its character and status change through various social fields in which it is manifested: art, science, religion, jurisdiction, or everyday speech.

In the domain of religion, second-hand knowledge is mostly perceived to be basic knowledge. Its validity rests on the fact that in the majority of religions the source is absent, and in its absence the trust in its mediators – like the first disciples, scribes of the holy scripts, and then priests – is unconditional. An important example or an exception that confirms the rule can be found in St Augustine's *Confessions*. His interior struggle was based on the fact that, as a former pagan thinker, he could not bear to have only second-hand knowledge, as was common in Christianity. He was therefore desperately seeking knowledge at first-hand: to obtain answers on God from God himself. The magnificence of his struggle, from a Christian point of view, is precisely in the fact that he was struggling against his own disbelief.

In law and jurisdiction, second-hand knowledge plays a great role and at the same time has an ambivalent status: it is necessary, but its credibility is always subject to doubt. A typical example is testimony. All testifying is second-hand knowledge since it is a story told by witnesses. Here we can see how the testimony acquires the status of "performative", to which we assign "juridical" power as if it has it itself.[6] Namely, its illocutory dimension owes exactly to the protocol and conventional situation in which it is performed, and here lays its power and weakness at the same time. The characteristic situation is a trial, in which the testimony is given the status of a statement that is constitutive of the event reconstruction, under the obligation of telling the truth, where the promise, we know it, may be kept or not. Or, speaking in a wider perspective one can find testimony in the form of media report, which is based on the premises of objectivity and credibility of journalism, even though increasingly doubted, as well as in everyday communication, where its performativity is based on the voluntary trust in someone who is reporting an event, for example, an authority or a friend.[7] Elisabeth Fricker, whose analysis is focused on the differentiation between the perception and the testimony, conceives of the testimony as a paradigm of second-hand knowledge that characterizes most of how we learn:

> One issue concerns the depth and extent of our epistemic dependence on testimony, as we may label this broad epistemic source: Do we have any knowledge at all that is free of epistemic dependence on what we have learned from others?[8]

> Conceptually speaking, if not epistemically, we climb up the ladder of testimony, to then throw it away. Mummy saying "red" was how I learned what is called "red". But as I become a master of folk physics and folk psychology, I appreciate that Mummy's saying something is red is one thing, its being so another – even if she is in fact always truthful and accurate.[9]

Keeping the Fricker's thesis in mind, I would move now to the terrain of everyday speech. There, second-hand knowledge has negative connotations, meaning: unverified knowledge, knowledge that is not based on factual insight, entailing the lack of basic understanding of the facts and similar. I would ponder this a little, assuming that the commonsense is nothing but an internalized pattern of ideologically instilled way of thinking. On epistemological level, these negative connotations also indicate faith in the objective, positive knowledge gained in a direct, empirical way: by perception and factual insight, experience, and analysis. That is exactly the definition of first-hand knowledge, with its imperatives of objectivity, neutrality, and positivity. And from that viewpoint, all interpretation is undesirable, since

---

[6] I refer here to the J. L. Austin's theory of performative utterances and speech acts. See John L. Austin, *How to do things with Words*, Clarendon, Oxford 1962.
[7] See further in Elizabeth Fricker, "Second-Hand Knowledge," *Philosophy and Phenomenological Research*, 73: 3 (2006), pp. 592-618.
[8] Elizabeth Fricker, "Second-Hand Knowledge," p. 592.
[9] Ibidem, p. 611.

it distorts the "image of reality" as it really is. However, this everyday use of the term is not naive or simply inaccurate. We should understand that it has been firmly tied to the basic ideology of modern Western epistemology since the moment when it gave preference to scientific insight over all other types of knowledge – religious, intuitive, or artistic. On the other side, there is the entire legacy of 20th-century relativist and constructivist theory in social sciences and humanities, indicating that all experience or first-hand knowledge is subject both to perceptive errors or slips and to our own interpretation, determined by the subject's position, her social context, interests, ideology that operate in her cognitive political unconscious etc. Such arguments can be traced back even to the Marxist theory, followed by the Frankfurt school, then hermeneutics, poststructuralism, and cultural studies. Within these theoretical frameworks, second-hand knowledge is both important and necessary, since it enlarges, complements, and transforms our experience, making it possible for us to gain abundant insight, even when we are not prepared for its acquisition or capable of it at the given moment.

Considering the fact that second-hand knowledge is not based on personal experience and perception, but rather communicated to us, one of its essential aspects is the social situation. Patrick Wilson, author of the book *Second-Hand Knowledge; An Inquiry into Cognitive Authority* has delineated a social epistemology that centres on the notion and the mechanisms of functioning of the "cognitive authority".[10] In the context of information society – characterized by the hyper-production of information – Wilson has begun by analyzing the generation of cognitive material in an individual and its relationship with expertise, after which he has dealt with the mechanisms of knowledge industry, ending with the issue of control of (the content of) information. Although the author maintains the dichotomy between the first-hand and the second-hand knowledge, he at the same time destabilizes the border by locating the learning in social contexts and processes, which we are sometimes aware of and quite often not. According to Wilson, cognitive authority is a function that always operates in the process of gaining knowledge in a social situation. In defining it the author tries to distinguish between the cognitive (or epistemic) authority, predicated on claims to certain knowledge, such as a specialist, an expert on specific matters and the "performatory" (or administrative) authority, who is entitled to occupy a position or is authorized to judge, to forbid or command something, like a judge.[11] However, the demarcation line becomes somewhat unstable when Wilson infers that the cognitive authority is dependent on social perception and recognition. That is to say, there is no cognitive authority *per se*, while our recognition and appreciation of the authority relies on such things as

---

10   Patrick Wilson, *Second-Hand Knowledge; An Inquiry into Cognitive Authority*, Greenwood Press, Westport CT 1983.
11   Ibidem, pp. 13-35.

the reputation, the public opinion, and the performance of the speaker. At that point the cognitive authority becomes "performatory" as well, so what differentiates her from the other sort of authority may be only the official, administrative entitlement. In any case, in my viewpoint the most important Wilson's question in regard to cognitive authority may be formulated in the following way: given the abundance of "texts" (in poststructuralist sense) that surround me, that are accessible to me, which one will become the authority as the source of knowledge (for me)? Which one will give me a key and make it possible for me to systematize and understand the complex nets of signifying hyper-production? In the current context of Internet expansion, with numerous other information and communication media enabled by digital technologies, this question becomes ever more urgent and more complex, since hyper-production has been greatly accompanied or even substituted by hyper-exchange of information and knowledge. In that situation, where we are overwhelmed with various net portals, platforms, blogs, generators and aggregators, the source is "normally" lost, and the exchange, recombination, editing, sharing, etc. is becoming the production itself.

I hope that the outline of argumentation that I have presented here offers sufficient material for attempting a reinterpretation of second-hand knowledge as a poetic term of Yugoslav cultural scene, and perhaps also for understanding its negative connotations as a habit of everyday speech. On the one hand, as I pointed out above, that habit is rooted in modern Western epistemology, which has already been thoroughly examined and contested, while on the other hand it reductively and paradoxically refers to the practices of learning that are regularly used even by those who speak of second-hand knowledge as a negative term. For instance, if the ideological lens is suddenly turned inside out, one can see that the fact that we have illegally shared and photocopied books or pirated VHSs, CDs and DVDs is not specific for this context of periphery at all but is something that is also done both by the millions of "ordinary consumers" worldwide and by leftist Western circles and their cultural-artistic scene, from Pirate Cinema Berlin to Pirate Bay and numerous "free online libraries", with the purpose of resisting the neoliberal market of art and culture, encouraging principles of sharing and of alternative distribution of knowledge.

Although we cannot conclude from this deconstruction that second-hand knowledge is better than the first-hand one – nor is my aim to advocate this inversion – we can conclude that second hand knowledge is not specific for the artistic and cultural context of the margins, but exists both on the East and West, as a regular and common type of knowledge, and that today, after all contemporary theory in social sciences and humanities from the 1960s on, there is no satisfying epistemic argument that could discard second-hand knowledge as less authentic, objective, and reliable type of knowledge comparing to the first-hand one.

After these dichotomies are contested this way, it seems that the reason for still predominant negative connotation of the notion and its substantializing linkage to the cultural peripheries lies somewhere else. I would say that it could be found only in the social categories, the categories of having opportunity and being privileged to access the real, or even always imaginary *source*, which by itself marks the centre. Thus, whenever we use the notion second-hand knowledge this way we should be aware of and take responsibility for its ideological legacy and stake into a cognitive colonization or into an internalized self-victimization, which are the two sides of a coin. Since, what is crucial in the social sense, even the social sense of art, is that the hierarchical relationship between first-hand and second-hand knowledge symptomatically reflects the hierarchical order of centre and periphery in the global process of knowledge production, distribution, and exchange. Thus, if we say that in the region of Yugoslavia second-hand knowledge has always been the dominant form of knowledge, that statement also has a negative connotation, since its function is precisely to place the region in a subordinate position with respect to the centre. It is only in this way that the periphery is actually interpellated and becomes periphery, which is how it comes into the position of importing knowledge (concepts, technologies, information, paradigms, trends, etc.) with smaller or larger distortions and delays.

However, I would like to add something at the end.

It is not quite correct to say that the only knowledge we have ever had in our context is second-hand knowledge. If you go back to the beginning of the text, you will see that my framework is precise enough: all the while, I have been speaking only of the knowledge that is coming from abroad, from centre to periphery. But beside that, there is of course also specific, first-hand knowledge that has been and is produced here. I will mention here Zenitist movement within historical avant-garde and its provocative figure of artistic disobedient named "Balkan barbaric-genius", inter-media artistic practice from the 1996s called "verbo voco visual", or the Marxist philosophical movement Praxis school, among many other examples. But the thing is that this knowledge has almost never entered the global circulation of knowledge. This way, these discourses mostly rest outside of the Rancièrean "partition of the sensible" of the international Artworld – as invisible images, voices that are not heard, or that are heard only as a noise from the EAnd today, when I am trying to reopen that question I am doing it with the help of second-hand knowledge (here, by referring to western theory) again. It is necessary, I would say, as it forms a discursive platform for my activity when I want it to become widely (namely, so-called "internationally") recognizable. Perhaps that is the only possible relationship between centre and periphery, however cynical that may sound.

However, there is maybe something "good" in all that, something reminding of the Lacanian discourse of the master-servant in terms of constructing the models of knowledge and of the social predications of the value placed on knowledge. From this viewpoint, the master discourse is exactly that what puts the servant's one at work, and whose work will undermine it. Making a long leap, I would say that we should never forget that the servant must know both her own language and that of her master in order to survive, while the master, although his discourse is advantageous in all respects, and perhaps precisely because of that, remains always deprived of understanding the language of servants. Opening this issue here is not about the servants' secret gratification, not at all, but about reminding on the permanent threats to the master discourse and its hegemonic symbolic matrix of truth, whatever it is.

2012, CC BY-NC-SA 3.0 Srbija:
http://www.creativecommons.org.rs

Part II
MIS-INCORPORATIONS, MIS-PRESENTATIONS, MIS-SPECTATORSHIPS

Part II
MIS-INCORPORATIONS,
MIS-PRESENTATIONS
MIS-RECIPROCATIONS

Arseli Dokumacı
Misfires that Matter: Habitus of the Disabled Body

[T]he fundamental principles of the arbitrary contents of the culture…are placed beyond the grasp of consciousness, and hence cannot be touched by voluntary, deliberate transformation, cannot even be made explicit.[1]

As I type this letter, I feel the pressure that the top of my right middle and index fingers make with the keyboard; the effect that this pressure makes with their corresponding metacarpal bones; the warmth and tenderness of these bones and whatever is surrounding them. As I type this letter and move my fingers onto this one, the humeral head of my right shoulder reverberates with the pain accompanying this millisecond journey.[2]

Everyday life would turn into chaos, be almost impossible to inhabit, if we had to constantly rehearse our movements and attend to our moving body in each of its posture transformations. "It is a fundamental premise of cognitive psychology that the amount of attention that can be allocated to various activities is limited".[3] In a way, we need to ignore the movements of our eyeballs in their sockets so as to understand the meaning of these letters. In point of fact, to be able to function in daily life, we need to overlook what has animated us in the first place and let our bodies disappear from our awareness.[4]

The bodily "disappearance",[5] which characterizes one's being-in-the-world and which makes mundane life flow, is also what makes habitus so ef-

---

1 Pierre Bourdieu, *Outline of a Theory of Practice*, trans. R. Nice, Cambridge University Press, Cambridge 1977, p. 94.
2 Author's personal notes, 2013.
3 John Kihlstrom, "The cognitive unconscious", *Science*, 237 (1987), p. 1447.
4 See Drew Leder, *The Absent Body*, University of Chicago Press, Chicago, IL 1990.
5 Ibidem, p. 25.

fective in its trade. In letting routinized phenomena consume as little attentional capacity as possible, bodily unawareness allows phenomena that one has never willed or consciously engaged in to remain in operation beyond the reach of one's will and reflection. What ontologically makes habitus so effective in its trade, at the same time renders it methodologically so resistant, if not impossible, to investigate.[6] After all, how can one study what is "beyond the grasp of consciousness"[7] or "ask people to reflect on aspects of their lives they themselves are unaware of"?[8]

In the following, I take on this challenge of method and present an investigation of habitus qua invisible disabilities. I listen to what invisibly disabled people have to say about banal practices of the everyday which they, by way of their bodily image, are expected to perform and which they, due to an underlying impairment, often misperform. The series of testimonies[9] are taken from people who live with mobility-related pain, resulting from a chronic disease that affects their joints and movements. The testimonies are structured à la Marcel Mauss[10] in order to apply what he developed at a "program level" to actual cases of *body techniques*[11] and develop a theorization of habitus thereof.

Techniques of rest

Annick is in her 40's, unemployed (due to illness) and living with her husband in a country house in Quebec. She has no visible deformations but, at the time of interview, had severe pain and inflammation in her joints. In the following excerpt, we are talking about how the disease affects socializing with friends.

> ANNICK: If we go at friends for supper, you know at eight thirty, I am starting to yawn, I have a hard time staying sitting at the table with everybody. I want to lie on the couch but... It's very awkward so...

---

[6] Bourdieu's conceptualization of habitus is known to be strongly influenced by the work of Maurice Merleau-Ponty and his emphasis on a pre-reflexive self (see Raymond Lau, "Habitus and the Practical Logic of Practice: An Interpretation", *Sociology*, 38: 2 (2004), pp. 369-87). But Bourdieu's own empirical work is criticized for downplaying the importance of lived experience and individuals' phenomenal experiences of their bodies (see Abdellah Hammoudi, "Phenomenology and Ethnography: On Kabyle *Habitus* in the Work of Pierre Bourdieu", in eds J. Goodman and P. Silverstein, *Bourdieu in Algeria: Colonial Politics, Ethnographic Practices, Theoretical Developments*, University of Nebraska Press, Lincoln & London 2009, p. 220 and Chris Shilling, *The Body and Social Theory*, Sage, London 2012).

[7] Pierre Bourdieu, *Outline of a Theory of Practice*, p. 94

[8] Paul Sweetman, "Revealing habitus, illuminating practice: Bourdieu, photography and visual methods", *The Sociological Review*, 57: 3 (2009), p. 496

[9] Excerpts are taken from the materials of my ethnographic fieldwork that I conducted in 2009 (in İstanbul, Turkey and in various locations in Québec, Canada) with people who have rheumatoid arthritis-related invisible disabilities.

[10] Marcel Mauss "Techniques of the body", in eds M. Lock and J. Farquhar, *Beyond the Body Proper: Reading the Anthropology of Material Life*, Durham: Duke University Press, Durham 2007 [1935], pp. 50-68.

[11] The reader might be confused about my rather interchangeable use of the terms body techniques, movements, gestures, actions, acts, tasks, activities and practices. This is a deliberate shift I make to revoke any idea of distinctiveness among these units. In the temporality of *doing*, there exists no pause to action therefore no calculus that tells where a movement ends and a technique begins; where a technique ends an action beings and where an action ends and another begins. Such distinctions can only exist in conceptual thought.

ARSELI: Do you sometimes cancel appointments because you don't feel good, or do you go out less often?
ANNICK: Oh yes, a lot, a lot... [Pause] Or my husband goes, and I don't go with him. You know I say, "Go see your friends. It's good. I can't go." It's fine, you know. Sometimes, it is fine. Sometimes I wish... [Pause] Sometimes I wish, everybody would come here and we have supper in the bedroom and I can just be comfortable, like they are comfortable, you know. [Crying] [Pause] But that... it's crazy, you know... My friend Nancy sometimes has come. I was in bed, I couldn't get up and she sat on the bed and we had a good conversation. But at the same time, people are not comfortable with that, I can understand. You can't say, 'Come over, and I will be lying in my bed. We can have supper together'. You know, it doesn't work. It is just... impossible.

Referring to the deployments of "social" in sociology as if it were some form of an abstract force, Bruno Latour writes that social is not a kind of "glue" fixing things otherwise connectable but *"what is glued together by many other types of connectors"*.[12] Latour's statement could be understood better if one were to take out *things* from the event of "socializing" described above. Remove the tables, for instance, and guests would begin moving their chairs around and rarely keep the arrangement and face-to-face direction invoked by the presence of a table. Take the chairs out of the picture and people would be standing more and more ready to shift between different locations and actions. They might chat on the corner, in the middle; moving through circles of people; lingering in the kitchen; going to other rooms. Or they might lie on the couch as Annick herself wishes to be able to do. In a way, it is by way of being seated (and giving up the readiness to act implied by being on foot) and of being seated around a table (facing people in their plurality) that the likelihood of performing other actions at that moment is reduced and collective attention is more easily directed to a particular set of actions and gestures.

A report from the UK suggests that "67 per cent of children rock backwards and forwards on their chairs" in order to find a position that they are comfortable in and avoid assuming C-shape posture.[13] This indicates that sitting on chairs, especially sitting "properly", probably is not so good for the body if children instinctively seek ways of protecting themselves against it.[14] As a matter of fact 30 percent greater pressure is exerted on the spinal discs

---

12   Bruno Latour, *Reassembling the Social: An Introduction to Actor-Network-Theory*, Oxford University Press, Oxford 2005, p. 5.
13   G. Knight and J. Noyes, "Children's behavior and the design of school furniture", *Ergonomics*, 4: 5 (1999), pp. 755-67 quoted in P. Wilkin "Are you sitting comfortably? The political economy of the body", *Sociology of Health and Illness*, 31:1, pp. 35-50, p. 46.
14   A. C. Mandal, *The Seated Man: Homo Sedens*, Daffnia Publications, 1985, pp. 36-42 quoted in P. Wilkin 'Are you sitting comfortably? The political economy of the body', *Sociology of Health and Illness*, 31:1 (2009), pp. 35-50, p. 46.

when sitting than when standing[15] and it is no coincidence that longer hours spent on chairs are accompanied by increasing prevalence of low back pain complaints.[16] Why then, one wonders, do people keep sitting on chairs and continue to believe that "a better chair could solve our back problems – many of which were induced by the practice of chair sitting in the first place"?[17]

Sociologist of architecture, Galen Cranz, says "our biology, physiology and anatomy have less to do with our chairs than do pharaohs, kings and executives".[18] From the erect style of sitting adopted by the kings in antiquity[19] to medieval seats of grandeur in churches,[20] chairs were long the sole prerogative of royalty, religious dignitaries and the aristocracy in the pre-modern era. It was only in the 19th century, when industrialization had moved most of labour from fields to factories and offices[21] and mass manufacture made furniture more affordable[22] that chairs become available to those outside the ruling elite. But along with the device inherited from those in positions of authority, so were its traditional design; the erect and singular sitting style that this design induced and the symbolic meanings that this style had been associated with. In fact, there was a "contrast between the conservatism of chair design and the rapidity of social change during the nineteenth century".[23] Seating devices were rapidly entering into homes, classrooms, offices, spaces of leisure and transport, introducing collective sitting practices and seating arrangements. But this democratization was not met by a parallel expansion in seating codes and symbolic meanings. The emerging middle class emulated the seating codes and designs "previously restricted to the upper classes"[24] and chairs, where introduced (family unit, offices, etc.), continued to reflect hierarchies in the form of age, gender and status distinctions[25]. To participate in these emerging quotidian practices shaped around furniture, the new group of sitters "had to believe... [they] were sitting comfortably".[26]

Obviously this myth still continues in the now post-industrialized societies. But, from a historical perspective, one can say that it is less a

15 Galen Cranz, *The Chair: Rethinking culture, body, and design*, W.W. Norton and Company, New York 1998, p. 97.
16 See *Low Back Pain Initiative*, Department of Noncommunicable Disease Management, eds George Ehrlich and Nikolai Khaltaev, The World Health Organization, 1999, apps.who.int/iris/bitstream/10665/66296/1/WHO_NCD_NCM_CRA_99.1.pdf [last accessed: November, 2013] and Janet Freburger et al. "The rising prevalence of chronic low back pain", *Achieves of Internal Medicine*, 169: 3 (2009), pp. 251-8.
17 Galen Cranz, *The Chair: Rethinking culture, body, and design*, p. 18.
18 Ibidem, p. 23.
19 Peter Opsvik, *Rethinking Sitting*, Gaidoros Forlag AS, Oslo 2009, p. 22.
20 Peter Wilkin "Are you sitting comfortably? The political economy of the body", *Sociology of Health and Illness* 31:1 (2009), pp. 35-50, p. 42.
21 Galen Cranz, *The Chair: Rethinking culture, body, and design*, p. 45.
22 Jenny Pynt and Joy Higgs, *A History of Seating, 3000 BC to 2000 AD: Function Versus Aesthetics*, Cambria Press, New York 2010, p. 162-3.
23 Galen Cranz, *The Chair: Rethinking culture, body, and design*, p. 45.
24 Jenny Pynt and Joy Higgs, *A History of Seating, 3000 BC to 2000 AD: Function Versus Aesthetics*, Cambria Press, p. 163.
25 Galen Cranz, *The Chair: Rethinking culture, body, and design*, p. 50
26 Peter Wilkin "Are you sitting comfortably? The political economy of the body", *Sociology of Health and Illness* 31:1 (2009), pp. 35-50, p. 42.

matter of poor design or bad taste than "the ways in which people actively come to desire and identify with the very things that, in this instance, unknowingly cause them harm" that have made chairs have so much a part of the everyday.[27]

It is with this cultural myth of being comfortable on chairs that Annick's testimony takes issue with. As noted, objects invite people to perform a series of actions by assuming certain sets of movements (such as chairs making people sit in certain positions). But were it not for bodies that collectively accept these invitations (by way of their automated mechanisms) then these objects would remain simply pieces of wood glued and nailed together. It is because the tendons, ligaments, bones and muscles of a group of sitters mechanistically follow the movement and posture suggestions given by the formal features of chairs that multiple connectors of the scene (tables, chairs, cutleries, bodies, etc.) become tightly glued and the activity of "socializing" happens. Annick's cry of despair and her wish that people had suppers on the side of her bed reveal how tightly *glued* these connectors are. In fact the *collective belief* is so firmly in place that participants are unable to entertain, let alone offer, another physical configuration in which the "same" activity can take place. As Annick repeatedly says, a different performance is "awkward", "crazy" and "impossible". Her reiterated use of the phrase "you know" suggests that I, both as the addressee in her sentences and a co-participant in the same sedentary culture (who is sitting on the very chairs that we are talking about), should know this impossibility very well.

My aim here is certainly not to denigrate a piece of invention and make a naive call for its jettisoning from entire quotidian practices. Needless to say, not all bodies are disabled by their environments in the same way and not in all cases do chairs prove to be that harmful. As in the situation described below, chairs might turn out to be quite useful or even be, as in the case of wheelchairs, an integral part of an individual's mobility.

Ismail is in his early 30's and comes from a small village in a rural part of northern Turkey. He has had rheumatoid arthritis since early childhood, and as a child had to keep travelling for treatment, as there was no access to services in his hometown. Today, Ismail has severe disabilities, can hardly bend his knees and has to walk with the aid of crutches. He says that he visits his hometown from time to time and, in the following describes how he deals with the eating, resting and socializing habits adopted by the inhabitants of his hometown.

ISMAIL [I]: When I first enter a house or visit a neighbour, I immediately check where I can sit. A place not too low. I seek my comfort in

---

27   Ibidem, p. 42.

that respect.

ARSELI [A]: What sorts of places do you prefer not to sit?

I: Rigid, at a first glance. Places low and not too rigid.

A: Not too rigid?

I: Actually rigidity doesn't hurt me.

A: Is not it harder to get off soft surfaces?

I: No, not really. It doesn't much matter if rigid or soft. More if it is comfortable. I mean when you look at it as comfortable, psychologically... It can be soft, made of sponge, etc. I observe these things right away and ask myself: Where can I sit most comfortably? Food being eaten on the floor for instance... I cannot sit down to floor meals. At our places [referring to his hometown], our relatives always set up the meals on the floor [giggling]... I cannot sit down and tell them: "For me it is not floor table, it is the king's table please". [Laughing] ... This can be one of the obstacles I face for instance when visiting people... Eating on the floor...

A: Sofas? Any other things?

I: Sofas are not a problem. I mean it is the sitting that is problematic. Imagine if a house does not have chairs or sofas. And it often happens when I visit my village. There are floor cushions and things like that. I right away ask people "Please find me a chair, I cannot sit on the floor" [giggling]

In the case above where the person's knees do not bend easily and his body cannot easily switch between sitting and standing positions, it is not the chairs but the floor cushions that become the problem. This time, chairs do not inflict pain; to the contrary (as solid, knee-high surfaces) they take the strain off the sitter's knees, carry his body-weight and facilitate his switch between sitting and standing positions. In this entirely different material arrangement (than the one in Annick's case), sitting on chairs comes to be the aberrant body technique from the one normalized in the habitus. And Ismail, whose impairments are visibly recognized, experiences less difficulty in expressing and performing his 'aberrance' and disrupting the collective belief than Annick, whose impairments remain hidden behind an able-bodied image.

Techniques of Greeting

The activity of "socializing" might call for chairs or floor cushions but not all of its occurrences depend upon an external prop. After all the body is, as Mauss reiterates throughout his text, a most basic instrument itself.[28] Below

---

28   Marcel Mauss, "Techniques of the body", in eds M. Lock and J. Farquhar, *Beyond the Body Proper: Reading the Anthropology of Material Life*, Duke University Press, Durham 2007 [1935], p. 56.

are excerpts which show how the activity is put in motion by the codes surrounding its instrumentalization.

Susan is in her early 40's, has no visible impairments and lives by herself on the island of Montreal. Her friend was present during the interview.

> SUSAN [S]: I'm afraid of shaking people's hands since I have this.
> Susan's friend: Why?
> S: Because some people shake very strong and... a couple of weeks ago, a man... we were going out for a couple of drinks with friends. And this lady she knew a lot of people there. So this gentleman came and said "Oh, nice to meet you" and he really squeezed my hand hard and I jumped... I was so [unintelligible] and he was looking at me like [imitating his gesture of shock] "What's wrong?" and I said "Oh, I just have problems, uh..."

Extending one's arm to another person, grasping his hand as you let his hand grasp yours, exerting a certain pressure on the grasped hand and moving it and down are the notations of a common daily ritual that bring friendliness and trust into flesh. These gestures are so effective in what they do that any of their misperformances (such as jumping when one's hand is grasped) can raise suspicions about the trust being (per)formed (e.g. the man's reaction to Suzan's jumping in pain).

S.B.[29] is in her early 30's and after a major quarrel with her mother, decided to live by herself. She is an Orthodox Christian and lives in a one-room basement in a rather ethnically diverse region of İstanbul.

> S.B.: When I am in pain, I don't want to see or to talk to anybody. Sometimes, when I see people that I know and they greet me, I pretend that I didn't see them, because it is an excruciating, indescribable pain. You have to live through it to understand it. As I said, only people who have the same disease can understand.

What S.B. does not, or rather cannot do reveals that greetings co-performed not only with strangers that one meets for the first time but also with those that one already knows involve a certain degree of bodily commitment. From listening to her testimony, one realizes that you cannot call people acquaintances or friends and, upon bumping into them in the street, not interrupt your current action at the same time. As to the conventions of friendship, your recognition of the other rests in the bodily energy and capital you give to approach them, stand up to engage in conversation and remain on your feet until the talk reaches its minimum acceptable duration.

---

29 The participant preferred not to reveal her identity.

Techniques of Dressing

BRIAN [ANNICK'S HUSBAND]: It's something that just became natural. It's just a... [pause] just a routine. Like her, showing the store bag. [The bag that Annick prefers to use for carrying grocery] If it is in the way somewhere and I want to move it... That's why it was hanging on the post for the stairs [pointing] 'Cause it's easier for her to reach [showing the movement] To grab. She doesn't have to bend down. Her hands. Pick up and that's it...I guess I don't know, I find it hard to think about everything in the day that I might do. It's just, for some of the stuff, it's just routine. Yeah...

ANNICK [A]: For him it becomes routine. For me every time it hurts. You know. Every time it's me facing it. Even attaching my bra in my back. You know. I have to [showing the movement] tie it here [on the front, at her waist] twist it, put it on... And eeh... [turns to Brian] I ask you.

B: Yes [nodding].

A: You never... You don't mind. It's okay. You come right away, you are super nice. And me, I am thinking, "Oh my God, I have to ask him to tie up my bra."

Techniques of Moving in Clothes

ZARIFE: My social life ended. How did it end? In terms of dressing up for an event, say wearing a fancy shoe. As you see, the bones in my feet are in bad shape so I always have to walk around in sneakers. And I am so afraid that somebody would invite me to a special event or a gathering... Weddings let's say. I dread getting wedding invitations as it always makes me ask: "Oh no, what shoes am I going to wear!?"

MELIHA'S HUSBAND [MH]: We [meaning her wife] are done with fancy shoes. [Now] Always with soft things.

MELIHA [M]: More things like velcro.

MH: ...Soft leather and flat shoes.

M: Otherwise, it is difficult for me. When getting in and out of car...

MH: For instance, at the most, these [referring to the ones M. is wearing] wedged ones. They make you more comfortable. They are not too bad but others not any more...

M: Such as slim-shaped, much stylish. None of those any more.

MH: Because, it is really difficult to walk on high heels. You both need to exert force not to keep your balance...

M: And then your ankles are locked [meaning stiff with pain]

MH: But these ones [wedged] directly spread to the sole of the foot instead so she is not too uncomfortable walking or standing with these ones.

In "Techniques of the body" Mauss refers to the *"onioni"*, a way of walking adopted by the Maori women that Elsdon Best (1924) elaborates on in his study of the Maori customs.[30] The technique involves an exaggerated swinging of the hips which mothers drill into their daughters, often through the verbal reprimands of its misperformances, such as: *"'Ha! Kaore koe e onioni'* (you are not doing the *onioni*)".[31] The swaying movement, obviously, has no anatomical motivation. In fact it must be so discomforting that its training has to be supported by verbal injunctions.[32] But as the movement is practiced and repeated for the –nth time, the discomfort it causes is forgotten and the trauma that it once created "on the knees and feet and lower back will be eventually naturalized as part of what it feels like to be a woman, or to have a woman's body".[33]

Similar observations could be made about the movements and actions mentioned by Zarife, Meliha and Annick above. But in their case pain hits back. Their bodies resist kinesthetic amnesia. They cannot attach a bra, wear heels or slim-fit shoes without feeling the pain that the doing of these actions cause in their joints. It becomes harder to feel "womanly", "fancy", "elegant" or "well-mannered". The unrelenting presence of pain prevents the experience of performing (an action) from disappearing from the awareness to be later on colonized by meaning[34]. Precisely because it does so, meanings of femininity and meanings of being socially proper become stripped of their taken-for-granted gestural and somatic counterparts with which they pass as facts and necessities. If gendered movement cultures semanticize women's experiences of their bodies, one could (in light of the testimonies) above say that proprioceptive awareness of chronic pain de-neutralizes and de-naturalizes the made body. Below are further examples of such de-naturalizations.

Techniques of Cooking

Meliha and her husband are both retired, living in a two-story house in İstanbul together with their son. Ünzile is in her 50's, living with her husband and teenager son. Both women live in families with conventional and patriarchal structures in which the upkeep of the household is considered the duty of the women. Meliha's husband's emphasis on the pronoun *her* that he puts before each everyday work he counts (it is "her" washing, "her"

---

30 Marcel Mauss, "Techniques of the body, in *Beyond the Body Proper: Reading the Anthropology of Material Life*, eds M. Lock and J. Farquhar, Duke University Press, Durham 2007 [1935], p. 54.
31 Ibidem, p. 54.
32 Carrie Noland, *Agency & Embodiment: Performing Gestures/Producing Culture*, Harvard University Press, Cambridge, MA, 2009, p. 28.
33 Ibidem, p. 28.
34 Carrie Noland writes about the role of somatic awareness in disrupting the discursive layers of actions. Referring to the act of curtsy, she notes: "What if the socially established meaning of the act were overwhelmed, at least momentarily, by the somatic experiences of pressure, friction and pain?" (*Agency and Embodiment*, p. 194). Noland's elaborate reading does not, however, go onto explore the further implications of such disturbances.

cleaning) attests to that. The household tasks that these women have to undertake on a day-to-day basis, despite the labour they take, have no visibility, no recognition because, when completed, they do not bring about a change in the state of things.[35] Instead, their completion helps to keep things as they are, in the routine. In other words, it is not their execution but only the absence of their execution that "garners attention".[36]

ARSELI [A]: What about cooking?
MELIHA [M]: I try to do my cooking but it is too hard.
MELIHA'S HUSBAND [MH]: She does the cooking and things like that out of necessity.
M: I have difficulty stirring and things like that...
A: [to M.'s husband] Do you sometimes give a hand?
MH: Yes I do. But to some extent. I mean the extent that men can do.
M: Especially the pressure cooker and other heavy pans. I find them quite hard to wash. Yet I still wash them, despite the pain. I mean I literally sweat in pain when doing it. But I still try to do it. Because if I don't do those, then I would altogether... I don't know... Not now, perhaps in the future someone professional can come and help for a few hours...

Techniques of Cleaning

ÜNZILE'S NEIGHBOR: I know her for a long time, for 18-19 years long. I know her healthy days before the disease. Um... She is very hardworking, very good at keeping the house. She was really like that. Lacework, handicraft, you name it... She even sold them. With this disease, all these came to a halt. She cannot accept this and feels its frustration inside...
[Continued at later part of the same interview]
ÜNZILE'S NEIGHBOR: Normally, we [women] get together and if she thinks this place is dirty, then it eats her up inside. For instance, if there is something [dirt] on the carpet... We [women] were reading the Quran altogether [the other day]. This is very interesting... We are altogether reciting the Quran and Ünzile is staring at the carpet. She saw some dust there. She cannot pick it up but by staring at it, she means that we should pick it up. Imagine, even when we are immersed in reading the Quran. Like I said, it is interesting. Household, which she is unable to do. She was very good at keeping the house and when

---

35   Luce Giard, "The Nourishing Arts", trans. T.J. Tomasik, in *The Practice of Everyday Life Volume 2: Living & Cooking*, eds M. de Certeau, L. Giard and P. Mayol, University of Minnesota Press, Minneapolis 1998, p. 156.
36   Ibidem, p. 156.

it all suddenly stopped, when she was no longer able to do those... She resents that. "Oh I wasn't like this in the past."
MELIHA [M]: I cannot really squeeze out rags and things like that as I used to do in the past. Before the onset of the disease I used to clean the house from top to bottom. The windows, carpets, sofas, anything you can think of. All my tasks were done....
MELIHA'S HUSBAND: Oh the squeezing out task is terrible.
M: Oh yes, it is terrible.
ARSELI: So, you don't do it then?...
M: No. I still do it even if it hurts.
ZARIFE: All women, cause this disease mostly effects women, tend to deform. Probably because of their bone structure... [waits a second and then] Also um... Because you do things around [pointing around, meaning household], like you squeeze out rags, etc. Cause you are not like a man. Most often, their [women's] fingers are all deformed, check yourself next time.

Gendered movement regimes, as I noted above, suture cultural meanings to bodily behaviors and actions. The above excerpts further this insight by showing how the suturing of the somatic and the semantic could even make the absence of assumed bodily conducts significant.

Inability to clean up the dirt, wash the dishes, or squeeze rags garners attention. In these instances, there is something *the matter*[37] with the female body. There is *the matter* because they point at the failure of "her" gender. As could be sensed in the feelings of guilt and psychic pain that infiltrate Ünzile's, Annick's, Zarife's and Meliha's testimonies, a gendered matrix frames these failures, to use Butler's phrasing, as a "site of dreaded identification", as "'unlivable' and 'uninhabitable' zones of social life" [38] which then help constitute the domain of bodies that really matter (area of importance). In not attaching her bra by herself, in not wearing the clothing that a ceremony needs, in not cleaning the dirt off the carpet, in not doing lacework, in not keeping the house, the female body perhaps avoids the physical pain that the performance of these tasks would cause. But at the same time the person deeply suffers from the psychic pain of not fulfilling her birthright duties, of having failed "her" gender. Non-performances come with public embarrassment, a shame of dependency, resentment at being helped and the guilt of living an "uninhabitable" body. Sometimes the failures are so strongly feared that, the female body, as in Meliha's case, prefers to experience the actual physical pain that the performance of the actions inflicts (she sweats in pain but still does the washing). Gendered movement re-

---

37 Here I use the word in the following meaning: "The condition of or state of things regarding a person or thing, esp. as a subject of concern or wonder. Chiefly colloq. in what is the matter?" (OED, 2013).
38 Judith Butler, *Bodies that Matter: On the Discursive Limits of Sex*, Routledge, London and New York: p. 3.

gimes indeed punish "those who fail to do their gender right".³⁹ And in each of the testimonies above, one can hear in the background an indistinct voice shouting another version of "'*Ha! Kaore koe e onioni*'"!

Techniques of Preparing Food

LOUISE: I don't have a big knife for cutting cabbage. And since the cabbage is pretty big, I slice it into small pieces… [Gripping the knife reversely with a locked fist where the blade points downward and opposes the thumb] And sometimes I use the knife like this to cut it. It's not very elegant but it is only my kitchen that sees me! [laughing]
MARTINEZ: [At the moment she is in the kitchen slicing bacon] The pressure needed for cutting the bacon, the force you need to exert to cut it like this [imitating the gesture, moving her L-shaped arm backward and forward] is hard on my wrist.

Techniques of Eating

LOUISE: One time I went into a restaurant and I was not able to chew my steak. My jaw was not moving.
ANNICK: You know like when you eat soup and you have to extend your chin forward. Oh my god, that's very hard. Sometimes I forget but after second or third (showing the movement). Ahhh! I forgot to be careful and now the pain is there that's it.
ARSELI: When you go out do you order food easier to eat? For example steak is too…
ANNICK: I love meat a lot. I eat a lot less then before but… I ask Brian before "if I order this, are you gonna help me?" If it's okay with him, I order it. If there is nobody around [to ask for help]… if there is other people around, then I don't ask…. If there are other people around, I never ask you to do that, huh [talking to Brian]?
BRIAN [B]: Very rarely.
ANNICK: I think it happened once with J. & B. very close friends.
B: Yeah, yeah but you can count them like…
A: Yeah, only that time. That's it! [waits]… And if I am here [home], and if I have a really hard time and Brian is not there, I just take the whole thing [imitating the movement of grabbing the food and biting it] and go like that

---

39   Judith Butler, "Performative Acts and Gender Constitution: An Essay in Phenomenology and Feminist Theory", *Theatre Journal*, 40: 4 (1988), p. 522.

AYMENUR: Also I have difficulties eating out. Börek, for instance, you need to cut it with your knife. But I can't use the knife. Can you use it?
ARSELI: Not really. When you don't use it though, it looks rude. I eat it holding it like a piece of pizza.
AYMENUR: Me too. Or I directly stab my fork into the food. They may call me rude if they wish. I do have manners but... unfortunately you cannot eat it like that.

Techniques of Drinking

MARTINEZ: [Holding a plastic bottle containing liquid yogurt and pulling the peelable foil lid on top with her teeth] I open these with my teeth.
ARSELI: What if you are unable to open jars, bottles and things like that?
RUKIYE: If I can't open such things, then I push under the cap with a knife and rip it off. Or I twist and turn it with my teeth.

Techniques of Sleeping

ROGER: [Talking about a period in his life where he had an rheumatoid attack] You see like... Um, with the inflammation or with all the broken ribs that I had during a period of ten years... Um, I, I... for a while, I stopped sleeping in my bed. Because in my bed I move and if I move, I'd hurt myself and I'd wake up and not have a good night sleep. So for a while, I started sleeping on my sofa and the way I was set up, I was sort of stuck in the corner of the sofa [showing with hand gestures] so during the night I would not move and... That made it so that I could sleep better nights. So for a long time, sofa is my bed.

After the previous techniques where the actions in question were not necessarily essential to the living, one may ask "What about the techniques performed for biomechanical, physiochemical needs? What could ever be punitive, made or learned about them?". To answer, I turn to the elementary relation between a body and its physical environment.

The environment, despite the stillness of its materiality, is in a constant state of alteration – one that is gradual and extended over centuries. Its furnishings carry within their features the imprints of centuries-long interactions that have taken place throughout its history. Any object, built structure or form of the landscape, from this majestic perspective, appears as the crystalized version of a past act, of a long gone movement. In point of fact, the entire landscape appears as "a pattern of activities 'collapsed' into an array of features".[40] A past that an ephemeral present has distilled into and thus handed itself over to a future... This coagulation of a disappearing present into a material present has two main implications for the current argument. First it means "life must be lived amidst that which was made before"[41] Second it means life-to-be-lived-in-point-A of the world's transformation would, in a most physiological sense, not be the same as life-to-be-lived-in-point-B.[42] What does this mean?

Everything in the environment (from infrastructures to tools, from words to food) has "a mode", "a form which is at once common to large numbers of people and chosen by them from among other possible forms".[43] These modes and forms are "found only here or there, and only at such-or-such time periods"[44] and they draw people of their time into performing common actions and movements.[45] No action, even those actions that are considered to be of an anatomical necessity, escapes this rule of historicity because all actions have to take place under specific conditions, through the mediation of place, objects, technologies, and infrastructures – all of which carry in their materiality the work of a history and the work of a collective will. Think of drinking for instance. Where pipes, storage reservoirs, valves, faucet handles, bottles and caps mediate the flow of and access to water, techniques of drinking become much about gripping, twisting, turning and exerting a certain amount of force. But, in an imagined place, where water resources are directly available to drinkers without the mediation of supply networks; a whole system of production, packing and distribution and without the control mechanisms of quality and cleanliness standards, drinking might involve quite a different choreography... Even the action of chewing (which literally happens inside the body and could therefore be thought to be less contingent on historical variables) could take on a variety of forms depending on the type, texture, form and chemical composition of what is being chewed (see Louise's excerpt above about her experience of chewing a steak).

If, as the previous paragraph emphasizes, the very doing of an action is given a form by the physical conditions of the setting in which it takes place, it must then follow that there is no definition, no "essence" of an

40   Tim Ingold, *The Perception of the Environment: Essays on Livelihood, Dwelling and Skill*, Routledge, London and New York 2000, p. 198.
41   D. W. Meinig, "The beholding eye: ten versions of the same scene" in *The interpretation of ordinary landscapes*, ed. D. W. Meinig, Oxford University Press, Oxford 1979, pp. 33-48, p. 44 in Tim Ingold, *The Perception of the Environment: Essays on Livelihood, Dwelling and Skill*, Routledge, London and New York 2000, p. 191.
42   See Tim Ingold, *The Perception of the Environment*, p. 376.
43   Marcel Mauss, "Civilizations, Their Elements and Forms", trans. J. R. Redding, in ed. N. Schlanger , *Techniques, Technology and Civilization*, Berghahn, New York 2006 [1929/1930]), pp. 67-8
44   Ibidem, p. 67.
45   Emma Williams and Alan Costall "Taking Things More Seriously: Psychological Theories of Autism and the Material-Social Divide" in *Matter, Materiality, and Modern Culture*, ed. P. M. Graves-Brown, Routledge, London and New York 2000, p. 99.

action "that can be isolated from the real-time performance of the action itself".[46] No real-time performance of an action stands for a universal definition of that action against which variations or misperformances can be cast. This is what the previous testimonies of disabled individuals help us to understand. An action exists in its many different ways of performing it and "mis"-performances of disabled subjects do not point at its failure but at *the arbitrariness of what is thought to have just failed*. In seeing the movements of an arthritic hand that eliminate the use of knives and forks; in observing how one's teeth could replace the function of fingers; in hearing the stories of paraplegics and quadriplegics who "can have orgasm in any part of their bodies where they feel touch",[47] one comes to realize that things could have been performed *otherwise*.

No action exists in and of itself somewhere for its actual happenings across times and places to count as mere cultural, historical or individual variations. If it appears to do so, this is solely because a collective will has come to prioritize one way of doing over others and accepted it as the default mode that everyone recognizes and abides by. This is why the experiences, accounts and misperformances of disabled subjects *matter*. They err, misfire and do not abide by these modes. In so doing, they remind us that the temporality of per-*form*-ance is always a formation, a creation itself. Their so-called misperformances are the living proof that per-form-ance itself is a phenomena that is always *in movement* towards the forms that it is yet to take.

Conclusion

The technique of an action, Mauss writes, has to be traditional but also *effective* and *efficient*.[48] In being performed, it needs to successfully yield an already established meaning and incarnate a set of conventions that have made its transmission necessary. But how does a technique become effective and efficient?

Bourdieu gives the answer: "It is because agents never know completely what they are doing that what they do has more sense than they know".[49] A body technique becomes efficient because the agents are unaware of the citational quality of their actions at the very moment of executing them. In fact, the more ignorant they are (of bringing a tradition into life), the more non-historical and the more "real" their actions feel and the more effective the tradition becomes. So does "the performative magic of the social"[50] happen. But then how come the agents become so captivated by its magic? How

---

46   E. Thelen, "Motor development: a new synthesis", *American Psychologist*, 50 (1995), pp. 79-95, p. 83.
47   *Sexuality and physical disability*, eds David G. Bullard and Susan E. Knight, C. V. Mosby, St. Louis 1981, quoted in T. Ingold, *The Perception of the Enviroment: Essays on Livelihood, Dwelling and Skill*, Routledge, London and New York 2000, p. 378.
48   Mauss, "Techniques of the body", p. 55.
49   Pierre Bourdieu, *The Logic of Practice*, trans. R. Nice, Stanford University Press, Stanford, CA 1990, p. 69.
50   Ibidem, p. 57.

could they ever be so immersed in the illusion that the past-enacted-in-the-present manages to drop its re- quality (representation, repetition, reenactment) and pass as *the* irrefutable real?

"The human body is not ready-made for anything, but undergoes continuous change throughout the life-cycle as it is pressed into the performance of diverse tasks".[51] When it is born, it is born as a body (as substance). But this body-as-substance lives solely because it "learns to be affected"; it learns to "register and become sensitive to what the world is made of".[52] The presence of intrinsic developmental schedules (or lack thereof) is no guarantee that it will (or will not) eventually perform the actions that it is supposed to. The infant *learns to* do things, as it engages with the environment, enacts, practices and repeats actions – actions that were already in practice in the environment before its arrival. It will not, for instance, walk unless it *learns* to do so in the presence of "a variety of supporting objects and a certain terrain" and "with the help of other persons, already competent in the art".[53] Or it may begin to do things that it was hitherto thought to be not capable of when provided with matching environmental counterparts. For instance, research suggests that when "normal" staircases that babies usually encounter in their daily environments are scaled down, they begin to ascend and descend the stairs (and to do so by alternating their feet) at much earlier ages than the norms that textbooks on motor development indicate.[54]

As the emphasis on learning-through-performing reveals, habit literally condenses, compacts and "skeletalizes action".[55] In other words, habit is "not simply acquired habit, but habit that is contracted, owing to a change, with respect to the very change that gave birth to it".[56] For example, the "facts that no novice has succeeded in sustaining balance and co-ordination on a first attempt, and that the knack of riding a bicycle, once learned, is never lost indicate that the exercise of the requisite sensory and motor skills leave an indelible anatomical impression, if only in the normally invisible architecture of the brain".[57] Learning, or training or acquisition of habit, if

---

51   Tim Ingold, *The Perception of the Environment*, p. 376.
52   Bruno Latour , "How to talk about the Body? The Normative Dimension of Science Studies", p. 206.
53   Tim Ingold, *The Perception of the Environment*, p. 375.
54   Josep Roca, Lizandra Mireia Martinez,Anna Fabregas Mireia and Anna Cordoner, "Registres evolutius motors: Una observacio critica", *Apunts*, 6 (1986), pp. 61-64, quoted in A. Costall, "On being the right size: Affordances and the meaning of scale", in *Confronting Scale in Archaeology: Issues of theory and practice*, eds Gary Lock and Brian Molyneaux, Springer, New York 2006, pp. 15-26, pp. 19-20.
55   Elisabeth Grosz, "Habit Today: Ravaisson, Bergson, Deleuze and Us", *Body & Society*, 19: 2&3 (2013), pp. 217-239, p. 221.
56   Félix Ravaisson, *Of Habit*, trans. C. Carlisle and M. Sinclair, Continuum, London 2008 [1933], p. 25.
57   Tim Ingold, *The Perception of Environment*, p. 376. It is not for no reason the word 'know' may suggest such a shift, a slippage. In German, *können* (to know) and *ich kann* (I can) are inevitably linked and knowing is "coextensive with the word power or being able to" (Paul Ricoeur, *Freedom and Nature: The Voluntary and the Involuntary*, trans. E.V. Kohak, Northwestern University Press, Evanston 1966). In French, to know not only covers *connaitre* (to know through the senses, to recognize or perceive) and *savoir* (to know in the mind)" but also "actively shifts" between the two (G. Bateson, *Steps to an Ecology of Mind*, Jason Aronson Inc., Northvale 1972, p. 157). For Bateson, this shift indicates that "[t]hat which we know through the senses can become knowledge in the mind" (p. 157). Of course, a kind of obscure knowledge that is not readily accessible to conscious inspection.

you will, is what it means to have a body because each single doing of an action (movement, gesture, etc.); each single repetition of a sensation slips from a disappearing presence – the temporality of performance – into an active past and assumes a change in the very somatic stratum that has brought it into being. The reiterated performances of the body literally distil into its materiality in the form of motor schemes, neural pathways, perceptual automatisms and anatomical traces.

It is through this sedimentation process that the life history of the body overlaps with the larger history of the movement regime that it has found itself in. With the doing of habitual actions, not only a history is kept alive (the history of collectively engaged bodily practices) but is also archived into the very biology and physiology of its authors, as are their semantic accompaniments. As reiterated undertakings slip from ephemerality into materiality, performances become performative; habits turn into habitus and the habitus gains dual functions of being "formed" and being "formative".[58] In the end, what was once the work of a collective will appears as if it were the work of nature and this is where the "performative magic of the social" happens. The body, which could have been *learned* otherwise, passes as the irrefutable real.

The agents themselves remain inherently blinded to this magic and to the arbitrariness of their bodies' materiality exactly because "[w]hat is learned body is not something that one has, like knowledge that can be brandished, but something that one is".[59] Habituation erases the distance needed to reflect upon the form-generating relationship between the body, its locale and history, and as long as automatic processes continue to perform micro movements, gestures and actions *in silence*, the body continues to believe "what it plays at".[60] Thus does the "performative magic" continue.

Misperformances of disabled subjects offer rare examples of instances when this spell is broken. It is broken because when the disabled body executes banal actions and automated movements with the painful awareness of executing them, it can no longer be immersed in what it plays at (to be later on blinded to it). Pain and suffering "happen to" the body.[61] As a bodily phenomenon that resists being suppressed or forgotten, pain distances the body from its own materiality and its taken-for-grantedness. While its experience is highly unpleasant, an opportunity emerges at the same time to reflect on the choreographies of everyday: why we move in the ways we do and whether we could have done things differently. At least, this is what the stories of the individuals quoted here appear to offer.[62]

58   Judith Butler, "Performativity's Social Magic", in *The Social and Political Body*, ed. T. R. Schatzki, Guilford Press, New York 1996, pp. 29-48, p. 33.
59   Pierre Bourdieu, *The Logic of Practice*, p. 73.
60   Ibidem.
61   Paul Ricoeur, *Freedom and Nature: The Voluntary and the Involuntary*, p. 215.
62   Needless to say disability is not an over-arching homogenous category. It may be visible or invisible; congenital or

Perhaps one does not need to be a "trained" sociologist or wait for a major political and social upheaval to happen for habitus to open itself up to scrutiny.[63] Misfires of ordinariness and banality in disabled people's *extraordinary* lives have a lot to offer in this regard. It is with this final note, I ask whether there could be ways of approaching disability as a methodology; modes of considering the disabled body as something to *think with* rather than to think about...

ACKNOWLEDGEMENTS:
This paper uses the materials of the author's PhD research, undertaken at the Department of Theatre Film and Television Studies at Aberystwyth University. I would like to thank Mike Pearson for his supervision and support during this research. I also thank to Hasan Yazıcı and Mine Batumlu at İstanbul University Cerrahpaşa Hospital and Henri Ménard and Elizabeth Hazel at McGill University Health Center for their support during the fieldwork process.

---

acquired; fluctuating or permanent; it may or may not involve pain or an underlying medical condition; the pain may or may not relate to movement, etc. Each type of disability generates a different mode and level of bodily awareness. For instance, when individuals are disabled by physical barriers, such as "[t]he cripple before the stairs, the blind person before the printed page, the deaf person before the radio, the amputee before the typewriter, and the dwarf before the counter" (R. Garland-Thomson, *Extraordinary Bodies: Figuring Physical Disability in American Culture and Literature*, Columbia University Press, New York 1997, p. 24.), it is the absence of performance that brings a material awareness. In these instances, subjects do not have the luxury of being unaware of habitual activities that they cannot even perform.

In other instances where disability involves pain or an underlying physical condition, habitus can be confronted via both non-performances and misperformances. The latter often happen in cases of invisible disabilities where the individuals look able-bodied and are expected to fulfill their attributed functions even though doing so results in suffering from physical pain, discomfort or mental disorientation. This is slightly different than the first case in that it is not necessarily structural barriers that exclude the person from participating "in the everyday, mundane, sensate minutiae of the lifeworld" but the ways of conduct that prioritize "carnal performance" of certain bodies over others (Kevin Paterson and Bill Hughes, "Disability Studies and Phenomenology: The carnalpolitics of everyday life", *Disability & Society*, 14: 5 (2010), pp. 605).

63   See Crossley's critique of Bourdieu (Nick Crossley, "Habit and Habitus", *Body & Society*, 19: 2&3 (2013), p. 151).

Lada Čale Feldman
The Lecture and its Infelicities: Recovering Goffman's Legacy for (Mis)Performance Studies

Although Erving Goffman still figures prominently among the venerable predecessors of performance studies,[1] the importance of his work for this paradigm has recently been proclaimed to have "steadily declined".[2] Goffman does not fair better even in the recently published second edition of the *International encyclopedia of social sciences* (2010), where his work on performance is again presented as firmly entrenched in the past, no matter

---

1   Marvin Carlson, *Performance: a Critical Introduction*, Routledge, London and New York 1996.
2   Jon McKenzie, *Perform or Else, from discipline to performance*, Routledge, London and New York 2001, p. 41. McKenzie places this change in the reception of Goffman's work among the various „developments" within performance studies as a transdisciplinary field: the eclipse of Winnicott's and Piaget's psychology by Lacan's theory of the subject, as also that of anthropology by cultural studies - and Butler's renewal of interest in Austin. According to McKenzie, Goffman's demise is due to the fact that the very "notion of the social has been fragmented and dispersed among multiple and competing voices" (ibidem). I will later mention in passing to what extent Goffman's theory of the subject is compatible with Lacan's. Besides Goffman's continued interest in facets of everyday life, his *Gender advertisements* (1979) make him an even more prominent precursor of both cultural studies and Butler's theory of gender performance. Also, having "absorbed all that he could of J. L. Austin" (Tom Burns, *Erving Goffman*, Routledge, London and New York 1992, p. 354), and having frequently referred to this author's work, Goffman devoted to Austin's notion of felicity one of his very last, ambitiously argued and polemical essays, that could figure as one of the ground texts for *mis-performance studies* (Erving Goffman, "Felicity's condition", *American Journal of Sociology*, 89: 1 (July 1983)). As for "multiple and competing voices", it is curious to see Goffman's legacy dismissed on the ground of univocality, since in sociology he used to and continues to be both criticized and appreciated as a highly subjective writer, even the one using his own "voice as method" (see Ira J. Cohen and Mary F. Rogers, "Autonomy and Credibility: Voice as Method", *Sociological Theory*, 12: 3 (1994), pp. 304-318). Judith Posner notices that "it is ironic that Goffman gets into trouble for his cool objectivity when most of his critics accuse him of rampant subjectivity" (Judith Posner, "Erving Goffman: His presentation of self", *Philosophy of the Social Sciences*, 8 (1978), pp. 67-78, p. 75). Here is, in contrast to Mckenzie's judgment, what Hazelrigg states: "Today the possiblities of argumentation must contend with a certain 'crisis' of voice (i.e. of authority, legitimacy, etc.) which generalizes relentlessly. Goffman's 'playfulness' marks recognition of an argument that is implicated in the issues it seeks to address – issues of knowledge, power, voice, issues that unsettle and even derange customary possiblities of argumentation" (Lawrence Hazelrigg, "Reading Goffman's framing as provocation of a discipline", *Human Studies* 15 (1992), pp. 239-264, p. 240).

how fundamental it surely remains to "recent developments".[3] There are, however, even more focused discussions which "interrogate the myth and legacy of Erving Goffman", thoroughly dismissing his "contributions to a critical, performative sociology", with the argument that his approach is ideologically suspect, since it avoided "issues of social injustice, war or violence under capitalism".[4] "Preoccupied with illusion and reality", Goffman's work is shown to rely on a "concept of performance as mimesis", which was severely contested by performance studies in the nineties by such important names of performative theory as Kirschenblatt-Gimblett, Schechner or Butler, who all, as Denzin states, stress that performances are "actualities that matter" and therefore "critical sites of power".[5] Moreover, Goffman's findings are judged as being inoperative for the much needed "militant utopianism" and "educated hope" propagated by a "radical pedagogy" of performance studies that, according to Denzin, "insists on immediacy and involvement, on partial, plural, incomplete, and contingent understanding, not analytical distance or detachment"[6] presumably governing Goffman's sardonic comments on human face-to-face interaction.[7]

It is my contention that such an unfair view of Goffman's limitations, especially when it comes to performance studies, stems from a rather reductive reading of his *Presentation of Self in Everyday Life* (1959) - an early

---

3   Found to be lacking in macro-sociological interest, Goffman's inshights are declared to be, as in Mckenzie's book, superseded by Judith Butler's notion of (gender) performativity.
4   Norman Denzin, "Much ado about Goffman" in *Goffman's Legacy*, ed. A. Javier Treviño, Rowman & Littlefield Publishers, Lanham-Boulder-New York-Toronto-Oxford 2003, pp. 127-143, p. 130. For the continuity of this reproach among Goffman's contemporary and later critics, see Gary Allan Fine "Claiming the text: parsing the sardonic visions of Erving Goffman and Thorstein Veblen", in *Goffman and Social Organisation*, ed. G. Smith, Routledge, New York 1999, p. 177-197. Posner also emphasizes how his "nihilism is not popular in academic circles, where [...] at least the rhetoric of political liberalism constitutes the proper posture" (Judith Posner, "Erving Goffman: His presentation of self", p. 75). Having started his work in rebellious sixties, Goffman was fully aware of the probability of this counter-argument to his often understated social criticism. One can therefore only quote his answer to his alleged conservatism from his *Frame analysis*, imbued by his characteristic irony: "The analysis developed does not catch at the difference between the advantaged and disadvantaged classes and can be said to direct attention away from such matters. I think that is true. I can only suggest that he who would combat false consciousness and awaken people to their true interests has much to do, because the sleep is very deep. And I do not intend here to provide a lullaby but merely to sneak in and watch the way the people snore" (Erving Goffman, *Frame Analysis, An Essay on the Organization of Experience*, Cambridge: Harvard University Press, Cambridge 1974, p. 14.)
5   Norman Denzin, "Much Ado about Goffman" Denzin, p. 136)
6   Ibidem, pp. 137-138.
7   This is not the first attack Norman Denzin launched against Goffman, for it is he who initiated the most virulent polemic Goffman ever engaged in, after Denzin and Keller published an unfavorable review of *Frame Analysis* (see N. K. Denzin and C. M. Keller, "Frame Analysis Reconsidered", *Contemporary Sociology*, 10: 1 (1981), pp. 52-60). Back in the eighties Denzin attacked Goffman for his alleged adherence to French structuralism, insisting that his „concept of reality was illusive and blurred" (ibidem, p. 59). Goffman replied with condescension, horrified by the authors' "tone of a theological or political denunciation", and refused to be "subscribed to a particular doctrine", let alone "structuralism" to which he had always preferred the "crude empiricist" tradition in which he was raised (Erving Goffman, "A reply to Denzin and Keller", *Contemporary Sociology*, 10: 1 (1981), pp. 60-68, pp. 61-62.) The most interesting part of his vicious reply for our discussion touches, however, precisely a certain attitude he diagnosed behind Denzin's and Keller's "style": "I appreciate that graduate students in sociology might have need for this ideological format (a need also for schools of thought and of "paradigms"), in order to show their examiner that they have sociological convictions and some sense of sociology as a field, and I appreciate that their instructors might have recourse to the same slogans in order to establish standing in the classroom; but I feel sad about the recent tendency to make a publication out of these necessities" (ibidem, p. 61).

announcement of what Thomas Scheff finally acknowledged as being a full-blown deconstructive social theory[8] - as well as from a relative neglect of Goffman's subsequent writings *sub specie performativitatis*. Convinced that "in accounting for the disciplinary position of writing" one often surrenders to various "effects of communities of interest that accept or reject the author and the work",[9] I propose here to revalue some central tenets of performance studies in the light of Goffman's skepticism towards academy. In my view, Goffman's theoretical strength was and continues to be on a par with the major contributions of post-structuralist theory - precisely with its branch that was relentlessly questioning the limits of (social) representation and the idea of self, from Foucault and Lacan to Derrida,[10] who were all accused for undermining activist positions on roughly the same ground of giving too much power to inhuman instances of "discourse", "symbolic structure" or "language". In Goffman's case, such relentless questioning of selfhood led to him being equally accused of perverting the very idea of the Normal.[11] Nevertheless, contrary to all the quoted statements regarding the out-datedness of Goffman's notion of the social, contemporary sociology[12] does not hesitate to call for a radical re-evaluation of the revolutionary potential of his "quirky" and "enigmatic" opus which, although often cited, for long remained, according to Judith Posner, "mis-understood" and elusive, even taken to be "impossible to understand or apply".[13]

8 Cf. Thomas J. Scheff, *Goffman Unbound! A New Paradigm for Social Science*, Boulder: Paradigm Press, London 2006.
9 Gary Allan Fine, "Claiming the text: parsing the sardonic visions of Erving Goffman and Thorstein Veblen", p. 195.
10 It would be rather pretentious to engage here in a thorough argumentation of this link, and I can only point to connections already made, between Foucault and Goffman, by Ian Hacking, "Between Michel Foucault and Erving Goffman: between discourse in the abstract and face-to-face interaction", *Economy and Society*, 33: 3 (2004), pp. 277-302 and, between Goffman and Derrida, by Patricia Ticineto Clough, *The Ends of Ethnography: From Realism to Social Criticism*, Sage Publications 1999. As for Lacan, the conception of a „looking-glass self" derived from Goffman's writings (cf. Tom Burns, *Erving Goffman*, Routledge, London and New York 1992, pp. 270- 297; Scheff, 2006, Thomas J. Scheff, Thomas J. [2006] *Goffman Unbound! A New Paradigm for Social Science*, Boulder: Paradigm Press, London 2006, pp. 33-50) strongly associates the American sociologist's penetration into what we could term the social unconscious with the French psychoanalyst's theory on „the mirror stage". Lacan's idea of the human subject as something arising out from the chain of signification, as a „signifier functioning as the subject for another signifier" could also easily be read in-between, for instance, the following humoristic lines of Goffman's „Deference and demeanor": „Each individual is responsible for the demeanor image of himself and the deference image of others, so that for the complete man to be expressed, individuals must hold hands in a chain of ceremony, each giving deferentially with proper demeanor to the one on the right what will be received deferentially from the one on the left" (Erving Goffman, *Interaction Ritual: Essays on Face-to-Face Behavior*, Pantheon Books, New York 1967, pp. 84-85).
11 Charles Lemert, "Goffman's Enigma: Series Editor's Foreword", in: *Goffman's Legacy*, ed. Javier A. Trevino, Rowman & Littlefield, Lanham, Boulder, New York, Toronto, Oxford 2003, pp. xi-xvii, p. xvi. "Normality" was first attacked by Goffman in *Asylums* (1961) and *Stigma* (1963), where it was shown to be a constantly sliding social ideal, a cluster of social values dependent upon varying situations, largely construed by the privileged and the powerful, and ultimately embracing –at least in the Anglo-American world - only "young, married, white, urban, northern, heterosexual Protestant father of college education, fully employed, of good complexion, weight, and height, and a recent record in sports" (Erving Goffman, *Stigma*, Prentice Hall, Englewood Cliffs, NJ 1963, p. 128). On the other hand, one of his most famous essays, "Normal appearances", published in *Relations in public* (1971), demonstrated that the idea of normalcy is something humans construct on the basis of their most elementary, animal instincts of survival: behaving "normally" here turns into not emitting any signs of potential threat to the other's "territory of self".
12 Gary Smith, *Erving Goffman*, Routledge, Taylor & Francis Group, London and New York 2006; *Goffman's Legacy*, ed. Javier A. Trevino, Rowman & Littlefield, Lanham, Boulder, New York, Toronto, Oxford 2003; Thomas J. Scheff, *Goffman Unbound! A New Paradigm for Social Science*, Boulder: Paradigm Press, London 2006; Michael Hviid Jacobsen, *The Contemporary Goffman*, Routledge, New York 2010.
13 Judith Posner, "Erving Goffman: His presentation of self", *Philosophy of the Social Sciences*, 8 (1978), pp. 67-78, p. 76.

Indeed, the eventual misunderstandings, just as the current lack of any pronounced or more systematic interest in Goffman's work within the performance studies paradigm, may perhaps be recuperated through a possible attention to the proliferation of mis-prefixed notions and concepts that populate and even rule both Goffman's "poetics"[14] and the negative social ontology he ambiguously draws - both projecting and disavowing the validity of interactional frames, "bracketings" and "keyings" which fall under his scrutiny. His idiosyncratic terminology bristles with such simple and disturbing, sometimes even self-contradicting words and wordings as "mis-representations", "mis-haps", "infractions", "errors", "infelicities", "disruptions", "disengagements", "breaches of constraints", "frame-breaks", "mis-framings", "out-of-frame activities", "misalignments", "civil inattentions", "improper moves", "accurately improper moves" and "calculated unintentionalities", "non-persons" or "negational selves", who all turn our attention to the fragilities of the daily social contracts humans consider to be sealed in order to "keep the world from unsettling them".[15] His highly individual style intentionally provokes conceptual "embarassments" of the pre-conceptions about social reality in general and academic procedures that contribute to it in particular. In fact, it is precisely through the detection of the aforementioned ruptures as occasions of "poking through the thin sleeve of immediate reality" that Goffman could suggest his performative vision of "the normal course of life" as being "replete with deviations that depend entirely on the centrality of Lie"[16] – or rather, on desperate attempts to maintain a refined design of social architecture in order to avoid the awareness of a fundamental vulnerability of our looking-glass selves. The interest in endlessly proliferating "mis-framings" humans fall prey to in search for stable "structures of experience" made Goffman sensitive to obsessive, repetitive tacit coverings of possible neuralgic gaps in human interaction, and point to the ontological void which even the most intimate social relations verge on. The second aspect that will be important to what follows here, and that was also taken for granted in the reception of Goffman's work within performance studies, is the pivotal role of human embodiment - whether intentionally or unintentionally put to performative use – in establishing not only sociality itself, but also one's own daily chances to build up a respectable or at least satisfying "moral career". This focus on the body - not only on its "impression management" or "behavior" in private and public places, from social kisses and handshaking to bumping into each other in the streets, but also on its sometimes ineradicable social "stigmas" (race, gender or disability included) - is in Goffman's opus a crucial methodological choice, to

---

14   Paul Atkinson, "Goffman's Poetics", *Human Studies*, 12 (1989), pp. 59-76.
15   Erving Goffman, *Frame Analysis, An Essay on the Organization of Experience*, Cambridge: Harvard University Press, 1974, p. 15.
16   Charles Lemert, "Goffman's Enigma", p. xvi.

which not enough attention has been paid, especially having in mind that it is there that for Goffman most of "embarrassments" and "infelicities" of interaction find their common ground.[17]

Among the somewhat mis-treated writings of the American sociologist there is a study that gave critics some "trouble in following Goffman's argument",[18] and entitled "The Lecture", published in Goffman's last book, *Forms of Talk* (1981), which was generally perceived as "a highly technical book on language"[19] and thus, perhaps, not of such urgent interest for performance studies. "The Lecture" minutely analyses the performative features of the central event which still persists in maintaining its status of "the dominant performance of modern pedagogics", taking place at the lectern as the "emblem of knowledge and power [....] separating the one presumed to know and thus empowered to speak the truth from the one presumed not to know and thus empowered to seek the truth".[20] This is despite the much more complex resources offered by contemporary technology of an entire "lecture machine", so poignantly evoked by McKenzie in its proliferation of uncontrollable pathways and growingly intricate networks of the distribution of knowledge, that could, or so it seems, easily dispense with such old-fashioned and authoritarian way of imparting wisdom as lectures growingly seem to be. Even though "The Lecture" is occasionally referred to in literature on education and incidentally praised for its "brilliancy",[21] it has rarely attracted critical attention in its own right.[22] It represents a culmination of Goffman's numerous anti-disciplinary "provocations"[23] that point to rituals permeating and regulating the institutionalized production of knowledge, and denounce their aim of concealing precisely the "partial-

17 Neither Burns (Tom Burns, *Erving Goffman*, Routledge, London and New York 1992) nor Smith (Greg Smith, *Erving Goffman*, Routledge, London 2006) did include in their monographs the body among their different headings under which they discussed different aspects of Goffman's opus. Smart (Barry Smart, "Facing the Body – Goffman, Levinas and the Subject of Ethics", *Body & Society*, 2: 2 [1996], pp. 67-78) pointed out that Goffman could be seen as one of the first to introduce embodiment to sociology in general, particularly to its interests in moral matters, but I do not agree with Smart's recurrence to repeated devaluations of Goffman as social cynic, especially since this qualification, at least in Smart's study, again relies only on the *Presentation of Self in Everyday Life* and the essay "On Face-Work", published in the book *Interaction Order* (1972). In the most recent collection devoted to "the contemporary Goffman", however, both Hviid Jacobsen and Lemert insist on Goffman's politics being precisely a "body politics" (see Michael Hviid Jacobsen, *The Contemporary Goffman*, pp. 12 and 154).
18 William A. Corsaro, Forms of Talk (review), *American Journal of Sociology*, 89: 1 (1983), p. 220.
19 Yves Winkin, "Erving Goffman: what is a life? The uneasy making of an intellectual biography", *Goffman and Social Organization, studies in a sociological legacy*, ed. by G. Smith, Routledge, London and New York 1999, pp.19-41, p. 36.
20 Jon McKenzie, *Perform or Else*, p. 21.
21 Rod Watson, Erving Goffman, Forms of Talk (review), *British Journal of Sociology*, 35: 1 (1984), pp. 155-156, p. 155.
22 Significantly, the monograph devoted to Goffman as a "key sociological thinker" by Greg Smith, *Erving Goffman* (2006) barely mentions the piece, but the same author will later join Michael Hviid Jacobsen in praising Goffman's irony regarding "the verbal and non-verbal manoeuvres involved in academic lectures" (see Hviid Jacobsen, *The Contemporary Goffman*, p. 136). For a more detailed account of The Lecture, see Tom Burns, *Erving Goffman* (1992), although I cannot help but finding the essay somewhat purified by Burns's analysis, that is, deprived of its most salient, performative features. It is interesting for the discussion that follows here to note how Corsaro defends his inability to grasp the Lecture in its full potentiality: „It is possible that this paper was more successful in its original presentation as a lecture than it is in the print" (William A. Corsaro, Forms of Talk [a review], p. 220).
23 Cf. Lawrence Hazelrigg, "Reading Goffman's framing as provocation of a discipline", *Human Studies*, 15 (1992), pp. 239-264.

ity, plurality, incompleteness and contingency" of any "understanding",[24] even if these values are now proudly espoused as a pedagogical ideal. As we shall see, Goffman nourishes no hope for Denzin's project of "radical pedagogy", carried out in the spirit of "militant optimism", however openly partial, incomplete and contingent it may present itself to be. For Goffman, as for Derrida's *corps enseignant*,[25] the role of the lecturer presupposes and supports the very "notion of intellectual authority in general", regardless of what kind of cognitive establishment, let alone socio-political power, governs and remains hidden behind its corporeal representation in the lecture-hall. Suspicious of the ideal of "immediacy and involvement" stripped of any such compromising clothes, Goffman claims that during a lecture, "the external must be melded to the internal, coupled in some way, if only to be systematically disattended".[26] This "disattention" to the external – to "the structural features of society" such as "relationships of power and status"[27] – is for Goffman, however, a matter of coquettish performing versatility that cannot in itself undermine the contingent rigidities of the social script, or at least not that much as the writings of the social analyst keen on exposing the ways these abstract structures find their way to embodiment and thus to their own inadvertent fallibility as well.

Because "The Lecture" presents itself as a verbatim reproduction of a lecture delivered by Goffman himself, it provides additional possible interests of (mis)performance studies in the way a transcription of a performance-piece manages to engender a (mis)performance of its own. Not only does Goffman explicitly link the practice of lecturing to specific instances of artistic or entertainment performing (contemporary avant-guard performances, poetry readings, stand-up comedies, animal displays and live concerts, i. e. various "stage activities"), but he also intentionally blurs the difference between its spoken and written version that it purportedly endeavors to clearly define and refine with ulterior differentiations, which appear as a presupposed generally valid "truth" the author is speaking in the content of his lecture. In fact, the very designation of the topic - "the lecture" - is said to obscure the matter, "sometimes referring to a spoken text, sometimes to the embracing social event in which its delivery occurs".[28] While reading the (presumably) "spoken text" of Goffman's own lecture, we soon realize that the huge, second section of it will indeed concentrate upon the lecture as a celebrative occasion, as organized and mediatized

---

24   Norman Denzin, "Much ado about Goffman", in *Goffman's Legacy*, ed. A. Javier Treviño, Rowman & Littlefield, Lanham-Boulder-New York-Toronto-Oxford 2003, pp. 127-143, p. 137.
25   Jacques Derrida, "Où commence et comment finit un corps enseignant" in *Politiques de la philosophie*, ed. D. Grisoni, Grasset, Paris 1976, pp. 55-99.
26   Erving Goffman, "The Lecture" in: *Forms of Talk*, University of Pennsylvania Press, Philadelphia 1981, pp. 160-196, p. 193.
27   Tom Burns, *Erving Goffman*, Routlege, London and New York 1992, p. 338.
28   Erving Goffman, "The Lecture", p. 167.

"social event", which is shown to be largely taking over the apparent attention that the audience accords to the text. Not only do speakers, institutions and sponsoring organizations profit from the lecture's often celebratory and advertising character - thus according preeminence one to the other in an "unholy alliance" that "may be sustained at the expense of lecture itself",[29] but the members of the audience are also said to "handle whatever they do become involved in so as not to openly embarrass the understanding that it's the text they are involved in".[30] Although "there is the truth in saying that audiences become involved in spite of the text, not because of it" - no matter how threatening this could be to the "precarious ideal" of the lecture, the assumption namely that its impact should not depend on "the felicities or infelicities of the presentation"[31] - it would hardly be possible to make the text completely surrender its symbolic powers to the behavioral and social frame.

The lecture, obviously – Goffman's own included – requires from the lecturer to be "a performer, but not merely a performer", since even the very "felicities or infelicities of the presentation" cannot be squarely placed, either in the presentational frame, or in the textual content, whether the written or the spoken one. The mentioned "precarious ideal" of the lecture seems to be internally split: the lecture must "carry away the audience into the special realm of being", as if the public were assisting a game or a theater performance. At the same time, it must not "be frankly presented as if engrossment were the controlling intent",[32] since there are some "format-specific limits"[33] to any redirection of the attention of the audience to the fact, for instance, that the lecturer has either a skillful or a fallible body at all, let alone the one performing in this specifically coded face-to-face interaction. What kind of (mis)performance, then, is a performance that must carefully negotiate the amount of awareness of it being a performance if it is to succeed as a performance? Reversing the usual assumption drawn on the example of dramatic theatre – that performance is here to sustain an illusion - Goffman seems to imply that, during a lecture, illusionistic aspects of a performance are here to underpin its performative success, which may have nothing to do with the amount of knowledge produced. For what kind of success does it count on - of producing the knowledge (the "special realm of being" in which both the lecturer and his or her audience will feel knowledgeable) or of producing a specific genre of social encounter, with all the ritual satisfaction that goes with it?[34]

---

29   Ibidem, p. 170.
30   Ibidem, p. 166.
31   Ibidem.
32   Ibidem.
33   Ibidem, p. 185.
34   Goffman is in fact quite adamant at convincing us that "a text allows a speaker a cover for the rituals of performance" ("The Lecture", p. 194), but we should never take him too seriously, there is more to his text of "The Lecture" for us to do so.

A look at the introductory and concluding paragraphs of Goffman's essay suffices to understand that here Goffman outgoffmans himself, taking the opportunity of the frame his authorial voice is both in, and in making, to discuss the justification of his entire theoretical opus which, however varied in its "naturalistic observation" of human interaction, could be defined as an endless discussion of the reflexive, if not abyssal character of the social frame[35]. Each and every sentence that is embedded in this frame of "The Lecture" is thus inevitably ambiguously situated, being both within and outside the frame of the text that we already started to read, or listen, if we were there, duly warned that, due to special circumstances, something will inevitably "leak out".[36] Goffman's first disclaimer in particular achieves this with: "I am not trying to wriggle out of my contract with you by using my situation at the podium to talk about something ready to hand, my situation at the podium".[37] Of course, he both is and is not doing precisely what he is saying: the issue is undecidable - moreover, undecidable as any self-reflexive performance of the self, here mockingly named "puerile opportunism we have had quite enough", embracing, among other things, "the John Cage school of performance rip-offs".[38] The lecture will ensue, and it will offer something more substantial than a sheer rip-off: it will be both a proper lecture (on the lecture) and a proper rip-off of its investments in performative efficiency, since the final paragraph – the (dis)closure of the frame - will dispel any illusion that the lecture is or produces anything more than *a performance* of "immediacy and involvement" relying on an agreement between the speaker and the audience, and serving the same cause, regardless of the "substantive domain" on which the lecturer is lecturing. The final paragraph, namely, tells us that the lecture intends "to protect us from the wind, to stand up and seriously project the assumption that through lecturing, a meaningful picture of some part of the world can be conveyed, and that the talker can have access to a picture worth conveying". For, the ritual of this "shared proposition" ended, "the speaker and the audience rightfully return to the flickering, cross-purposed, messy irresolution of their unknowable circumstances",[39] together with the messy irresolution of lecturing, lectured upon in Goffman's *Lecture*.

But then you may well ask what is or was the content taking place within this quickly outlined frame, and what is or was its relationship with the frame itself? The content, to be sure, refers to the lecture as a "form of

---

35   See how he manoeuvres the demonstration of this abyss in the introduction to his *Frame analysis* (Erving Goffman, *Frame Analysis, An Essay on the Organization of Experience*, Harvard University Press, Cambridge 1974, pp. 16-20) right after he warns against thorough „methodological self-consciousness" that leads to an excessive concentration on „the reflexive problem itself, thereby displacing fields of inquiry instead of contributing to them" (ibidem, p. 12). Ten years after, it seems, he opted for just such a „displacement" in the *Lecture*, proving once more how serious he takes his own warnings to be.
36   Goffman, "The Lecture", p. 164.
37   Ibidem, p. 162.
38   Ibidem. This is an allusion to Cage's famous *Lecture on nothing* (1950).
39   Ibidem, p. 195.

talk", alluding thereby to the lack of any content in this particular, as perhaps in any such, "form of talk", if it is not the very form, that is, frame, within which the talk on the form occurs, but whose exact limits are very hard to pin down, since they constantly slide, from chapter to chapter, in infinite regress of realms to be distinguished, and rightly or falsely attributed to either the liveness or the premeditated character of the event/text of the lecture. In this respect, Goffman does nothing but follow the admonishments of his initial, early intrusion into the linguistics of speech: as he already warned linguists in "The Neglected situation" (1964),[40] no analysis of speech behavior, let alone the one determined to account for all the "semantic, expressive, paralinguistic and kinesic features of behavior involving speech", can do away with "the microecological orbit" in which the speakers find themselves, that is, the human and material setting in which all the features of the speakers' behavior take their particular and changing value. It is therefore that "The Lecture" is careful to describe its own social frame, and the values that stabilize it: its institutional setting, its roles, the text of the lecture and its "serious and slightly impersonal" style, the controlling intent and effect, the warrant of the statements in truth, "appearing as something to be cultivated and developed from a distance, coolly, as an end in itself",[41] even while the distance is being abolished by the very immersion of the speaker in the "truth" by which his sentences are warranted, that is, his own lecture.

But this is not the only thin sleeve of immediate reality Goffman is poking fun at. The crucial thin line our author draws in the essay - however "insulated" it may appear by his self-reflexive puns - concerns, as we already said, the fragile distinction between writing and speaking, and, by inference, reading on one hand, and listening to/watching the performer on the other. The lecture approaches in that respect the ontological status of the text of a play: a text, that is, written with a performance in mind, in an endeavor, as Goffman formulates, to tie the lecturer in advance to its upcoming audience "with a typewriter ribbon" through the use of some "contextualizing devices",[42] and further, to allow the author-playwright to step out from the shade and assume the role of the actor, to accept to be the focus of "the staring-at attention".[43] Once put in front of the public, the lecturer, however, engages in multi-layered, additional illusionistic work – above all, in creating the illusion of himself as not only a knowledgeable person and eloquent writer/speaker, but an efficient performer as well, wholly devoted to the occasion at hand.

It is here, I think, that "The Lecture"'s contribution fruitfully joins the most daring discussions of one of the delicate problems that buttressed the

---

40 Ibidem, p. 195.
41 Ibidem, p. 165.
42 Ibidem, p. 188.
43 Ibidem, p. 165.

performance studies paradigm, whose legitimization is still entangled in contestations and discussions over the dichotomies of speech versus writing, and text versus performance.[44] The mischievous mis-performance of Goffman's lecture consists precisely in dismantling not only the idea of a successful, felicitous lecturing performance – the one presumably delivering a truth through its text – but also the reverse idea of its complete immersion in the actuality of performance: "the pleasure and the displeasure of the occasion" is determined by a "membrane", a "boundary" between the two, that serves as "a tickler".[45] The lecture thus emerges as indeed a specific generic instance of performing a text, with Goffman's own lecture as a case in point, proving that, in this case, it is impossible to ontologically distinguish between talk and printed word (especially if the author later insists – as Goffman did – to print the lecture apparently devoid of any additional editorial work).[46] Impossible, that is, up to a point in live interaction in which a simple mistake, some "minor hitch"[47] and its subsequent correction "expose the speaker as having all along faked the appearance of being in touch with the thoughts his utterances were conveying".[48] This "embarassement", of course, can hardly happen in the written version, the better to serve the illusion of a present self, entirely devoted to his audience (of readers, or listeners?)! Paradoxically, then, the liveness of the body of the lecturer, revealed through his/her misperformance, both endangers the illusion of "being in touch" – as if the lecturer were indeed a character he/she performs,[49] and not the playwright of that performance – and makes his/her exposure an attraction secretly preyed on, a welcome symptom of the lecturer being actu-

---

[44] See William Worthen, "Antigone's Bones", *The Drama Review*, 52: 3 (T 199) (2008), pp. 10-33.
[45] Ibidem, p. 173.
[46] The *Lecture* is framed by multiple frames and disclaimers, one of them forming a kind of preface that explains to the reader the circumstances that occasioned such a curious mixture of self-reflexive and substantive discoursing, defining a special „form of talk". Here Goffman states it was his intention to „provide an actual instance" of „differences between talk and the printed word", and only secondarily to discuss the format of the lecture. Moreover, from this preface it is clear that the lecture provided an excellent opportunity to consciously „abuse" both the actual audience of its delivery and the later readership of its printed version as to where the aforementioned „differences" actually lie. Goffman namely mischevously declares in the preface that „this version" (the printed one) was also meant to „instantiate" the same difference, but „this time from the other side", that is, from the perspective of the printed word. Since he openly admits, however, that he both did not rework the text for reading and "had not forborne to change a word or add a line", a reader can only realize his intention was to do quite the contrary: to demonstrate that no definite differences can ever be instantiated, at least not the ones a clever lecturer/writer could not play with and cheat us into believing in. We should therefore take him for his word when he admits at the end of the preface: "Thus, however much the original talk was in bad faith, this edited documentation of it is more so" (p. 161).
[47] Goffman, "The Lecture", p. 188.
[48] Ibidem, p. 191.
[49] A word is needed about that curious personage projected during the occasion, for in Goffman's talk one can find a fairly thick, rounded description of his or her ideal *moral* features, that builds up a model-lecturer-as-stock- character. Elbowing his or her way through the six chapters of the piece, a lecturer appears across various discussions of "footings" and selves projected with the latters' help, and then shines through the final passages as a true "star" of the occasion, providing he or she has successfully managed all the possible trappings. Here are the "sterling attributes" he or she is expected to exhibit: not merely: scholarship, office, reputation, institutional status, intelligence, wit and charm (even capacity to tell anecdotes, be ironic and sarcastic), but also a talent to present him or herself as "a person just like ourselves", and to "relax the distance", to wear his or her "authority lightly", and to seem "unimpressed by his or her own quality", since all these provide for a "stage-limited performance of approachability", and make for an "audience usable self" – a self giving the impression that the audience could handle his business as easily as himself.

ally there, with or without the text to deliver, with or without the knowledge to convey.

While self-referentially engaging with issues and values of "immediacy and involvement", Goffman's essay therefore shows his lecturer - both the one talked about and the one once actually impersonated - grapple with various further possible disturbances, "production crises" and eventual improprieties of his "script", if only to demonstrate to what extent the performance of the lecture derives its charm precisely from its own misdeeds. These range from awkward illustrations of the subject matter, humorously exposed in his "bracketing" introduction, to various "liberties taken with the audience" usually censored in the printed version – colloquialisms, irreverences, untrue or undocumented statements, sarcasms, *sotto voce* asides and other "crude devices", "setting the lecturer and the audience in collusion against absent figures".[50] In Goffman's text, all these simultaneously uphold and dismantle, or rather, as the author would put it, "insulate" in the process what is tacitly held to be both "The Lecture"'s and its audience's over-arching and ever-lasting knowledge -"profit". The self-referential loop that is thus produced somewhere in-between the un-locatable roles of the author, the principal – the one who actually endorses opinions that he expresses – and the animator of the text, offers a performance surplus value. It engages Goffman's reader in an inadvertent guesswork of reconstruction of his actual delivery of the piece, (misleadingly or not) referred to in the text as lacking in histrionic competence to enact a model lecturer, the one presenting himself as "just another humble member of the gathering",[51] and speaking "intimately and comradely".[52] That is, at least, what we infer from his text, confronted as we are with the performative capacity of his verbal "brilliancy", which manages to carry out even those segments of the lecture that in the text figure as something belonging exclusively to its oral delivery and as something necessarily requiring platform skills of a true performer. In this, one of his very last interventions, Goffman thus engaged precisely in what McKenzie himself pleads for if one wants to fulfill "the task of theory" - that is, in "allowing one's generalizations to deviate itself into idiosyncratic passages of experience, something that can only be done with immanent partiality and detachment" since "it can only take place by taking part while simultaneously taking apart one's own part in the unfolding machinations of generalization".[53]

Goffman distinguishes "three main modes of animating spoken words: memorization, aloud reading (such as I had been doing up to now),

---

50   Goffman, "The Lecture", p. 190.
51   Ibidem, p.192.
52   Ibidem, p. 193.
53   Jon McKenzie, *Perform or Else*.

and fresh talk".⁵⁴ Note immediately that the bracketed words suggest a possibility that Goffman interrupted his declared "aloud reading" for a moment, but we can never be quite sure what section of the text has been delivered as "fresh talk" from that moment on. Perhaps we could have known this if we were there when Goffman was actually delivering his lecture, but as soon as the distinction between the mentioned three "production modes" is established, it will reveal itself to be untenable, even for the audience actually assisting the spoken delivery. Memorization is, Goffman says, never employed admittedly, so that although fresh talk is "the general ideal" and "quite common",⁵⁵ we can never know how much of this talk was in fact memorized in advance, as if the lecturer was just playing "the theatrical part" during whose display we keep our knowledge of memorization "in abeyance" in order to enjoy the "fresh talk" of the characters.⁵⁶ This however does not mean that the lecture can analytically collapse into theater performance, since its generic specificity is precisely the skilful maneuvering of the performer between the three modes - that is, apparent maneuvering, without the audience ever being capable of guessing which of the three is the authentic one, particularly if the lecturers manage to avoid any "production crisis" or disturbances by their "backstage considerations". These include "giving thoughts to how they seem to be doing, where they stand in terms of finishing too soon or too late, and what they plan to do after the talk".⁵⁷ All these are instances that, on one hand, could break the illusion that the lecturers "are properly involved in communicating", and on the other, are necessary concerns if one is to pay attention to the generic requirements of this social occasion. Such concerns are therefore indelibly incrusted into the text of the lecture – its length, the number of its digressions and illustrations, the addresses to the audience, and so forth.

If we were silly enough to follow Goffman's initial "recommendation that a lecture contains a text that could just as well be imparted through a print"⁵⁸ – as his is - we would be led to believe that we are only missing "the form, the interactional encasement, the box, not the cake"⁵⁹ of his actual delivery of the text we are reading. But why is it that we fall into the trap of his excuses when he states that the issue of "speaker's handling of himself" is something "easy to write about circumspectly but hard to lecture on without abusing one's podium position"?⁶⁰ Are we thereby invited to attend to the writing or to the speaking "self" of Goffman's lecture?⁶¹ Chapter IV of the

54 Ibidem, p. 171.
55 Ibidem, p. 172.
56 Ibidem.
57 Ibidem.
58 Ibidem.
59 Ibidem, p. 173.
60 Ibidem.
61 A „self" is for Goffman an entity projected by concurrent or shifting „footings". For instance, a „textual self", representing the knowledgeable author, just as a „historical-experiential" one, which can decorate his text with personal anecdotes, are

lecture will endeavor to provide an answer, albeit with further intricacies: once we put the undetectable boundaries between memorization, aloud reading and fresh talk aside, the lecturer will provide new nuances in the delivery, additional, peformative "footings", "distance-altering alignments" and various paralinguistic "keyings", particularly the one needed by text brackets and text parenthetical remarks, which should be delivered in such a way that a "speaker appears to have arrived at" these "qualifying thoughts" just "at the very moment"[62] – as the ones in Goffman's lecture itself, warning us that he does not imply "that as of now these paralinguistic markers can be satisfactorily identified, let alone transcribed".[63] "As of now"? What is the moment referred to in the text? The moment we are reading in, he is writing in, or he has been speaking in? If we choose the latter, we are free, for lack of transcription, to imagine Goffman's various "keyings" of all the funny textual trappings we have been led into so far, free, that is, or should I say forced, to perform his performance.

For it is what the occasion of lecturing finally offers, a performance of the lecturer's self that "allows him to fall back from his textual self into one that is intimately responsive to the current situation".[64] And what is Goffman's lecture – even the one we are reading, long after the occurrence itself – if not this "fancy footwork" of constant "falling back" of the lecturer into a self "intimately responsive to the current situation"?[65] The same performative appropriation of a general rule will happen just after the use of the digressions is discussed. Once established as those moments in which "the speaker seems most alive to the ambience of the occasion", proving "how fully he has mobilized his spirit and mind for the moment at hand", digressions are immediately denounced as "the moments to most suspect" of being just a "simulated fresh talk".[66] Having said so, Goffman continues unabashedly: "May I digress for a moment?", and the fact that he does allow himself to digress only confirms that bracketing and parenthetical remarks, along with keyings imposed on the ongoing text, only seem to bear more on the occasion of the lecture than on the situation the lecture is about. Furthermore, they simulate to be out of the boundaries of the text and are in

---

generally held to be the ones we are, during a lecture, most interested in – but they can also very easily be projected by a printed text. Why, then, do we invest so much into his live presence, if not to enjoy his performative illusions of spontaneity and/or in return to triumphantly witness his eventual embarassments?

62   Goffman, "The Lecture", p. 177.
63   Ibidem, p. 175.
64   Ibidem, p. 175.
65   One must bear in mind that by constantly referring to the situation he himself is placed in while discoursing on it, Goffman makes fun of his adversaries, since he was typically accused of relying too much on his own "intuition as to what typical instances" of his analysis "look like" (Rod Watson, "Erving Goffman, *Forms of Talk*" [review], *British Journal of Sociology*, 35:1[1984], p. 156), and not on any palpable, verifiable examples. "The Lecture" is in that respect a satire of "the rigorous methodological tradition [...] of using recorded and transcribed data" and of all the claims that Goffman "remains dependent on analyzing made-up scenarios rather than using naturally occurring phenomena that could more forcefully substantiate his claims" (David T. Helm, "Talk's Form: Comments on Goffman's *Forms of Talk*", Human Studies 5 [1982], pp. 147-157, p. 148).
66   Goffman, "The Lecture", p. 178

fact, as in his lecture, premeditated, textual "stage directions" and "parts" of "theatrical parts".

The final tackling issue that should undoubtedly prove that lecture is indeed a specific kind of performance – something fundamentally unpredictable, produced in the very moment, no matter how well rehearsed, memorized or simply prepared in advance by writing a text – is the lecturer's management of performance contingencies, which are a potential source of "noise" occurring during any live communication – a noise, indeed, "from the perspective of the text", which is at the same time "the music of the interaction",[67] the very precious prove that during the lecture we have access to the living mind and body of the one who prepared it, and are therefore equally willing to "affect unconcern" for all the disturbances as the lecturer is to proceed with lecturing, even though he may have recourse to apologies concerning his "remedial actions" in order to relieve us of this ritual duty.[68] Here again we might suspect that we as readers of Goffman's lecture are deprived of experiencing all the "equipment and encoding faults" he enumerates as the ones that "imply that a living body is behind the communication", "a self in terms of which the speaker is present and active, although not relevantly so".[69] The body, therefore, is not only responsible for vocal and gesturing modulations of the text, but figures above all as a disturbing source of an infinite array of potential "noise" – "breathing, fidgeting, scratching, coughing, brushing back one's hair, straightening one's skirt, sniffling, fingering one's pearls, cleaning one's glasses, burping, shifting from one foot to the other, swaying, manneristically buttoning or unbuttoning a jacket, turning the pages, squaring them off, mispronouncing words", etc. – that is supposed to distract the audience from the main purpose of the lecture.[70]

And yet this "self" for which a place is made in lecturing, and which is allowed to perform side-involvements such as clearing his throat or taking a drink of water - providing that these are "performed in speech-segment junctures" - suddenly appears in Goffman's text as the one which both actually performs one such side-involvement improperly, out of his own speech-segment juncture, and, as the text says, gives its self to another, textual one, that will refer to the incident as "some overcute theatricality", performed

---

67   Ibidem, p. 186.
68   Ibidem, p. 182.
69   Ibidem, p. 184.
70   The body nevertheless, as the primary carrier of the lecturer "self", turns out to be the main focus and motivation of the audience's arrival, presence and attention given to the lecture. Already informed of the lecturer's "writings or other activities", the audience is sure their view will be "modified when they can see him in flesh and watch and listen to him handle the transmission of his text over the course of the delivery", ibidem, p. 187. Curiously enough, one of Goffman's most frequently evoked predecessors, Georg Simmel, who often gave not only university lectures but also public ones – considering himself to be some kind of "wandering priest" of his philosophy – allegedly owed the fame of his lectures precisely to a very striking manner in which he gave embodiment to his texts (cf. Janet Stewart, "Georg Simmel at the Lectern. The Lecture as the Embodiment of Text", *Body and Society*, 5: 4 [1999], pp. 1-16).

in order to provide a "frame-analytical illustration of how to go wrong in performances".⁷¹ This excuse being pronounced in the text, the excuses of this kind are declared to be "split off from the mainstream of the official textual communication" and to belong to the speakers' "structural position to betray their obligation to transmit their texts",⁷² that is, to refer to the lecture in their capacity of animators, not authors of the text. It is a kind of "reflexive frame-braking" (ibid) allowed to a certain, fine balanced extent, in any delivery of the lecture, but what about the written one we are reading, whose structural core is such intermittent reflexive frame-braking? Does it remain a sheer transcription of a lecture, a trace after the fact, or induce a reception-performance guided and induced by non-distinguishable layers of Goffman's performance, only seemingly confirming the distinctions hypothesized in the content of the lecture in a form of some non-admitted "overcute theatricalities"?

All suggestions of "The Lecture"'s written-in performativity notwithstanding, audiences usually cannot content themselves with written performances of the sort provided by Goffman's printed text of "The Lecture" (and that is perhaps why Corsaro had such trouble in following Goffman's argument, and so mourned, as a true character of Goffman's satires, the fact that he had missed "the original presentation").⁷³ There is something that draws them to the occasion even when they feel that listening to text transmission is just "a price they have to pay",⁷⁴ in the same way in which "a manifest content" allows for secret, latent enjoyments⁷⁵ – here, enjoyments of the access to the author and to his authority, the "preferential contact with an entity held to be of value", as well as a "ritual access to the subject matter"⁷⁶ of the lecture. Note that it is only a ritual access, "substantive" one being, as Goffman states in parenthesis, "quite another matter". If, however, the lecture's success and the "pleasure" it provides is to be judged according to the way the lecturer balances a precarious "partition between the inside and the outside of words, between a realm of being sustained through the meaning of a discourse and the mechanics of discoursing",⁷⁷ Goffman's *The Lecture* should be judged a successful failure, or, as he would perhaps formulate, "an accurately improper move". Apparently left with nothing but the text and the "meaning" of its "discourse", we are left with a meaning of "the mechanics of discoursing". Curiously, though, even devoid of any chance to have ritual access to the body of the author and his knowledge, we are equally left with the impression of having known his personal self for what he claimed

71   Goffman, "The Lecture", p. 184.
72   Ibidem, p. 185.
73   See footnote number 3.
74   Goffman, "The Lecture", p. 186.
75   Ibidem, p. 191.
76   Ibidem, p. 187.
77   Ibidem, p. 173.

a personal self is: a product of "syntactical relations" among acts of social language, and of "fancy footwork" in-between various social and performative frames of experience, unavoidable in even the most viscerally engaging circumstances, or in situations in which we are forced to give off information about ourselves most unconsciously (even if only apparently, Goffman would hurry to add).

My return to Goffman's deconstructive claims should not, I insist, be read as a plead against lecturing (let alone against its subsequent printing): in contrast, the (mis)performance a lecture occasions – the value of the live human encounter that empowers the very idea of knowledge - may be much more important as "the actuality that matters" than any "truth" the lecture pretends to transmit, and a much more responsible task for any lecturer to deliver - a task that no "lecture-machine", no matter how sophisticated and informed it may be, can thoroughly absorb, fulfill or replace. Nevertheless, let us not underestimate Goffman's nuanced warning that, while righteously raging against the ideological presuppositions of the lecture's old fashioned variant, we may have reversed its former ideal and invested too much - in the moral sense of the term - into its capacity to provide not "calmly considered understanding", but the very effects that Goffman, in his characteristically ironic insinuation, enumerated as standing at the opposite end: "mere entertainment, emotional impact", or "immediate action".[78] We could therefore perhaps reconsider what misperforming the present ideals of our lecture-halls might mean.

Appendix

In search for some profitable academic interest, one could easily correlate "The Lecture" to a marvelous piece of dramatic fiction, Chekhov's *On the Harmful Effects of Tobacco*, since I am convinced the latter would truly profit of some insights of the former (or vice-versa). However, my work on this plead for remembrance of Goffman's half-humorous, half-bitter denouncement of the lecture as a central academic (mis)performance practice he himself used to avoid as much as he could[79] was framed by an unexpected corroboration, that arrived with the rebellion that took place on the Faculty of Humanities and Social Sciences in Zagreb precisely during the preparations for the 15th PSi conference (whose topic was, ironically enough, *Misperformance:*

---

[78] Ibidem, p. 105.
[79] There are testimonies to this fact, as to a relative unpopularity of his delivered lectures, see Yves Winkin, "Erving Goffman: what is a life? The uneasy making of an intellectual biography" and Anne Warfield Rawls, "Language, self, and social order: A reformulation of Goffman and Sacks", *Human Studies*, 12 (1989), pp. 147-172, p. 168. Gary Marx, however, testifies to Goffman's „subtle wit, sarcasm, poker-faced delivery, and understatement" that „had one on the edge of the seat", and states that „the class was entertaining" (sic!), since "Goffman's humour and sharpness were without parallel", and not an end in itself, but "a means to revealing some hidden and poignant truth", and "offered a searing moral message regarding individual dignity" (Gary Marx, "Role models and role distance: A remembrance of Erving Goffman", *Theory and Society*, 13 [1984], pp. 649-662, p. 655).

Misfitting, Misfiring, Misreading). A large group of students took over the Faculty for a period of 5 weeks in order to pressure the University, the Ministry of Education and the Government to legally proclaim all levels of education free of any charge whatsoever. During this protest against the commercialization of knowledge the lectures were suspended, their obligatory attendance having been designated by students as "a system of control" to which they offered an alternative: a daily program of free-attendance lectures delivered not only by some willing professors of the faculty, but also by several independent scholars and intellectuals, as well as visiting professors from Croatia and Slovenia. These included even the famous Slovenian philosopher Slavoj Žižek, whose audience usually counts in hundreds, counter to the almost universally shared judgment of his lectures being just a montage of mental tricks, disconnected anecdotes, jokes and punch-lines, deprived of any intellectual merit.

Despite the fact that the protest was primarily directed against power structures dictating the educational policy from the outside, and having apparently nothing to do with the actual way the knowledge was produced inside the faculty, the very means of protesting – blocking the regular course of lecturing – soon sprang to the media surface as the most contested aspect of the student's action. Almost everybody – including the Dean, the Faculty's Council, and even the Minister of Education – immediately declared their principled allegiance to the student's goals, but strongly disagreed with what was called their "method", claiming that interrupting lectures and preventing other's freedom to attend them was an act of violence putting the whole academic enterprise into question. An enterprise it soon indeed revealed itself to be: the major argument in the attempt to persuade the students to de-block the faculty was the possible suit by those students who paid their right to attend the lectures. This client-service logic finally pressed the authorities to resolve the situation the students produced in a manner finely fitting Goffman's mordant insight into the "unholy alliance" between speakers, institutions and sponsoring organizations that, as he somewhat astonishingly insisted, "may be sustained at the expense of lecture itself".[80] After two weeks of the Dean's unsuccessful negotiation with the students, the web-page of the faculty announced that the lectures were displaced all over various and distant teaching institutions in the city. This was done with no regard for the actual combination of courses which forced some students to be at two locations at the same time, and with no real care if the lectures were attended at all, either by students or by their profes-

---

80 Goffman, "The Lecture", p. 170.

sors, particularly those who declared their solidarity with the student's cause. What mattered was to preserve what Goffman called "the form, the interactional encasement, the box, not the cake" of the lecture, and, of course, the right to charge for it, if only by providing a virtual image of the actual ritual access to the "authority" of the professors and their various "subject matters" whose "substantive" side they did not even have to produce.

The regular course of lecturing thus acquired two alternative modes, two of its doubles, one virtual and the other actual, a free-attendance one, supposedly relying much more on a "truth" worth listening to and delivering for free. However, by substituting the kind of lectures one might be held accountable for delivering and attending by a parallel course of rather randomly organized, free-chosen ones, the students only fortified the insidious workings of the frame of the lecture as a celebrative occasion and an advertised social event, attracting its eventual audience by the authority of the speaker's name,[81] and by the very protesting gesture of civil disobedience both the attendance and the delivery implied. This brings us back to the nauseating feeling that Goffman's work induces, and that cost his opus such resistance and criticism: we cannot break the frames by their more "militantly optimistic" multiplication, since multiplication and compulsory repetition belong to their pernicious, socially unconscious nature.

---

[81] A Goffman axiom here applied: "In a sense...an institution's advertising isn't done in response to the anticipated presence of a well-known figure, rather a well-known figure is useful in order to have something present that warrants wide advertising" (p. 170). Once found, however, the figure only "sells association" with something that currently catches audience's "fleeting attention" (p. 187).

Joe Kelleher
On Misattention

The image we are concerned with may be visible enough, distinctive enough and legible enough. It may even be repeated, as it were inside and outside the performance, so that there is no opportunity either to miss it or forget it. It appears, for example, as several large-format colour photographs suspended behind the audience around the four-sided playing area. These photographs show citizens of a contemporary city in various everyday settings – a library, a railway platform, the aisles of a supermarket, the foyer of a bank, a public swimming pool – paired off, or in groups, hugging each other, chest to chest. This same action will be reproduced on stage for about a minute or so towards the end of the three and a half hour show, the entire cast of more than a dozen actors embracing each other in pairs, holding onto each other like that as if the rest of the watching world could hereafter by all means be ignored. An image, I would have to say, that is striking for its combination of outright banality and insidious weirdness. The banality of the group hug as a basic expression of human sociality, alongside the utter abandonment of everything that gives that sociality its grain and context: the built world, its peculiar places and devices and structures and institutions, let alone the peculiarities and particularities of human difference (which remain conspicuous on stage and in the photographs, even if the production appears not to want to 'make' anything of these differences, except for occasional organization of the action around gendered groupings).

Except, this image of human sociality will turn out to have been a mis-reading – at least at the level of the dramatic fiction. My mis-reading has to do with taking this as an image of anything *human* at all. The performance in question, *Ice. A Collective Reading of the Book with the Help of Imagination in Riga*, by Alvis Hermanis' ensemble company New Riga Theatre, which I saw in Brussels at the Kunstenfestivaldesarts in 2007, is an adaptation of Russian author Vladimir Sorokin's dystopian 2002 sci-fi novel *Ice*.[1] The huggers in fact, according to the story, are a non-human species in human form deposited on earth by means of some stray inter-stellar block of meteoric ice, who recognize each other by communicating, literally, heart to heart. Hence the hugging. They have little use for this planet or its inhabitants – 'meat machines' is how they refer to our particular species. Nothing, then, to do with human sociality at all: at least at the level of the fable. So much for the dramatic fiction, although in a sense what is at work here, as far as the theatrical image goes, is a familiar and fundamental theatrical illusion, or parallax effect as Slavoj Žižek might call it, whereby human being – or indeed any sort of being – distinguishes itself and draws our attention by virtue of registering a minimal difference from itself, shining out as it were with an alien likeness. So it is, in any theatre, with a frame to move against and a fiction to inhabit, that the actor's strangeness can strike us, and so it is that the image we construct upon that strangeness can continue to follow us, however hard we pull away.[2]

Which is to say, the image may be not an effect of a mis-reading – or not only that – so much as something like a mis-spectating, although mis-spectating itself can be a pretty banal matter also. I speak of the banality of the spectator; and I confess. The production of *Ice* I saw that afternoon in Brussels was long and full of talk – it is after all basically a collective reading of a novel – and the talk was in a foreign language (foreign to me that is), i.e. Latvian. There was indeed simultaneous translation in a choice of two other foreign languages, Flemish and French, but only one of which I speak, and that not too well, and the voice in my earphones was soporific, I was tired from travel and, well, to cut the story short, I found myself nodding off through parts of the show. Nodding off and, from time to time, as I do in such situations, hallucinating: by which I mean suffering the sort of image-disturbances, the sort of hypnagogic delusions that come on us as we cross between waking and sleeping but continue to "hug the boundary of the crossing" as we do so.[3]

It is an odd sort of experience, in that these theatre hallucinations can seem personal, as if image were some animate substance oozing from the

---

1   New Riga Theatre's production was made in 2006. Sorokin's novel was published in English translation as *Ice*, trans. Jamey Gambrell, New York Review of Books, New York 2007.
2   Žižek reads a classic literary example, the hallucinatory "stolen boat" episode of Wordsworth's long autobiographical poem *The Prelude*. Some pages later, on related material, he writes: "We are dealing here not with a substantial difference between two particular contents but with a 'pure' difference that separates an object from itself and that, as such, marks the point at which the subject's gaze is inscribed into the perceived object." *The Parallax View*, MIT Press, London 2009, p. 154 (see pp. 151-55).
3   Pavel Florensky, *Iconostasis*, trans. Donald Sheehan and Olga Andrejev, Crestwood, St Vladimir's Seminary Press, New York 2000, p. 44.

representational form and seeking me out, setting up odd little repetition patterns to distract me, pulling out a thread of my distracted thought and giving voice and shape to it there on the stage, whispering to me, confronting me with something, as if "the ground of the image" – to appropriate a phrase from Jean-Luc Nancy – "rises to us in the image".[4] At such times I wonder how it is for everyone else in the theatre. It is a strange form of detachment after all, from one's fellow spectators and from the spectacle that we are all there to witness, involving as it does such an intense adherence of the individual spectator to the images that appear to appear. I presume, though, that the experience is by no means unusual. For instance, I've long wondered whether this was the sort of thing Gertrude Stein meant in her lecture "Plays" of 1935 – a text which deals with the problematic derivation of theatrical "sight and sound" from dramatic literature – when she wrote about how "your emotion as a member of the audience is never going on at the same time as the action of the play".[5] For Jean-Paul Sartre also – to wander further into the literature on the matter – hypnagogic hallucination is an ordinary enough experience, although again there is some sort of temporal displacement at work, some displacement of what is read against what is known or felt. In Sartre's analysis it is not a matter of mis-spectating or mis-perceiving an image that is already there to be encountered, so much as the conjuring of an appearance, a phenomenal form, a vision, to account for a passing idea, a notion, an intention. Hypnagogic images, he writes, "are never prior to knowledge. Rather, all of a sudden one is abruptly seized by the certitude of seeing a rose, a square, a face. Up to that point one did not take notice there: now *one knows*".[6] A particular line of nineteenth century French speculation took a similar tack. Physician Alfred Maury, in his 1865 volume *Le Sommeil et les rêves* [*Sleep and Dreams*] writes that "[a]s soon as the mind rests on an idea, a corresponding hypnagogic hallucination is produced, if the eye be closed[...]. The state of hallucination is nothing more than an intensity of the image-idea, owing to the internal parts of the sensorial apparatus having become more delicate and more readily excitable, and consequently undergoing, in the operation of conception, a more vigorous shock than in the healthy state – a shock, however, of the same nature as that which accompanies thought." This passage from Maury is cited in Hippolyte Taine's 1870 *De L'Intelligence*, a book that also relays some of the author's correspondence with noted hallucinator Gustave Flaubert,[7] although Flaubert appears to put some distance between hallucinations proper and the sort of "poetic vision[s]" that provoke practitioners of the

---

4   Jean-Luc Nancy, *The Ground of the Image*, trans. Jeff Fort, Fordham University Press, New York 2005, p. 13.
5   Gertrude Stein, *Last Operas and Plays*, Johns Hopkins University Press, Baltimore 1995, p. xxix.
6   Jean-Paul Sartre, *The Imaginary* [1940], trans. Jonathan Webber, Routledge, London and New York 2004, p. 39.
7   See Paolo Tortonese, "Au delà de l'illusion: l'art sans lacunes", in *Les arts de l'hallucination*, eds Donata Presenti Campagnoni and Paolo Tortonese, Museo Nazionale del Cinema, Turin 2001, pp. 33-49.

creative arts, such as himself. He writes: "I know both states perfectly; there is a chasm between them. In strict hallucination, there is always fear; you feel your personality escaping you; you think you are about to die. In poetic vision, on the contrary, there is pleasure; it is something which enters into you. It is none the less true that one loses consciousness of where he is." The novelist goes on to say, however, that this poetic vision can itself often be "fugitive, like the hallucinations preceding sleep. Something passes before your eyes; you must seize it on the spot, greedily."

That said, to get back to the production before us, there is nothing particularly hallucinatory or elusive about *Ice*. If anything, the show would appear committed to a documentary procedure, worked through a whole set of dramaturgical strategies that would fix our imagining of the novelistic narrative in images that one way or another *remain*; and which can be seized – literally – in the hand as well as they can be held in mind. Simply put, these dramaturgical strategies include the cast's group reading of Sorokin's novel around the stage perimeter; the performance of selected actions in the space between them; and – a particular innovation of this show – the distribution to the spectators of various picture books that illustrate the action according to specific genres of visual representation. Let me say something of what I remember. The performance takes place "in the round", the cast seated on a ring of chairs encircling the performance space, from where they read out the text from typescript copies that look like rehearsal scripts. Occasionally one or more performers will go into the central space and sketch out a rudimentary action that relates – or so the linguistically challenged spectator must assume – to the action being narrated from the text. The actors are wearing everyday clothes. It all has the look of an open rehearsal, a text workshop. A few props and pieces of furniture are brought into play. A couple of chairs are made to serve as a motorcar. A table and a bathtub appear to be doing service as a table and a bathtub, and sometimes as other things: a bed, a boat, maybe a mortuary slab. From time to time there is some business involving actors slamming each other on the chest with ice-hammers. I don't know what that is about, or at least I didn't then, but it suggests that the story involves some rough violence, interspersed it would appear with moments of tenderness: as I say, couples just standing there, hugging each other, chest to chest, for what seems minutes at a time. Call this, i.e. the action that takes place on stage, a first order of images, a rehearsal of what is to be imagined, gestures towards a more embodied narrative, something to be worked up later but good to be going on with for now. The second order of images, however, is more demanding. The spectators are given aides to provoke our imagination, picture books basically, handed out by the cast, as if to nudge us into capability right now, while the images can still be gathered up amongst us, rather than later when we go home and think about it all in private, if that is what we do. The first book is an album containing photographic snaps of the same actors that we see on stage before us, except "in character" and "on location", in real world settings, wearing proper costumes and pulling "action" poses, again presumably 'rehearsing' scenes from Sorokin's novel; although now that we have the images in our hands and are able to flick through at will, a possibility of displacement is opened up between what is said, what is to be seen, and what may be made of it "with the help of imagination." Our mimetic capacities, so provoked, might then contribute a third order of images to the spectacle, whether or not we consider such a contribution to be made collectively or individually. I imagine, for instance, given a suitably alert and linguistically adept group of spectators, the production of something like a collective hallucination: some sort of supplementary image-substance in, around and beyond the recited text and the rudimentary visual representations, co-habiting with whatever intentional images are given on stage. I imagine myself, or the person sitting next to me, putting our imaginations to work, invisibly, inaudibly, conjuring whatever companionable – or not so companionable – presences we may.[8] All the same, different sorts of visual aide may provoke different sorts of 'creative' thinking, or even delimit the imagination, as well as calling into question the practicalities of a collective reading of the book: whether that is the book being recited around the stage, or a book of images in the hands of members of the audience. The second volume we are given, which we are obliged to share with our neighbor, whoever our neighbor happens to be, and which accompanies a period of the show when the men in the cast leave the performance space and the reading is continued only by the women, consists of a specially commissioned volume of comic-book drawings expressing the argument of the tale through the medium of vividly pornographic Nazi kitsch. "Sharing" these images with the stranger sitting next to me is no more straightforward than the task of measuring the degree of excess deployed in the representational means, not only in relation to the story that the women on stage are currently telling, but also in relation to them "as people". Them and ourselves, human presences amongst whom we find ourselves, visible to each other and conscious of our proximity, aware of what our eyes are seeing, and our hands are touching, imagining, as far as we can or are inclined to do so, each other's imagination to be at work. The third and last book, which accompanies a more elaborate passage of on-stage activity involving bath-water, and the hugging couples, and ice skates, and motorized whetstones on which the skates are being sharpened by the entire cast, sending up showers of orange sparks as the theatre lights come down at the end of the show, is another photograph album. This one contains sepia tinted snaps of uniformed figures in some icy landscape

---

[8]   For a fine essay on adjacent themes see Dan Rebellato's "When We Talk of Horses, Or, what do we see when we see a play?", *Performance Research*, 14:1 (2009), pp. 17-28.

maybe a century ago, posing for the record as people do in old photos, looking a little bit called to attention, and at the same time a little bit lost. To cite Nancy again, "in a photograph there is always something hallucinatory, something that has lost its way or is out of place".[9] I am feeling a little bit lost and out of place myself at this point, trying, but largely failing to put one thing together with another and make a whole that makes coherent sense. It may be that there is some sort of order of images here that might be organized, with the help of imagination, into a representational synthesis, but that's not how it feels. How it feels is I don't know what is there to be seized at, or how to seize it, even though I am pretty sure that these are all, as one might say, "representational" images.[10] Instead I allow the images, the sounds, to adhere themselves to me, if they will: the screeching of the whetstones, the flying sparks at the conclusion of the show, this strange and strangely moving spectacle of a shared and at the same time divided action, each performer, behind their goggles, attentively focused on sharpening their skates. For a journey north I presume; unless they are making ready for a time when the ice comes south, as soon it might. Again, I am wondering how it is, how it will be, for everyone else.

There was, anyway, whatever mis-reading or mis-spectating may have been going on, no lack of attention involved. However, this was not – to deploy briefly a more technical vocabulary – so much a drawing of attention towards a particular synthesis of perception and understanding, but rather an "analytic" dispersal or "decomposition"[11] of attention around various imaginary possibilities. For instance, in and around a perceptual experience that is felt to shift between what belongs to one's sole self and what can be shared, or be imagined to be shared, with others who happen to be there also. There are then, with respect to the theatrical situation where what is given to be perceived is spatially and temporally bounded, further shifts – shifts in how we value what we produce and consume as spectators – between what we are "supposed" to see and hear and make sense of over the course of a show, and whatever it is we are actually capable of perceiving on that particular occasion. Indeed, not just what we are capable of taking in, but what we would *rather* take in: notwithstanding that one may experience all sorts of ambivalences – or say it more straightforwardly, all sorts of guilt – over such preferences and one's "right" to indulge one's desire in such a fashion.

Much of what interests me here is touched on in a recent book by Rei Terada, *Looking Away: Phenomenality and Dissatisfaction, Kant to Adorno*. Terada explores tensions between private and shared – or collective – expe-

9   Nancy, *op. cit.*, p. 106.
10   Representational, for instance, of recent Latvian theatre practice. "For Hermanis, these three assemblages represent the current collocation of theatrical motifs in vogue in Latvia: everyday social concerns [...], titillating voyeurism (decadent attempts at prurient entertainment), and traditional depictions of historical theatre [...]." See Jeff Johnson, *The New Theatre of the Baltics: From Soviet to Western Influence in Estonia, Latvia and Lithuania*, McFarland, Jefferson and London 2007, p. 179f.
11   Cristina Campo, *Gli imperdonabili*, Adelphi Edizioni, Milan 1987, p. 167.

rience through an examination of what she calls "phenomenophilia". She is interested in distraction, and the troubled ethics that go with it: the giving of one's attention to transient, ephemeral, "pointless" phenomena – things that flicker momentarily and insubstantially on the edge of more important stuff, things that appear to appear as it were apart from the main scene, whatever that scene is supposed to be. In the philosophical and poetic examples that Terada considers, phenomenophilia is a deliberate practice, cultivated if not exactly as a means of turning away from the real world, then a way of avoiding – at least for a while – the felt obligation to accept the world "as is". Such experiences, given that the world "as is" is the one we share with other people, tend to be private; we might even say "selfish". They tend to suit those occasions when we don't want to think of others as sharing our perceptions, experiences that we seek out – Terada suggests – as a response to dissatisfaction: dissatisfaction with the world and our relations to the people in it, and with what we might feel as a coercion – not only to *accept* things as they are, to accept that is to say the facts of life, but to *value* those facts within certain normative frameworks.

I should say at this point that much of the pleasure of reading Terada's book – appropriately enough perhaps given the sorts of experience she addresses – is the delicacy of her own attention to conceptual distinctions. It is worth observing, however, that the issue through much of her argument is not just that we experience dissatisfaction in life but that we 'mind' these feelings when we recognize them, finding them in some ways unworthy of us and inappropriate to share, which is why perhaps there is something self-withdrawn in those moments when we look away to the film of ash, the "stranger", flickering in the grate of the fire; or focus our attention on the patch of grass outside the Wal-mart supermarket rather than having to deal with the Wal-mart itself.[12]

There are, of course, freedoms to be found in looking away. Terada writes about the promise of non-coercive relations that the objects of phenomenophilia can hold out, and about the liberating or faux-liberating effects of the appearance of appearance and its temporary suspension – a sort of rhetorical suspension she calls it – of fact perception.[13] She also points out that these experiences are indeed short-lived. As she says, the hope for freedom surfaces, but then it is timed out.[14] In part this is to prevent others from intruding on our experience; but it is also a sort of self-policing, to the extent we do not believe in this hope, or do not trust our belief, or we feel we are betraying something in such activity, betraying the world, betraying

---

12   Both are examples that Terada discusses, from Samuel Taylor Coleridge the 19th century poet and Michael Vahrenwald the 21st century photographer (Rei Terada, *Looking Away: Phenomenality and Dissatisfaction, Kant to Adorno*, Harvard University Press, Cambridge, Mass. and London 2009).
13   Ibidem, p. 21.
14   Ibidem, p. 203.

the others who share it with us, and that we don't deserve such relief from our obligations to the world, or at least don't deserve so much of it. And, as Terada brings out, many of the key texts in which phenomenophilia is attested to tend to be cross-genre literary-philosophical texts – caught as it were between the rigors and distractions of thinking and feeling – and often fragmentary texts at that: like incomplete or fanciful conversations, cracking open a solitude in the company of others who might – after all, or so we choose to imagine – still be there.

I enjoy Terada's book and I am grateful for it, not only for what it tells me and gives me to think about the various concerns explored there, but for what it allows me to understand about my own experience, as a theatre spectator let's say. And also then for what it helps me to translate of that experience– let's say now as a theatre scholar and teacher – into a declared interest in what I take to be legitimate professional concerns, to do with appearance and the appearance of appearance and how all this functions, in Terada's words, as "a temporary phenomenological event and rhetorical effect".[15] I suppose I am saying I like what the text acknowledges about the role of partiality, distraction and incompletion in familiar experience;[16] while acknowledging in turn ways in which I allow my pleasure and interest to defer in this instance to the authority of a theoretical text, in itself a way of measuring up the value of what appears to appear. At the same time I am mindful of what Terada says about 'minding' throughout her book, about a certain sense we may have that not only our familiar experience, but even the interest we take in that experience, might still be illegitimate in some way or other: as illegitimate, if you like, as nodding off and letting your attention wander in the theatre, when the work has been made on your behalf – the work of the words, of the actors, of the books of images – when you have paid for your ticket and everything.

Other authors come to mind. One is the poet, essayist and translator Cristina Campo who writes, in a text entitled "Attention and Poetry", that "truly every human, poetic or spiritual error is nothing, in essence, if not disattention".[17] Another is the philosopher Gillian Rose who, in her unfinished late book *Paradiso*, names attention – the ability to be rapt by what is in front of you without having to seize it – as one of the three qualities needed to become a philosopher, along with eros (a curiosity for all things) and acceptance (of pathlessness and aporia, from which there is no way out only a deepening of the questions that draw you on).[18] Interestingly, in a

15   Ibidem, p. 21.
16   Familiar experience is of course historicisable. Terada makes the point about the historicisation of (mis)attention, specifically Marxist historicisations, on p. 152. As she notes, one of the key figures here is Jonathan Crary. See his *Suspensions of Perception: Attention, Spectacle, and Modern Culture*, MIT Press, Cambridge, Mass 1999.
17   "Perché veramente ogni errore umano, poetico, spiritual, non è, in essenza, se non disattenzione", Campo, op. cit., p. 170
18   Gillian Rose, *Paradiso*, Menard Press, London 1999, pp. 42-3.

passage from one of the essays collected in Mourning Becomes the Law, Rose speaks again of attention in relation to philosophy as a living – which is to say political – practice, as opposed to the coercive authority, as she sees it, of a certain "postmodern" discursive regime. "Do we *assume* sleep, dreams, laughter, rage, sadness?" she writes. "Do we *assume* the moment looking out from the train, when the bare, charcoal landscape heaves a deep sigh, and takes on the hazy hues of brown? Is all knowing *mastery*, and not rather *attention*, the natural prayer of the soul?"[19] I am reminded also of a passage from an essay by Maurice Blanchot on Simone Weill, where attention is figured again as a sort of impersonal suspending of the need to know, the need to possess and make sense of things, although not without keeping open the intermittencies of the heart to desire and whatever other disturbance may be visited upon it, even perhaps a latent panic: "Attention is waiting: not the effort, the tension, or the mobilization of knowledge around something with which one might concern oneself. Attention waits. It waits without precipitation, leaving empty what is empty and keeping our haste, our impatient desire, and, even more, our horror of emptiness from prematurely filling it up. Attention is the emptiness of thought oriented by a gentle force and maintained in an accord with the empty intimacy of time".[20]

Terada – to return to her – proposes a not dissimilar response to the aporias and dissatisfactions that generate phenomenophiliac behavior, although in the end her concern is indeed with those things "with which one might concern oneself". Borrowing images and figures from Adorno and Freud respectively, she rehearses notions of infinite justice and infinite patience: that is to say, the infinite justice of a court of appeal that that would attend to every *particular* resentment; and the infinite patience of a therapist who would attend to the discontents of an entire civilization. The individual resentments involved are, in the example taken from Adorno, those of the slighted or offended lover who knows that his unhappiness has nothing to do with fairness or unfairness, at least not in any universal conception, and who knows that the happiness of any depends upon the free choice and activity of all, but who *feels* hard done by even so. A similar awareness plays out at the level of a civilization – a point so obvious, Freud declares, it is a waste of pen and ink and of the compositor's and printer's labour even to write it down and have it published – that any pursuit of happiness will at some point impede the happiness of others, just as other people's pursuit of happiness can only get in the way of one's own satisfaction. As it is, no-one has the time or the patience for such impossible tasks, and it might be pretty scary if they did (that is to say, the idea is as much dystopian as utopian) although Terada proposes at the end that such figures are worth considering

19 Gillian Rose, *Mourning Becomes the Law*, Cambridge University Press, Cambridge 1996, pp. 136-7.
20 Maurice Blanchot, *The Infinite Conversation*, trans. Susan Hanson, University of Minnesota Press, Minneapolis, 1993 [1969], p. 121.

if they help us understand better "whether and how to think about impossible projects" and why "an unconditional space is a better idea than the few seconds of tolerance we usually give ourselves".[21]

Fair enough, we may say, although another objection to be made to the proposal is that the sessions of such a court, the practice of such a therapy would have to take place – as it were – outside the city, since the only perspective that would enable such justice – such infinite attention – to exercise itself, would be a perspective from 'outside "the human species"'.[22] Except then, we might add, one way of imagining ourselves from outside the city has long been through the framework of the theatre, whether the theatre itself is located at the civic centre or somewhere out towards its margins. I am applying a fair amount of leverage here, doubtless, but I do want to get back to the theatre, because those publicity images for New Riga Theatre's production of *Ice*, which re-appear as billboards within the theatrical space itself, depicting a civic space abandoned to an all-consuming – or should that be self-consuming – species-attention, and the weird un-humanness of that, won't go out of mind. And, while I may have been mis-spectating that afternoon in Brussels, I am not sure it was a matter altogether of mis-interpreting; at least, I don't think it was a matter of misunderstanding the codes. If anything, the codes are over-familiar, speaking as they do of a fundamental cruelty – something obscenely impersonal – in the mechanisms of theatrical representation, whatever the "collectivity" of intention or the means of production. In that sense the whole "alien invasion" theme is always already given. At the same time, though, there are no aliens. The aliens are a fiction. Or rather, the aliens are ourselves, and there is only our familiar and unfamiliar selves: there on the stage, there in the words and the picture books and photograph albums, there in the auditorium, and here in the places where we go over it all again. And on that basis, it is possible, with the help of imagination, to read the literary adaptation as it were against the grain of the literary text, to see passing before one's eyes, like one of the hallucinations preceding sleep, an image of "our" connectivity and collectivity, how it is for the likes of us, a momentarily material image you feel you could indeed reach out and seize.

If I imagine for now what it is that the theatre might have to contribute to these considerations, it would not be the dignity of the judge in their infinite justice nor the authority of the analyst in their infinite patience, but rather the chance-would-have-it passage of the actor-thief across the bounded time of the illuminated stage. I'm thinking, as it happens, of another production by Hermanis' New Riga Theatre company, and another adaptation from Russian literature, their staging of Tatyana Tolstaya's story

---

21   Terada, op. cit., p. 204.
22   Ibidem, p. 204.

Sonia.[23] This involves two stocking-masked performers 'breaking in' to disturb the hyper-realistic scenography: a meticulously detailed reconstruction of a 1940s Leningrad apartment, where the actor-thieves restore to brief existence Sonia herself, one of them reciting pretty much the entirety of Tolstaya's text ("A person lived – a person died. Only the name remains – Sonya"[24]) while the other dresses up in clothes found in the wardrobe and plays out her life in dumb-show. One cannot even call it historical existence, although it seems something more than literary existence, and history I suppose is where she disappears to when her story is done.

It is as if the thieves – thieves first and then actors, or is it the other way round? – get distracted from their original task, whatever it was they came here for (we must presume that task was to steal something), and instead allow their attention to be drawn by all the detail around them – the ingeniously sourced period furniture, the hatboxes, the hyacinths in a glass jar on the tablecloth, the rag dolls lined up across the pillow in order of size, the real jam in the stage jam-jar, the kitchen spoons, the one shapeless dress in the wardrobe – allowing themselves to be drawn into conjuring an image, a phantom, an hallucination of sorts, and attempting to give that phantom a form of life. As it happens, Sonia – the core of her story is that she spends almost her entire life the victim of a long-running practical joke, tricked into corresponding with a non-existent, or rather cruelly fabricated, secret admirer – herself does something pretty similar. She falls for a figment of her imagining. In a way, though, this is what saves her. Her affection is not stolen from her after all; rather it blooms upon the delusion. As for the thieves, they open a bureau at the end of the show and an avalanche of paper falls out, which they stuff into their swag-bag. Presumably this is Sonia's correspondence with her imaginary lover. Evidence, of sorts, of something known, something felt, something conjured out of poverty, if after the fact. They take the paper away with them, as much of it as they can. It might be worth something later.

---

23 First produced by New Riga Theatre, Latvia, 2006, dir. Alvis Hermanis.
24 Tatyana Tolstaya, "Sonya", *White Walls, Collected Stories*, trans. Antonia W. Bouis and Jamey Gambrell, New York Review Books, New York 2007, p. 141.

Part III
MIS(SING)-AESTHETICS, ETHICS, POLITICS

Annalisa Sacchi
Mi(s)mesis, or the Theatrical Way to the Stars

I. LIKE THE STAR-DANCE OF THE HEAVENS

It is a characteristic of thinking about theatre and performance that it must continually confront the question of mimesis. However, whether mimesis has been taken as "imitation" – be that the "imitation of the Ancients" or simple mimicry – or a manifestation of *poiesis* as in the Aristotelian legacy, there is one element that has remained less well known. This has been the case in the debates we have witnessed throughout the last century, over the adoption or the evacuation of mimesis, whether mimesis has been criticized, deconstructed, or ridiculed. What remains overlooked – and something therefore I would like to draw attention to – is the fact that one of the most ancient approaches to mimesis is related to the stars. This understanding of mimesis, which is external to the tradition deriving from the Plato-Aristotle diptych, I shall call mi(s)mesis, by which I mean to indicate a distinction, rather than an error or a radical difference.

The purpose of these remarks is twofold. Firstly, I will show that mi(s)mesis, or a certain interpretation of mimesis, is the origin or the matrix of what, in the wake of Benjamin's thought, has been called the mimetic faculty. In reconstructing this movement one can detect, with a certain precision, the pre-history of mimesis as understood by Benjamin and then by Köller and Gadamer among others. Secondly, I will propose that a consideration of the mimetic process as a regulator of the law of recognition of immaterial similarities offers a strategy for the spectator to engage in the work of a theatre maker such as Romeo Castellucci.

For Walter Benjamin and Theodor Adorno mimesis is a bio-anthropological behaviour rooted in adaptive mimicry and magic and completely divorced from any truth-model matrix. In Frankfurt School mythopoesis, mimesis reaches 'back' beyond the 'mimetic taboo' that was put in place by Plato and Aristotle when they subordinated artistic play to philosophical truth, and sensuousness to rationality. As Elin Diamond puts in: "In their different ways Brecht and Benjamin situate their materialist truths within, not anterior to, mimetic practice. Given the reification of human and commodity relations under capitalism, mimetic truth must be pried open through interpretative labor. Mimesis is this labor: a sensuous critical receptivity to, and transformation of, the object".[1]

In 1933 Benjamin wrote two articles, "On the Mimetic Capability" and "Doctrine of the Similar", where he describes the mimetic capacity as an adaptation to the environment.

These two works articulated in different ways the same set of considerations: the role of nature as a realm that produces similarities, mankind's ability to interpret them, and the resurgence of mimesis within modernity. This discovery of the importance of the mimetic is itself testimony – as Michael Taussig has underlined – to Benjamin's enduring theme: the surfacing of "the primitive" within modernity as a consequence of modernity itself, in particular through everyday-life rhythms of montage and shock as these have been felt alongside the revelation of the optical unconscious, made possible by mimetic machineries such as the camera and the movies.[2] By definition, this notion of a resurfacing or refocusing of the mimetic rests on the assumption that "once upon a time" mankind was mimetically adept. In this regard Benjamin refers specifically to mimicry in dance, to cosmologies of microcosms and macrocosms, and to divination by means of correspondences revealed in the entrails of animals and in constellations of stars.

Constellations of stars: here is the focus of these remarks, more specifically, how the constellations of the stars influenced the idea of mi(s)mesis in general and in particular the theatre work *Inferno*, inspired by Dante Alighieri and directed by Romeo Castellucci in 2008.

Twenty years after Benjamin's speculations, the classics scholar, Hermann Köller, in an extensive research project on mimesis, *Die Mimesis in der Antike*, noted that the original meaning of mimesis "is dance". *Mimeisthai* means primarily "to bring to representation through dance";[3] more precisely, as Hans-George Gadamer pointed out, it is derived from the star-dance of the heavens. According to the Pythagoreans, the stars represent the pure mathematical regularities and proportions that constitute the heavenly order. Thus the history of mimesis can be said

[1] Elin Diamond, *Unmaking Mimesis: Essays on Feminism and Theater*, Routledge, 1997, p. ix.
[2] See Michael Taussig, *Mimesis and alterity: a particular history of the senses*, Routledge, 1993.
[3] Hermann Köller, *Die Mimesis in der Antike, Nachahmung, Darstellung, Ausdruck*, Bern 1954.

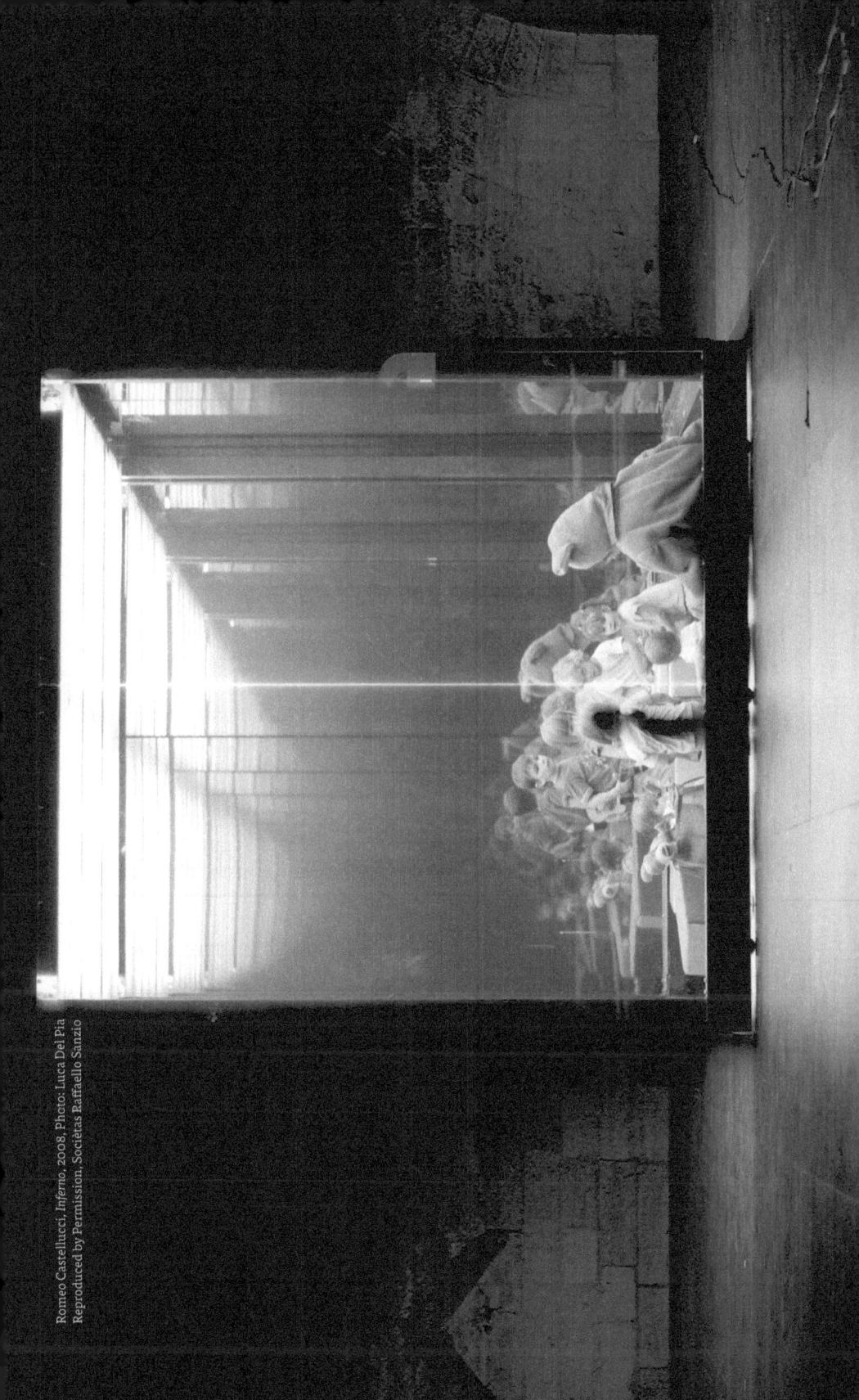

Romeo Castellucci, *Inferno*, 2008. Photo: Luca Del Pia
Reproduced by Permission, Sociétas Raffaello Sanzio

to begin not in making something after the model of something already known, but in bringing something to presentation so that it is present in its "sensual fullness".

In "On the Mimetic Faculty" Benjamin suggests that man's "gift of seeing resemblances is nothing other than a rudiment of the powerful compulsion in former times to become and behave like something".[4] Benjamin postulates that the mimetic faculty is evident in all of man's "higher functions" and that its history can be defined both phylogenetically and ontogenetically. Children's behavior is a prime example of the manner in which mimetic behavior is not restricted to man imitating man "in which the child plays at being not only a shopkeeper or teacher but also a windmill and a train". The mimetic faculty is formative for the child because it allows him to make himself similar to his surrounding environments through assimilation and play. Through physical and bodily acts of mimesis the distinction between self and other becomes porous and flexible. On the ontogenetic level mimesis, once a dominant practice, becomes a way of yielding to nature. Benjamin argues that in Western history mimesis has been transformed through modern science into a distorted, repressed, and hidden force. In ancient societies men would try to influence and control nature by imitating her moods and movements. Thus, in the time before human beings had begun to recognize themselves rationally in relation to nature, the law of similarity was alldominant.

Of course mimesis here has nothing to do with the mere imitation of something that is already familiar to us. Rather, it implies that something is represented in such a way that a similarity is found between a totally abstract order (a constellation) and a familiar figure who might be associated with a story and thus with a particular destiny (Cassiopea, the swan etc).

This appropriation and configuration are realized through a becoming-other, a mimicry: just as the insect becomes flower and so confounds itself with it, in the same way the child becomes the railway and only then does it know and experience it. Man makes the world through an exteriorization: the mimetic faculty is less a reproductive imitation than a process, an activity of interchange between man and the world. The mimetic faculty does not reproduce passively a world already made. On the contrary, it is that original relation with the world that comes to expression.

This is the reason why the similarities the mimetic faculty produces are immaterial: the relation that exists between the image and the thing might be described through the example of the map and the territory. The image is less a reproduction that has fidelity as its goal than a scheme, a drawing that captures essential traits, the borders or the silhouette of an event or a thing: similarity is a way of capturing one's own body through lines that are similar to those of the object. This is perhaps the reason why dance, which originally

---

4   Walter Benjamin, "On the Mimetic Faculty" (1933) in *Reflections*, Schocken Books, New York 1986, p. 333.

schematized the movements of the stars, was for Benjamin the perfect introduction to the comprehension of immaterial similarities.

In his history of the production of similarity, moreover, Benjamin proposes that thousands of years ago stellar constellations not only inspired imitation but were already objects whose mimetic character announced their relation to the possibility of meaning. "As inquirers into old traditions," he writes, "we must take into account the possibility that human beings might have perceived manifest formations, that is, that object had a mimetic character, where nowadays we would not even be capable of suspecting it. For example, in the constellation of stars".[5] Celestial processes were imitated, he suggests, because the possibility of imitation already contained the order to manipulate an existing similarity. In other words, the stars bore within them both the demand that they be imitated and the means - the existing similarity - whereby this demand could be met. The stellar constellations exerted "a powerful compulsion to become similar and also to behave mimetically".[6]

Stars are therefore another name for what makes similarity possible, for the process of mimetic reproduction. Astrology thus represents a subsequent, more advanced stage in the development of the mimetic faculty than simple imitation. The constellations signify an animistic relation to the cosmos. Personified, the stars are invested with the classical quality of the aura: the capacity to return the gaze. As Benjamin speculates: "Do relations exist between the experiences of the aura and those of astrology? Are there earthly creatures as well as things, which look back from the stars? Which from the heavens actually return their gaze? Are the stars, with their gaze from afar, the prototype of the aura?".[7] Within the constellations primitive man attempts to read the language of nature, to elicit its hidden meaning.

Astrology, indeed, interested Benjamin as a key to the personality: in particular, he regards astrology as an ancient proof of a link between humanity and the position of the stars: the "possibility of human imitation, that is, the mimetic faculty which human beings possess, may have to be regarded, for the time being, as the sole basis for astrology's experiential character".

II. PER ASPERA AD ASTRA

And the sky can still fall on our heads.
And the theater has been created to teach us that first of all.
—Antonin Artaud

---

5   Walter Benjamin, "Doctrine of the Similar" (1933), "New German Critique", 17, Special Walter Benjamin Issue, (1979), p. 66.
6   Ibidem, p. 69.
7   Walter Benjamin, "Doctrine of the Similar", p. 66.

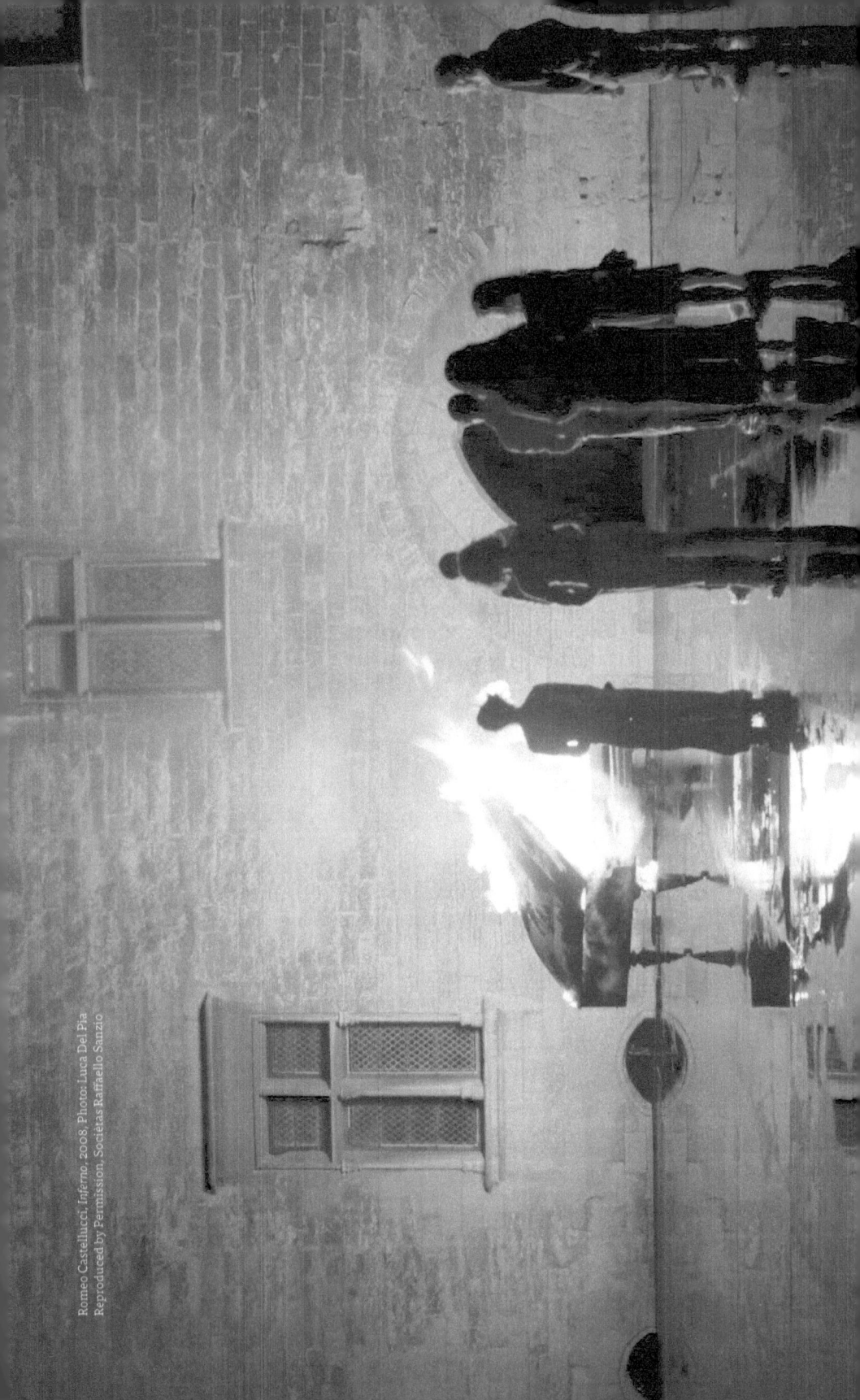

Romeo Castellucci, *Inferno*, 2008. Photo: Luca Del Pia
Reproduced by Permission, Sociétas Raffaello Sanzio

The constellation of figures that Benjamin sets into motion here – the gaze of the stars, reproduction, astrology, mimesis, image – is inscribed in the name that he associates most closely with the possibility of a revolutionary dismantling of the notion of history: the name of Auguste Blanqui. Celebrated as the most unrelenting insurrectionist of his age, Blanqui spent a great part of his life buried alive in the prisons of a monarchy, an empire, and two republics. Blanqui serves Benjamin as a figure not only of the arrest of history that makes revolution possible but of arrest in general. He was imprisoned in the Fort du Taureau during the Commune and it was there, near the end of his life, that he set down his cosmological speculations in *L'eternitè par les astres*. It is a short book, but it casts a very long shadow. Behind it looms the entire history of the revolutions of 1830, 1848, and 1870-71.

Benjamin calls this text – which he first read in 1937 and which, he states "presents the idea of eternal return ten years before Zarathustra, in a manner scarcely less moving and with an extreme hallucinatory power"[8] – the last phantasmagoria of the nineteenth century, claiming that it constitutes a criticism of all the others. Blanqui develops there his theory of the eternal return from his interpretation of celestial bodies and stellar formations. He argues that – given the infinity of time and space in the universe and the finite number of elements that can be combined – all the possibilities of the world are repeated endlessly an infinite number of times and in an infinite number of places throughout the universe.

This law of similitude and repetition has been described by Benjamin as "the mimesis of the stars" and it is decribed in this essential passage of Blanqui:

> The entire universe is composed of stellar systems. To create them, nature only has one hundred simple bodies at its disposal. Despite the prodigious advantage that it knows how to take from its resources and the incalculable number of combinations that they offer to its fecundity: the result is necessarily a finite number, like that of the elements themselves, and to the expanse, nature must infinitely repeat each of these original combinations or types. Every star [...] exists therefore in infinite number in time and space, not only under one of its aspects, but such as it is found at each of the seconds of its duration, from birth until death [...] The earth is one of these stars. Every human being is therefore eternal in each of the seconds of its existence. What l am writing in this moment in a prison cell in the Fort du Taureau, I have written and I will write for all eternity, on a table, with a pen, in these clothes, in circumstances wholly similar. And so it is for everyone. [...] The number of our doubles is infinite in time and space. In conscience

---

[8] Walter Benjamin, *The Arcade Project*, Belknap/Harvard University Press, 1999, p. 25.

one can scarcely ask for more. These doubles are in flesh and bone, indeed in pants and coat in crinoline and chignon. They are [...] the present eternalized.[9]

A revolutionary man, allergic to repentance, Blanqui didn't hesitate to ridicule the inexorable progress that, according to Socialist Ideologists, the temporal sequence would bring to the oppressed. But, as pointed out by Walter Benjamin (the philosopher who, more than others, has emphasised the non-progressive nature of Marxism), by repudiating superstitious faith in the singing tomorrows (Paul Éluard) the prisoner of Fort Tareau became radically sceptical about the possibility of an improved society. Blanqui wrote his book in exhaustion and hopelessness, describing the eternal return of the same which entangled his Epoch. As it was for the sky so it was for society: the inalterable constellations mirrored the inalterability of the dominance of the middle class.

In 2007 Franco Piperno wrote a book, *Lo spettacolo cosmico. Scrivere il cielo* [The Cosmic Spectacle. Writing the sky][10] which ideally represents a reply to Blanqui and to his treatise of cosmo-politics. Franco Piperno is a physician, professor, and a former political leader of Potere Operaio [Worker's Power], the organization of Italian workerism that gathered together a number of theorists (among them Toni Negri). By patiently observing the constellation of the stars – whose regularity is still much more trustworthy than any other repetitive phenomenon that we can experience on earth – Piperno deduces instructions for adopting a political way of living. The Cosmic Spectacle demonstrates that there is no need to fetishize the "new" in order to oppose, every time anew, present injustice. The study of astronomy induces us to pay attention to the complex relation between natural repetition and historical contingency, to the return of the same and the uniqueness of biographical experience. This cosmo-political reflection puts at a distance, in its turn, the myth of progress but with results radically different from those proposed by the disconsolate Blanqui. Piperno, who in his turn experienced his personal Fort Taureau at the time of the special laws that emanated in Italy against the political movement of the seventies, seems to adhere to a reflexion of the young Marx who, writing about ancient materialism, observed that the human aspiration to happiness could be realized also in the contemplation of meteors and in the study of the sky.

To recognize the shape of a bear or of a lion within the vault of heaven is not, according to Piperno, the proof of a naive behaviour or a poetical blunder. It is, on the contrary, the simplest (i.e. inexhaustible) way we know of to give a shape to the sky. A way based upon similarity, not upon

---

9 Auguste Blanqui, *L'eternité par les astres*, quoted in Walter Benjamin, *The Arcade Project*, pp. 25-26.
10 Franco Piperno, *Lo spettacolo cosmico. Scrivere il cielo*, DeriveApprodi, Roma 2007.

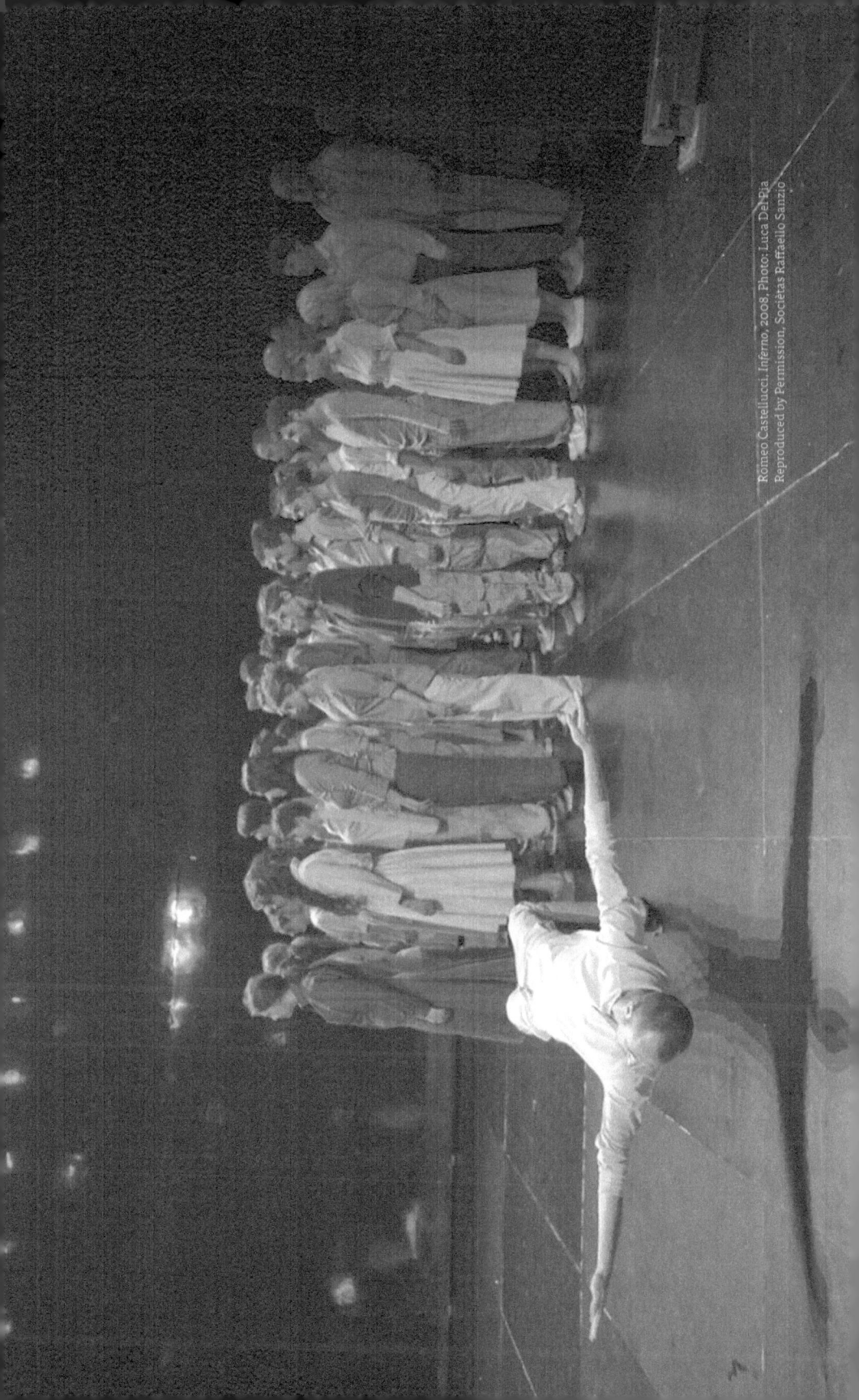

Romeo Castellucci, Inferno, 2008. Photo: Luca Del Pia. Reproduced by Permission, Sociètas Raffaello Sanzio

geometry or allegory. Constellations are the hieroglyphics of astronomical language: they are the superposition of linguistic forms on non-linguistic forms. These hieroglyphics are a patrimony for the whole of humankind. They are a powerful manifestation of the trans-individual – i.e. public – character of the human intellect. They are, at the same time, intuitions of the secret affinities between widely different materials.

Piperno's book is an academic text cast in the light of his political thought. Considered as a book for students it would appear to be at the same time highly specific but also very simple. It is, though, in fact composed for a wider community of readers. Piperno believes that enabling an individual to "read" the sky allows him or her to enter the realm of emancipated spectators. This reminds us that looking is an action and that "interpreting the world" is already a means of transforming and reconfiguring it. "The spectator is active, as the student or the scientist: he observes, he selects, compares, interprets".[11] The emancipated spectator postulated by Rancière is, thus, the spectator of the theatrical spectacle as well as the spectator of the cosmic spectacle.

But how could observing the sky produce political behaviour? According to Piperno, what is at stake is the feeling of impotence and confusion that one experiences while observing the heavens: more precisely, that feeling we traditionally call "sublime". It comes from the disproportion between immensity and our capacity to image it. Piperno believes that recognizing this disproportion allows men to start thinking non-banal thoughts and to perform magnanimous actions. Admitting the irrevocability of the necessary produces a comprehension of the whole range of possibilities held by every human being, raising the political question of *what we are capable of*. If one allows repetitive and impersonal events enter one's conscience, then we become much more sensitive to what is radically singular, unique, and labile.

This disproportion, although initially frustrating, becomes in the end an ethical and cognitive richness. The sublime works through the manifestation of greatness: the spectator, living an ordinary life, can then experience the sense of greatness which evokes, in its turn, elevated feelings. In other words, by observing the greatness of the constellations, the spectator of the cosmic spectacle becomes mimetic with a sense of eternity and absolute being that can be grasped by the mind.

This form of mimetic thinking creates a sensuous relation between the subject and the world. To the extent that *writing the sky* is possible through a form of pictographic script such as the hieroglyphic, it appears very close to the Artaudian idea of the actor's gesture in the Theatre of Cruelty. Indeed

---

11   Jacques Rancière, *The Emancipated Spectator*, www.tkh-generator.net/openedsource/the-emancipated-spectator [accessed 15 April 2014].

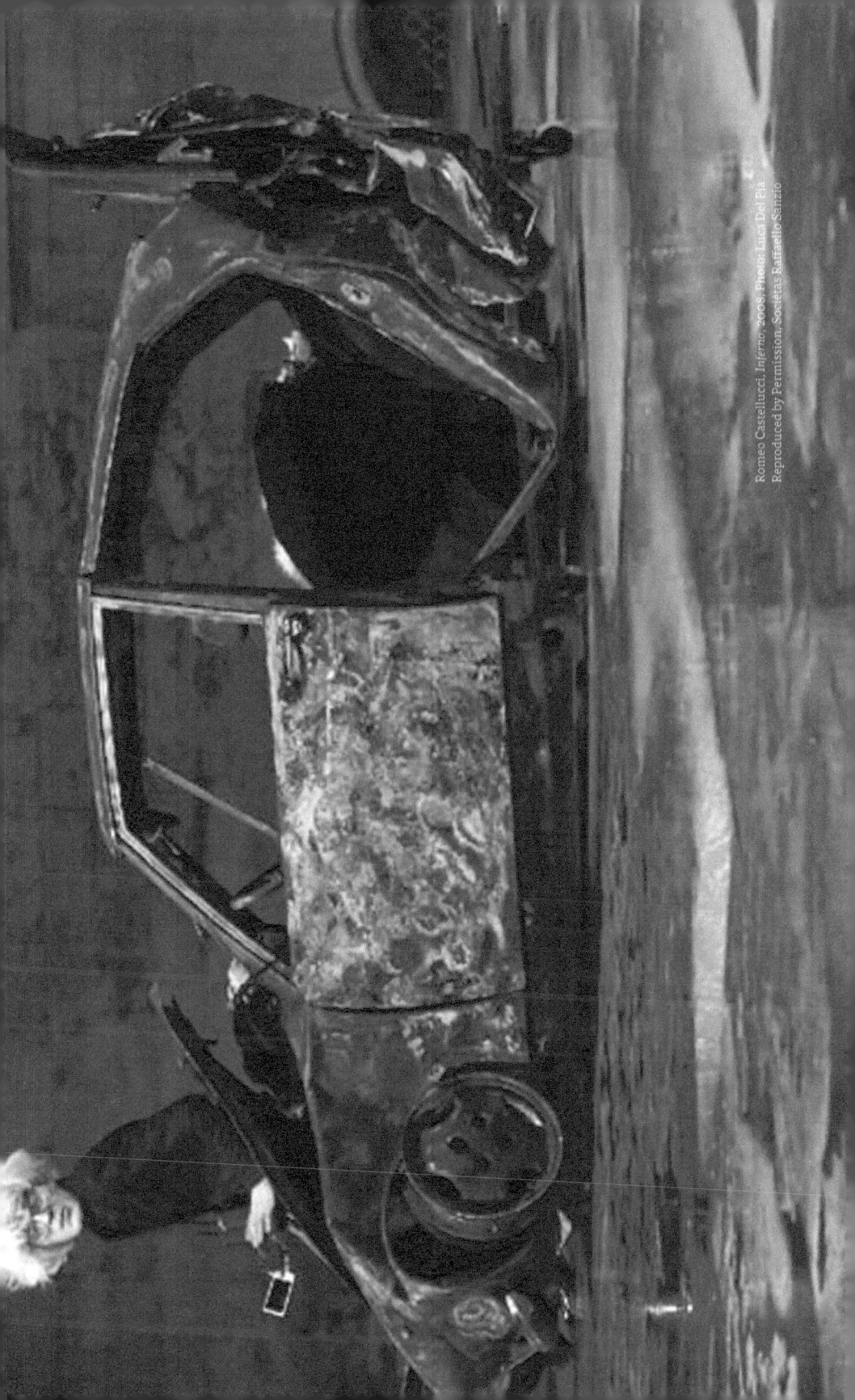

Romeo Castellucci, *Inferno*, 2008. Photo: Luca Del Pia. Reproduced by Permission, Socìetas Raffaello Sanzio

both Piperno and Artaud suggest that what has to be done (in making theatre and in writing the sky) is a work of translation that shows how astronomic formations and political discourses, as well as theatrical gestures and magical thought, translate each other through mimesis. "Those who have forgotten the communicative power and magical mimesis of a gesture, the theatre can reinstruct, because a gesture carries its energy with it, and there are still human beings in the theatre to manifest the force of the gesture made".[12] Artaud figures gesture in terms of work that the human being does so as to keep magic close to him or herself. This energy drives a passion for theatre as a place for knowledge, in which the communicative power and the magical mimesis of a gesture can appear.

This vision and this knowledge led to a sort of oxymoron, an active contemplation, where inoperativity is the organized field of community practices: a form of work and a form of negotiation between sites of agency (the individual spectators) and politically defined fields of possibility. Both the contemplation of the stars, and contemplation in theatre, are forms of inoperativity of the subject-spectator, and the "self" or "subject" is the void of inoperativity at the heart of all action. In inoperativity, "*bios* corresponds without residue with *zōē*." Thus we can understand the importance of contemplation in the Western tradition as:

> the metaphysical operator of anthropogenesis, which, liberating the living man from his biological and social destiny, assigns him to that indefinable dimension what we are accustomed to call political.... *Zōē aiōnios*, eternal life, is the name of that inoperative centre of the human, of that political "substance" of the West that the machine of economy and glory seeks incessantly to capture within itself.[13]

Active contemplation, inoperativity, the capability of seeing correspondences and activating the "mimetic faculty" are some of the most important elements for an emancipated spectatorship, and the basis for *the coming spectator* who, according to Romeo Castellucci, is God. "The spectator is God who sees under a figurative light. The Actor is his Creature".[14]

III. THE DIVINE MIMESIS

E quindi uscimmo a riveder le stelle
—Dante

---

[12] Antonin Artaud, *The Theatre and its double* (1938), Grove Press / Atlantic Monthly Press, 2000, p. 81.
[13] Giorgio Agamben, *Il regno e la gloria. Per una genealogia teologica dell'economia e del governo. Homo sacer*, 2:2, Neri Pozza, Vicenza 2007, p. 270.
[14] Romeo Castellucci in conversation with me. See Annalisa Sacchi, "L'estetica è tutto. Conversazione con Romeo Castellucci", *Biblioteca Teatrale*, 91-92 (2009), p. 130.

Inferno (2008) begins in presentification, mimesis and martyrdom.

Romeo Castellucci's work is inspired by Dante's text, but he does not deliver a literal "adaptation" of the first Canto of the *Divine Comedy*. As he writes in his working notes: "Read, reread, dilate, hammer at and study in depth The Divine Comedy so that it can be forgotten. Absorb it through the epidermis. Let it dry on me like a wet shirt". Rather, he aims at "becoming" Dante: "In this sense, being Dante. Taking on his behaviour as the start of a journey to the unknown." The creator enters the creation and introduces himself:

> I come onstage not as an actor but as myself, since I declare my identity and I say: "My name is Romeo Castellucci." I do not say "I am Romeo Castellucci." It is a name someone else has given me, so that the show becomes not an autobiography but a universal biography. This element is taken from Dante since he introduces himself in the beginning, and all of the reader's experiences go through his body. In a certain sense, Dante's body is always present throughout the journey. Dante very frequently addresses the reader, he calls him by name: "E tu, lettor" ["And you, reader"], so he turns his back to the representation and looks at us.[15]

While Castellucci stands onstage, seven German shepherd dogs are brought on, their leashes held by their respective trainers. Someone helps Castellucci put on a black reinforced protective suit and then the dogs are released. They attack and bite the artist. Romeo lets the dogs tear at him, he offers no resistance, his is a pure and patient passivity even if he must be feeling the urge to act.

The artist's vocation for the wounds of martyrdom, which he inflicts upon himself in the moment of overcoming the *principium individuationis*, substituting this with his losing of himself, his becoming Dante (the Other), is exhibited onstage. By entering the representation at its very beginning, he literally exposes himself to others, to the spectators: he leaves himself open to scandal, to ridicule, to reproof, and ultimately to death. Death is here an explosive and creative force, related to the cosmogonic myth of creation through sacrifice.

Another Italian artist also entered Hell once, an act that functioned like a prophecy. In 1963 Pier Paolo Pasolini started writing *La divina Mimesi* [*The Divine mimesis*] a project that remained unfinished. Pasolini rejected what he called "mala mimesi" [bad mimesis], the imitation of whatever model, in favour of a complex technique that textualizes reality through a

---

15 Romeo Castellucci in Margherita Laera, "Comedy, Tragedy, and 'Universal Structures': Societas Raffaello Sanzio's *Inferno, Purgatorio,* and *Paradiso*", http://findarticles.com/p/articles/mi_7180/is_200901/ai_n52370278/pg_3/ [accessed 15 April 2014]

contaminatio, a plurality of superimposed art works from the Western tradition, such as the *Divina Commedia*. The *Divina Commedia* thus represents for him, as it does for Castellucci, a pure structure for the coming of repetition. Just as for Castellucci, Pasolini's way of going through the *Divina Commedia* was to become a new pilgrim Dante following his memory and his ghosts through the circles of Hell.

In the *Divina Commedia* Dante constructs something that, in its entirety, works like a gigantic theatrical machine, where characters, stories and gestures return again and again. Characters here are individuals that both Dante and the reading public can recognize: famous poets, popes, kings etc. As Pasolini states: "The idea that death (a certain sort of death) gives a retroactive meaning to life is Dantesque. According to Dante, in fact, a biography or autobiography can only be written by starting with the perspective of the end, when nothing can happen to change the form of a life".[16] To put it differently: only after death is it possible for someone to return to the stage of a Comedy; that is to say of a theatre.

In Castellucci's *Inferno*, on the other hand, all of the figures are perfectly anonymous, all but one: Andy Warhol. Warhol is the figure of the inevitability of repetition: in other words, he has done with the idea of an "original" and "unique" work of art. What Castellucci declares, with the inscription of Warhol upon the stage, is not only the loss af the artwork's originality or singularity, but also the loss of that trascendent radiance which was at one time taken to define the essence of artistry.

Thus, the actor wearing Warhol's mask embodies neither a form of representation via imitation, nor a character. She simply performs the form and the movement of a return. The return of someone whom the spectator, just as Dante does in the *Divina Commedia*, can recognize. The return (paradoxically, or even in a certain sense literally) of one who had broken with the idea of uniqueness and origin, one who was himself the perfect illustration of a repetition machine.

Warhol is the central figure of the *Inferno* insofar as he turns the stage into what the stage has been since Greek tragedy: the place for a return. The entire history of theatre is traversed by this desire or pulsion of return, divided between the desire for a continual return of the thing or the subject (a problematic of repetition), and a return *within* the thing or the subject (a problematic of its, his or her [re]presentation).

It is no surprise, then, that in comments on *The Birth of Tragedy* and *Zarathustra*, Deleuze stated that these texts represent a nostalgia for the Greek theatre and, at the same time, the practical foundation for a theatre of the future, where repetition will replace representation. Theatre is for Deleuze and Guattari real movement, and it extracts real movement from

---

16   Pier Paolo Pasolini, *Empirismo eretico* (1972), Garzanti, Milano 2000, p. 254.

every art that it employs. This movement, the essence and the interiority of movement, is neither opposition nor mediation, but repetition. Deleuze and Guattari point out that they are not speaking of the effort of the actor who "repeats" because he has not yet learned the part:

> We have in mind [they write] the theatrical space, the emptiness of that space, and the manner in which it is filled and determined by the signs and masks through which the actor plays a role which plays other roles; we think of how repetition is woven from one distinctive point to another, including the differences within itself. [...] The theatre of repetition is opposed to the theatre of representation, just as movement is opposed to the concept and to representation which refers it back to the concept. In the theatre of repetition, we experience pure forces, dynamic lines in space which act without intermediary upon the spirit, and link it directly with nature and history, with a language which speaks before words, with gestures which develop before organised bodies, with masks before faces, with spectres and phantoms before characters - the whole apparatus of repetition as a "terrible power".[17]

One could say, somewhat elliptically, that this eternal return is the return of returning itself. Theatre – and the idea of theatre that is embodied by Warhol here – thus performs a desire for things to return.

It is fascinating then to remind ourselves that this desire has to do, in its turn, with the stars. The etymology of the word desire in fact brings us back to the book *De bello Gallico* by Julius Caesar: the *desiderantes* were the soldiers who used to wait at night for the return of those who had been fighting during the day. Here is the meaning of the verb desire: to wait under the stars for someone to come back.

High up on the back wall of the stage, during the performance, a sentence appears in the form of a commemoration: TO YOU ACTORS OF THE SOCÌETAS RAFFAELLO SANZIO WHO ARE NOT ANYMORE HERE TODAY. Then, the sentence is replaced by the word "*étoiles*", namely "stars".

Warhol is, then, literally under the stars, under the celestial bodies that exist only through an infinite process of reproduction and repetition. The fact that he himself was a "star" may be just an irony but it marks out the possibility of a correspondence, making the stage, the historical set with all its grandeur and the wrecked car that occupies centre stage, a kind of tomb in which subject and object are encrypted.

Warhol's final gesture is, then, the repetition of a gesture; or in Benjamin's terms, a continuous citation of a citable gesture. Like an ex-

---

17   Gilles Deleuze, *Difference and repetition* (1968) Continuum, London and New York 2009, p. 12.

hausted star, or more literally, like a falling star forced to repeat again and again the act of falling, Warhol thus reminds us that theatre is a matter of return and recognizability; it is the space where History, its images and its ghosts, fall.

A space opens around the question: "Do you recognize me?" an opening that ends with the prayer: "Remember me". Or, after Warhol, "Desire me to return". A space under the stars.

Edward Scheer
Recomposing the Social Drama: Myra's Olympic Snafu

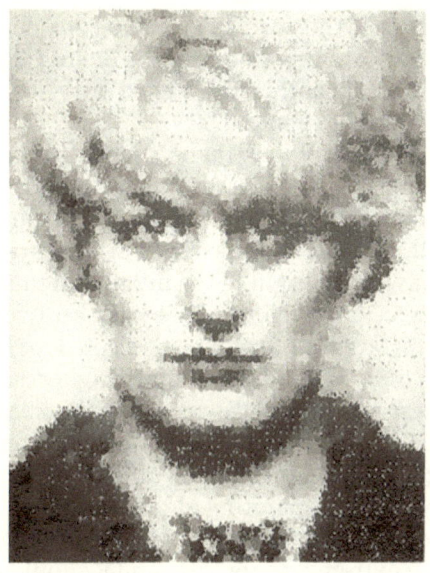

"SNAFU is an acronym that stands for *situation normal: all fucked up*. (...) *Snafu* also sometimes refers to a bad situation, mistake, or cause of trouble."[1]

"Thus, we can define an iconoclash as what happens when there is uncertainty about the exact role of the hand at work in the production of a mediator. Is it a hand with a hammer ready to expose, to denounce, to debunk, to show up, to disappoint, to disenchant, to dispel one's illusions, to let the air out? Or is it, on the contrary, a cautious and careful hand, palm turned as if to catch, to elicit, to educe, to welcome, to generate, to entertain, to maintain, to collect truth and sanctity?"[2]

---

1   http://en.wikipedia.org/wiki/SNAFU [accessed 14 April 2014].
2   Bruno Latour, "What Is Iconoclash? Or Is There a World Beyond the Image Wars? Prologue: A Typical Iconoclash" http://www.bruno-latour.fr/articles/article/084.html [accessed 15 April 2014].

Olympic games opening and closing ceremonies are expressly designed to perform the cultural identity of the host nation. In this sense they constitute ideal embodiments of the notion of cultural performance. The carefully staged limina around these events are similarly constructed as referential and even metonymic. In this sense the performativity of Olympic ceremonies is equally a question of the Butlerian (constitutive of the subject's "collective" identity) and the Austinian (the production by a subject). But what happens when these performances of communitarian ideals misfire? What is the effect of the misfire on the presentation and production (performativity) of community? To take this further I want to consider what happened in August 2008 after the closing ceremony at the Beijing Olympics. At London House in Beijing, the British authorities staged "an official party to celebrate the handover of the Games to London."

Among those at the party were then Prime Minister Gordon Brown and London Mayor Boris Johnson. According to *The Telegraph*: "While the two men each delivered a short speech to around 500 guests, a video screen behind them showed a series of quintessentially British images".[3]

The Star then has it that "right in the middle" of this promo which was "giving a taster of the city's rich cultural life was a portrait of one of Britain's most infamous killers, Myra Hindley, who was jailed for life for four child murders in 1963 and 1964." The admirable forthrightness of the reportage notwithstanding, there was no real discussion of the image in question. Instead the focus was entirely on its impact. The article continues on to note that "both Downing Street and the mayor's office have condemned London's tourist board for featuring the painting of the Moors Murderer, as Myra Hindley became known." It quotes a "Downing Street spokesperson": "The use of this image is in extremely poor taste and it should not have been used to promote London." Boris Johnson's office is quoted in the usual way: "The mayor is deeply concerned by the realisation that a shot of Myra Hindley was shown in a short video at London House and asked that it not be shown again." To complete the picture of confected outrage, even the Liberal Democrat Olympics spokesperson Tom Brake, was allowed to join the chorus in an absolutely typical Lib Dem fashion, an artful melding of parochialism and teacherly moral rectitude: "British art definitely represents some of the 'best of British', but of all the many masterpieces that could have been used, this was the most regrettable and the least inspired choice."

A "senior British government source" was alleged to have told *Sky News*: "This proud night for Britain has been sullied by this grotesque representation of London. Clearly, whoever was responsible must be found and fired immediately." Event organisers *Visit London* defended their inclusion

3   Rosa Prince, "Beijing Olympics: Myra Hindley Visit London 2012 image condemned" http://www.telegraph.co.uk/sport/othersports/olympics/2615247/Beijing-Olympics-Boris-Johnson-and-Downing-St-condemn-Myra-Hindley-London-2012-image.html?mobile=true [accessed 15 April 2014].

of the image, in the following manner: "This is a general three-minute video of London in which an artwork by Marcus Harvey very fleetingly appears. The video is not for general public use and has been used many times over the last few years to show to the tourism trade".[4] The context is broadened to focus on the status of the image as an artwork, which is only one of a number featured in the video.

All of this could be described readily enough as an example of what Stanley Cohen has called "moral panic" but more interestingly for my purposes perhaps it also perfectly highlights the idea of the "social drama". Neither of these are particularly new or fashionable ideas but the image of Myra appearing again in this promotional video requires a renewed discussion of this latter concept. The image itself references a moment of high social drama, a media photo of an infamous criminal but it is also a reworked image, part of the Young Brit Art movement which has redefined the visual identity of the UK. Its appearance in a corporate video for London at the liminal handover event of the Olympics places it again in a crucial gap in the symbolic. It is by no means clear how the image functions across these different registers of criminality, aesthetics and the performance of a national identity. Its traversal of global networked media spaces, national government dramaturgy and local (if London can be local) cultural politics might help us to determine whether the social drama is still a useful term to account for the sort of cultural forces the re-appearance of this image mobilises. It is in this sense of mobilising forces that I will refer to this image as a performative image. I will try here to outline some of the translations of its symbolic potential into different social enactments. I also wonder if this image can help to answer some of the following questions: whether the structure of social drama holds up in the age of the postdramatic? Is it meaningful to speak of a social drama if the stage drama is itself ossified as a form? To put the question differently, is a liquid state of modernity still amenable to such a linear pattern of events?

Returning to the social drama: it was and remains one of the defining concepts in what became performance theory in the then emerging field of PS. The social drama was Victor Turner's conception of the way that societies negotiate change especially violent change. He saw societies and their communities as processes rather than fixed entities. "Community is constituted by a set of practices, a series of 'performances,' through which claims are made about collective and inter-subjective identities".[5]

"Social dramas exist as a result of the conflict that is inherent in societies".[6]

---

[4] The Independent and Sapa-AFP, "Killer used in Olympic ad. Fury as London's 2012 promo uses face of notorious child murderess", 25 August 2008, http://www.thestar.co.za/?fArticleId=4576618. [accessed 14 April 2014].
[5] Victor Turner, *The Anthropology of Performance*, PAJ Publications, New York 1986.
[6] Beth Barrie, http://www.indiana.edu/~wanthro/turner.htm [accessed 15 April 2014]

Social drama and composition

M.D. Murphy describes it as "a concept devised by Victor Turner to study the dialectic of social transformation and continuity." Turner himself says that it should be understood as "a spontaneous unit of social process and a fact of everyone's experience in every human society".[7] This drama has four "acts." The first act is a breach or a rupture in social relations. The second is a crisis following from the breach. The third act is an attempt to redress or remedy the problem, and to re-establish normal social relations. The final act has two possible denouements: reintegration, the return to the status quo, or the recognition of a schism or separation, an alteration in the social arrangements).[8] Murphy adds that "In both of the resolutions there are symbolic displays in which the actors show their unity. These displays often take the form of rituals".[9]

The structure of Turner's social drama owes much to French folklorist Arnold van Gennep's division of rituals of passage into three stages: separation, liminality and re-aggregation (pre-liminal, liminal and post-liminal). The social drama proceeds according to a similar structure: breach, crisis, redressive action, separation/ re-aggregation in which the ritual/liminal phase is the redressive phase: judicial rites, war, other rites. For Turner, drama, theatre, ritual and art grow from this need to deal with crisis and to resolve the ruptures that open in social relations through acts of transgression. Transgression could take no more definitive form than the so called "Moors murders" which took place in the Greater Manchester area of the UK between 1963 and 1965 in which four children were sexually assaulted and slaughtered at the hands of Myra Hindley and her lover Ian Brady who were both convicted in 1966.

This case neatly maps onto the narrative structure of the social drama:

- Breach – the murders break open the social contract
- Crisis – the families' grief, the search for the victims and their killers
- Redressive action – the police procedures, collection of evidence and the trial
- Schism – the perpetrators are incarcerated for life.

At first glance, it's less clear how Myra's image functions in this regard but if we consider the history of *Myra* as image we find ourselves asking similar questions and returning to the language of social dramaturgy and especially the liminal phase of artistic response.

---

7   Victor W. Turner, "Social Dramas and Stories about Them", *Critical Inquiry* 7 (1980), pp. 141-168, p. 149.
8   Ibidem, p. 149.
9   Michael D. Murphy, "Anthropological Theories: A Guide Prepared By Students For Students" Department of Anthropology College of Arts and Sciences, The University of Alabama http://www.as.ua.edu/ant/Faculty/murphy/symbolic.htm [accessed 15 April 2014].

"so much defacement and so much 're-facement'" (Latour prologue)[10]

Myra was a prominent image in the *Sensation: Young British Artists from the Saatchi Collection* exhibition (1997-2000). The works comprising *Sensation* were all selected from the collection of Charles Saatchi who also funded the project. It attracted a record number of visitors in its inaugural presentation at the Royal Academy in London (18 September - 28 December 1997). Largely because of *Myra* it generated enormous controversy. *Sensation* then travelled via the Hamburger Bahnhof in Berlin (30 September 1998 - 21 February 1999) to the Brooklyn Museum of Art [BMA] in New York (2 October 1999 - 9 January 2000) where it became the subject of further controversy. It was then scheduled to appear at The National Gallery of Australia in Canberra (2 June – 13 August 2000) as well as the Toyota Municipal Museum of Art in Toyota, Japan (dates never finalised) but these were never realised. Senior political figures in Australia ensured that the works would never be seen in that country due to the controversies in London and Brooklyn.

Myra the painting is based on a famous mug shot taken at the time of her arrest and which was widely circulated in the British media. In it Hindley's face appears oddly "expressionless, [and] menacing in its impassivity",[11] The artist Marcus Harvey has said that, "The whole point of the painting is the photograph. That photograph. The iconic power that has come to it as a result of years of obsessive media reproduction".[12] His painting is a large scale monochrome 9 by 11 feet (2.7 by 3.4 m) entirely composed from a child's handprints. The image is formed out of the arrangement of hundreds of stencil outlines of the handprints.

For the *Guardian's* Jessica Lack it's all about the hands, "the power of this (image) was in the children's handprints that seemed to claw at Hindley's face, obliterating her features with their tiny grasping palms. It had the chill of horror we feel but can rarely express. In an interview at the time with the writer Gordon Burn, Harvey said: 'I just thought that the handprint was one of the most dignified images that I could find. The most simple image of innocence absorbed in all that pain'."[13] Of course its more than this, more than innocence V experience, the tiny handprints add an unbearable weight to the affectless media image of Myra, they deface not her image, but an image of British society (as a stable self sustaining entity constituted by communities of value).

Arthur Danto notes that when *Sensation* was in Brooklyn, "the Brooklynites, unfamiliar with British headlines, [gave] the painting an aes-

---

10   Bruno Latour, "What Is Iconoclash? Or Is There a World Beyond the Image Wars? Prologue: A Typical Iconoclash" http://www.bruno-latour.fr/articles/article/084.html [accessed 15 April 2014].
11   Anthony Julius, *Transgressions: The Offences of Art*, Thames & Hudson, London 2002, p. 165.
12   http://www.whitecube.com/artists/harvey/
13   Jessica Lack, "Censoring provocative art is the worst advert for 2012", *The Guardian*, 26 August 2008.

thetic once-over and [passed] on to the next work".[14] But Londoners were all too familiar with the notorious police photo of Myra. On *Sensation's* opening day in London vandals attacked *Myra*, in two separate incidents with ink and then eggs.[15] On the day following the incident, *The Mirror* featured the damaged painting in full colour on its front page accompanied by the caption: "Exhibited by the Royal Academy in the so-called Name of Art. Defaced by the people in the name of common decency", and a few pages later, "Attacked: The Evil Picture".[16] The painting had to be temporarily removed from the exhibition for cleaning purposes and was reinstated several weeks later behind perspex and with increased security.

A protest group called the Mothers Against Murder and Aggression picketed the opening, accompanied by Winnie Johnson, the mother of one of Hindley's victims, who reportedly demanded the portrait's removal saying: "Ask the head of the Royal Academy if he would go in and see the portrait of the person who murdered his child".[17] Unfortunately for Mrs Johnson, the then-director of the Royal Academy, Sir Norman Rosenthal, argued that Harvey's painting was the "single most important work of the *Sensation* exhibition"[18] and decided to include it even after Myra Hindley herself suggested that her portrait be removed from the exhibition. In a letter from jail she argued that the work was "a sole disregard not only for the emotional pain and trauma that would inevitably be experienced by the families of the Moors victims but also the families of any child victim".[19]

The Royal Academy's Secretary, David Gordon, defended the decision to let the portrait remain on show: "I have enormous sympathy with the protesters and with Winnie Johnson. We are not a bunch of heartless, unthinking people. The decision to hang the painting is *because* (my emphasis) Hindley is a horrific part of our history".[20] It seems that more than anything else it is the difficulty in reading the image, especially the uncertain pathos of the handprints, that generates the intensity of the response to the image. To return to Latour, it is the ambiguity of the artist's hand that disturbs: "Is it a hand with a hammer ready to expose, to denounce, to debunk, to show up, to disappoint, to disenchant, to dispel one's illusions...?"[21] It certainly looked that way to the

---

14 Arthur C. Danto, "Sensation in Brooklyn", *The Nation*, 1 November 1999. Review posted 14 October 1999. http://www.thenation.com/doc/19991101/danto [accessed 15 April 2014].
15 Dalya Alberge, "Controversial painting Vandalized", *The London Times*, 19 September 1997.
16 *The Mirror* (London), 19 September 1997, p 1.
17 Tamsin Blanchard, "Sensation as Ink and Eggs are Thrown...", *The Independent*, 19 September 1997, http://www.independent.co.uk/news/arts-sensation-as-ink-and-egg-are-thrown-at-hindley-portrait-1239892.html [accessed 22 April 2014]. Quoted in Teri J. Edelstein, "Sensational or Status Quo" in *Unsettling 'Sensation'*, ed. Lawrence Rothfield et al., Rutgers University Press, 2001, pp. 107-108.
18 Jessica Lack, "Censoring provocative art is the worst advert for 2012".
19 Sarah Lyall, "Art That Tweaks British Propriety", *New York Times*, 20 September 1997.
20 Quoted in Sandra Kemp, "'Myra, Myra on the wall': The fascination of faces", *Critical Quarterly*, 40: 1 (April 1998), pp. 38-69, p. 46.
21 Bruno Latour, "What Is Iconoclash? Or Is There a World Beyond the Image Wars? Prologue: A Typical Iconoclash" http://www.bruno-latour.fr/articles/article/084.html [accessed 15 April 2014].

Mama activists. "Or is it, on the contrary, a cautious and careful hand, palm turned as if to catch, to elicit, to educe, to welcome, to generate, to entertain?"[22] The latter would appear to be the reading preferred by the curatorium.

The Dramaturgy of *Sensation*

The Royal Academy used this disclaimer for those interested in viewing the exhibit:

> There will be works of art on display in the *Sensation* exhibition which some people may find distasteful. Parents should exercise their judgement in bringing their children to the exhibition. One gallery will not be open to those under the age of 18.[23]

Inside the gallery, at Burlington House, *Myra* was protected by two security guards.

Immediately following the attack, Tom Phillips, chairman of the Academy's exhibitions committee, reinforces the social dramaturgy behind the exhibition of this painting: "Do people want to throw an egg at Myra Hindley or at that painting? That picture is printed in every newspaper, so perhaps they should throw the egg at the newspaper that prints the biggest picture. There are other pictures to throw eggs at... bad ones, for example".[24]

This comment underlines the work's complex performativity, its remediation of an infamous killer's mug shot, its reawakening of the panic surrounding the murders, its putative celebration of the infamy of the killers in the style of the punk movement's embrace (YBA's most obvious precursors) of criminal transgression, the indexical connection to children's bodies, the subsequent amplification of affect which seems to have no clear object. "Unless you tell me it's withdrawn, I'm coming round to the academy and I'm going to stab the first person I see," was one of the anonymous threats received by the Royal Academy during the exhibition.[25] Here again the agonistic structure of the social drama is clear:

- Breach – the image of Myra in the exhibition in the Royal Academy
- Crisis – the anger and grief of the Mama rally and the public, the vandalism of the image
- Redressive action – the painting is removed and cleaned and returned with greater security
- Schism – the parties differ, 300,000 visit the exhibition.

22   Ibidem.
23   Press release text by Royal Academy of Arts, 12 September 1997, reprinted in http://www.artdesigncafe.com/sensation-royal-academy-of-arts-london-1997 [accessed 15 April 2014].
24   Quoted in Sandra Kemp, "'Myra, Myra on the wall': The fascination of faces", *Critical Quarterly*, 40: 1 (April 1998), pp. 38-69, p. 46.
25   Jessica Lack, "Censoring provocative art is the worst advert for 2012".

As an image *Myra* is primarily a trap for the gaze and a composition of the senses, bringing the viewer into a conceptual and perceptual relation with transgression. Perhaps this is simply to put in play a curiosity and a heightened sense of the potential meaningfulness of a media image. But the provocation inherent in the construction of this painting is also dramaturgical. The making of the portrait of a child murderer with the handprints of a child is designed to put into play this familiar drama. Or perhaps its purpose is to ask about the validity of this particular structure?

We cannot say the same for the replay of *Myra* in the *Visit London* promotional video in Beijing. Here the social drama has been triggered inadvertently:

- Breach – the image of Myra in video
- Crisis – panic about how people will perceive London and UK politicians
- Redressive action – all the politicians denounce the video and its makers
- Schism – the parties differ.

In attempting to assemble an affective composition that will speak to the essential sentimental nationalism of the Olympics, the editors of the video misread the image. That is they read it as a pure image without its essential performativity. They constructed it as an image *about* controversy and that promotes YBA art as yet more preposterous ornamentation in a society awash with extravagant imagery. In *The Guardian* Jessica Lack identifies the montage as a statement that "London may not have 40,000 drummers or an unlimited budget with which to herald the opening ceremony in 2012, but it does have a rich cultural heritage that is energising, all-embracing and supposedly uncensored." She adds: "Let us not jeopardise this at the first hurdle".[26]

Whatever the misfires of the editors of the *Visit London* video, the video itself certainly misfired in terms of its presentation of an image of British society and London in particular as a seat of Humanitarian values. The image of Myra also disrupted the smooth performance of the hand over by exposing the makers' hand, pulling focus onto the constructedness of the image of London in the video, revealing "the anthropology of a certain gesture, a certain movement of the hand".[27]

Latour asks: "what if hands were actually indispensable to reaching truth, to producing objectivity...?"[28]

26 Ibidem.
27 Bruno Latour, "What Is Iconoclash? Or Is There a World Beyond the Image Wars? Prologue: A Typical Iconoclash" http://www.bruno-latour.fr/articles/article/084.html [accessed 15 April 2014].
28 Ibidem.

The metastatic recomposition of the social drama

Following Latour again I want to continue to read *Myra*'s mis-performance by raising a question about the very terms I have been using here, that is, of the social dramaturgy itself. In his recent *Compositionist Manifesto*,[29] he identifies a need for the terms of our relations between knowledge and nature for example, to be entirely recomposed. In this current context, in relation to the work that is done by a media event such as *Myra* spiralling seemingly out of control, this would mean a new set of terms beyond the social drama to allow for a non-linear or discontinuous narrative of events. So the acts in the social drama are reconfigured to contain the notion of the composition of the social, the new dramaturgy in which the formation of the social as a media ecology moves into focus just as the environment itself moves into a state of advanced decomposition. A dramaturgy of the social will now have to address an ecology of relations which do not so much progress along a well ordered narrative path (breach, crisis etc.) but metastasise in the manner of cancerous cells or media stories.

In metastasis the structure of the social composition/decomposition pathway might be as follows:

- Division (of cells)
- Dispersion (in the bloodstream)
- Re-attachment (to the lining of blood vessels… to the channels or non places) and
- Replication (proliferation of cells).

What would this mean for *Myra*? What further displacements will she need to undergo?

- Division, the unified image of Great Britain divided by the image of a transgressor
- Dispersion (in the media)
- Re-attachment (the image is returned to the institutions of art)
- Replication (other artists continue the work of transgression)

"Division", like Turner's "Breach", contains the sense and status of a rupture but also suggests that something forms from the rupture beyond the break. The fact of division means that two or more entities must now be recognised and possibly reconciled. "Dispersion" clearly connotes a different order of event to Turner's "Crisis" but since there is no way of measuring the impact of the new divided state without recourse to a media

---

29   A draft version of *An Attempt at a Compositionist Manifesto* (*New Literary History*, 41 (2010), pp. 471–490) was posted on Latour's site at the above address at the time of writing. The final version does not contain the exact quotations from the draft which is no longer available.

which itself names, reproduces and distributes the event, then there is no sense in which it is a genuine crisis for the social and the media maintains its central governing function. The misfire of the media ritual of *Myra* is not therefore a crisis, as the power of the players is not questioned or displaced. Media and political figures are still the centre of the story and therefore continue to "manage" the meaning making processes of the social sphere. The image of *Myra* threatens the logic of the presentation in which it appears but is always contained and regulated. The dispersion of the divisive event is therefore potentially disruptive but largely at the level of affect. There may be a feeling of anxiety or discomfort at the image of *Myra* in the Video but what genuine threat is posed? So there is no crisis just a feeling of one always narrowly avoided. After the momentary moral panics have all died down *Myra* re-attaches to the media and art environments from which she sprang but this process of division and dispersion will always re-occur as long as art images continue to threaten their social and perceptual frames.

Myra's Olympic snafu then helps us articulate a minor recomposition of the social drama and one which reflects the recombinant nature of this structure in contemporary mediatised culture. A breach may be discernable in a solid structure but in a "liquid modernity" how can we be certain that the fabric is torn? We can see that formerly unified entities come apart and split and then go their different ways then reassemble with different properties and alternate valencies. As *Sensation* travelled beyond London, first to Berlin, *Myra* reattached to the bland apparatus of the fine arts. It returned to the world of painting. But when it went to New York USA, to the Brooklyn Museum of Art [BMA] (2 October 1999 – 9 January 2000) other images became controversial and the structure of the panic/drama/snafu started all over again (replication).[30]

The focus of the controversy this time was the Nigerian born artist Chris Ofili's painting *The Holy Virgin Mary*. This painting depicts an African Madonna surrounded by images "from blaxploitation movies and close-ups of female genitalia cut from pornographic magazines", and shapely lumps of elephant dung. The dung was supposedly "formed into shapes reminiscent of the cherubim and seraphim commonly depicted in images of the Immaculate conception and the Assumption of Mary".[31]

The replication of the perceived transgression and associated panic response was partly generated by the BMA itself by advertising *Sensation* with a message labelled as a "Health Warning" which read as follows: "The contents of this exhibition may cause shock, vomiting, confusion, panic, euphoria and anxiety. If you suffer from high blood pressure, a nervous dis-

---

30   In the following discussion I am indebted to Sarah Knopman who provided all the key references and conducted the principal research on *Sensation* for her own project.
31   http://en.wikipedia.org/wiki/Chris_Ofili [accessed 14 April 2014].

order, or palpitations, you should consult your doctor before viewing this exhibition".[32]

The President of the American "Catholic League for Religious and Civil Rights", William Donahue, responded by calling for a rally to take place outside the BMA on the exhibition's opening day, where vomit bags would be distributed, "in direct response to the exhibit's warning that seeing it may induce vomiting".[33] He wrote to New York City Council requesting that the museum have its public funds withdrawn and made the further point that "(n)ow that art has been reduced to dung and puke, there is no better time for public officials to stop all funding of the arts".[34] Other responses were similarly theatrical. Carol Becker notes that in September 1999 the artist Scott LoBaido threw horse manure at the BMA building, and later appeared at the museum with a 3-foot painting of the BMA Director, Arnold Lehman sucking a pig's behind.[35]

The then Mayor of New York, Rudy Giuliani, a staunch Catholic, took up the attack on the BMA and *Sensation* by threatening to sack the BMA's board of directors, to withhold all government financial funding from the BMA and to evict the museum from its city-owned premises. Giuliani claimed that "public funds are being used to aggressively bash the religious views of a significant number of people in this city and state and country. And the question is can tax payers' dollars be used for this kind of disgusting... anti-religious... demonstration?"[36]

Finally the crisis produced the same form of reverse iconoclasm that had befallen *Myra* in London. In December 1999, Ofili's *The Holy Virgin Mary* was vandalised, this time by a seventy-two year old "devout Catholic", Dennis Heiner, who "smuggled white latex paint into the museum in an empty hand-lotion container, slipped behind the plexiglass protecting Chris Ofili's elephant-dung-adorned *The Holy Virgin Mary*, squirted the painting, and smeared the paint around with his hands".[37] We see the same uncertainty about the hand of the "mediator" behind this instance of "iconoclash", the same intense ambiguity around Ofili's intentions and Heiner's response to those intentions: "Is it a hand with a hammer ready to expose, to denounce, to debunk, to show up, to disappoint, to disenchant, to dispel one's illusions,

---

32 Quoted in Robert R. MacDonald "Tolerance, Trust and the Meaning of Sensation," *Museum News*, 79: 3 (May-June 2000), p. 48.
33 William Donahue, "Vomit Bag Protest Mounts at Brooklyn Museum", Catholic League for Religious and Civil Rights archived release, 30 September 1999 http://www.catholicleague.org/99press_releases/pr0399.htm.
34 Ibidem.
35 Carol Becker, "The Brooklyn Controversy: A View From the Bridge" in *Unsettling "Sensation"*, ed. Lawrence Rothfield et.al., p. 16.
36 Giuliani, quoted in David Halle, "The Controversy over the Show 'Sensation' at the Brooklyn Museum, 1999-2000," in *Crossroads: Art and Religion in American Life*, eds Alberta Arthurs and Glenn Wallach, The New Press, New York 2001, p. 140.
37 Joshua Gamson, "The Culture wars", *The American Prospect*, 30 November 2002. http://prospect.org/cs/articles?article=the_culture_wars# [accessed 15 April 2014]. The white paint was water-soluble and was easily removed and did no damage to the composition.

to let the air out? Or is it, on the contrary, a cautious and careful hand, palm turned as if to catch, to elicit, to educe, to welcome, to generate, to entertain, to maintain, to collect truth and sanctity?"[38]

In the ensuing trial between the city of New York and the BMA, Judge Nina Gershon found in favour of the BMA and ordered Mayor Giuliani and the city to restore its funding and to cease attempts to evict it from its city-owned premises, citing First Amendment rights and adding: "There is no federal constitutional issue more grave than the effort by government officials to censor works of expression and threaten the vitality of a major cultural institution, as punishment for failing to abide by government demands for orthodoxy".[39]

This case more clearly describes the narrative of the social drama than *Myra*'s Olympic snafu:

- Breach – the image of *The Holy Virgin Mary* in the exhibition
- Crisis – moral panic about Catholic icons and values
- Redressive action – juridical action (trial between the city of New York and the BMA)
- Re-aggregation – the judge finds for the BMA

In terms of the metastatic recomposition of the social drama, we see the following structure:

- Division: "Jesus Christ to the right, freedom of expression to the left".[40]
- Dispersion (in the media)
- Re-attachment (the image is returned to the institutions of art)
- Replication (the work of transgression and taboo goes on... the show is scheduled to go to Australia)

The Absence of *Sensation*: an Australian drama

Then finally in Australia, the hand of god triumphed over the hand of man. The show was scheduled to be exhibited at the National Gallery of Australia in Canberra in the year 2000 as the major exhibit for the year but on 27 November 1999, the then gallery director of the NGA, Brian Kennedy, issued

---

38   Bruno Latour, "What Is Iconoclash? Or Is There a World Beyond the Image Wars? Prologue: A Typical Iconoclash" http://www.bruno-latour.fr/articles/article/084.html [accessed 15 April 2014].
39   Quoted in Stephanie Cash, "Brooklyn Museum Wins Round Against Mayor" in *Art in America*, 87: 12 (December 1999), p. 23.
40   Steven C. Dubin, "How Sensation Became a Scandal", *Art in America*, 88: 1 (January 2000), p. 53. Dubin describes the protests in New York the previous year against the production of Terrence McNally's *Corpus Christi*, which depicts the life of Jesus and the apostles as the story of a gay man and his friends in modern day Texas: "Cops kept the two groups [of opposing protesters] separated across a large no-man's-land. They directed newcomers with the command: 'Jesus Christ to the right, freedom of expression to the left'. Rarely has there been such a vivid and tangible embodiment of one of the deepest divisions in contemporary American society."

a press release announcing that the gallery had cancelled *Sensation*. The statement declared in part: "As a publicly funded institution, the Gallery will not proceed with a show which has been the centre of a furore in New York over issues which have obscured discussion of the artistic merit of the work of art".[41] Kennedy had earlier sought the views of Federal Arts Ministers Richard Alston and his deputy Peter McGauran - both extreme social conservatives – about *Sensation*. Kennedy later revealed that the subsequent decision to cancel the exhibition reflected their concerns.[42] This extreme act of censorship passed with barely a murmur in the Australia media. There was certainly some protest in the Arts pages but no widespread public discussion about the individual works in *Sensation* or their significance to an Australian context. So *Myra* and *The Holy Virgin Mary* returned to their quiet places on the wall.

In early 2010, on the occasion of a major retrospective of Ofili's work in London, *The Telegraph*'s Gareth Harris reported that "in a neat twist, the work *(The Holy Virgin Mary)* is now in the hands of David Walsh, a Tasmania-based millionaire mathematician and vineyard owner ... (who) bought the headline-hitting Ofili from Saatchi three years ago and plans to show the collage in his new private museum which is set to open in Hobart early next year (so *The Holy Virgin Mary* will get an Oz outing after all)".[43] In this final act of the post-social drama the hands of the collector are now at stake. Walsh's extraordinary private Museum MONA, which did indeed open in January 2011, showcases around 800 of the over 2000 works of a collection which is purposely celebratory of iconoclastic art. So far there have been no signs of moral panic concerning the collection though it is exhibited in Hobart, a small city at the bottom of Australia. Perhaps the distance diminishes the drama...

---

41   Gareth Harris, "Chris Ofili's The Holy Virgin Mary returns to London", *The Telegraph*, 28 January 2010, http://www.telegraph.co.uk/culture/art/art-news/7093216/Chris-Ofilis-The-Holy-Virgin-Mary-returns-to-London.html [accessed 14 April 2014].
42   This decision probably destroyed Kennedy's reputation in the sector and he did not remain in the job for much longer.
43   Gareth Harris, "Chris Ofili's The Holy Virgin Mary returns to London", *The Telegraph*, 28 January 2010, http://www.telegraph.co.uk/culture/art/art-news/7093216/Chris-Ofilis-The-Holy-Virgin-Mary-returns-to-London.html [accessed 14 April 2014].

Maaike Bleeker
Challenging forth the Truth: Rabih Mroué's *On Three Posters*. *Reflection on a Video-performance*

In 1999, Lebanese artist Rabih Mroué encountered the tapes of a video testimony recorded in 1985 by a Lebanese resistance fighter just hours before he left for his suicide mission. Mroué was familiar with such video messages as they used to be broadcast on the TV news after the successful completion of the fighters' mission. However, what was shown on TV had always been only one final version, or as Mroué puts it "an uncontestable and unequivocal document". The original tapes confronted him with things he had not seen on TV. The testimony appeared to have been shot in three versions and these versions showed what had been lacking from the clear statements on television: hesitations, errors and stuttering. These misperformances were revealing, Mroué observes, for "The instant we saw the stuttering we realized something so simple it was obvious: That the martyr was not a hero but a human being".[1] Mroué decided to make a performance based on the tapes in which he disentangles what he terms "the fabrication of the truth" in these tapes. This performance, titled *Three Posters* (2000) was performed with considerable success in Beirut and abroad until in 2004, Mroué and his collaborator Elias Khoury decided to stop performing it. Mroué created a new work, a video lecture (*On Three Posters. Reflection on a video-performance by Rabih Mroué*) in which he explains that the suicide mission carried out by the fighter who had recorded the testimony had been an act of a secular left

1   Rabih Mroué in *On Three Posters, a video-lecture by Rabih Mroué* (Rabih Mroué, 2004) and Rabih Mroué, "The Fabrication of Truth" in *Tamáss 1. Contemporary Arab Representations. Beirut/Lebanon*, ed. Catherine David, Fundació Antonio Tapies, Barcelona 2002, pp. 114-117.

wing resistance fighter directed against a foreign power (Israel) occupying his country. This action has nothing to do with the terrorist acts executed by Islamic fundamentalists that have come to dominate our understanding of suicide missions after 9/11. Nevertheless, after 9/11 this type of terrorism started to become increasingly part of how *Three Posters* was perceived. Considering this a misperformance, Mroué and Khoury decided to stop performing *Three Posters*. In the video lecture *On Three Posters*, Mroué blames this misperformance on the media framing the performance in inappropriate ways.

For Mroué, both the final version of the testimony and the post-9/11 perception of his own performance fail. The reason why they fail is that they do not do justice to the moment from which the tapes originate, i.e. the "there and then" in front of the camera. Both the edited version of the tape and the performance fail to reconnect us viewers, here and now, to the actuality and authenticity of that moment. Such misperformance however, I will argue, might actually be called characteristic for how media perform as part of what Jon McKenzie (2001) has termed the *performance stratum*. Performance, McKenzie argues, will be to the twentieth and twenty first century what discipline was to the eighteenth and nineteenth century, that is, a formation of power and knowledge. This formation is historical in that it is part and parcel of the global emergence of technological media and information technologies such as computers and electronic networks. "The emergence of this hypermediating media affects all cultures, all organizations, all technologies, for the digitalization of discourses and practices enables them to be recorded, edited and played back in new and uncanny ways".[2] These technological transformations, McKenzie observes, challenge forth the world in new ways. This situation requires that we take into account not only what we or others do with media, but also how media act, i.e. the performativity of the media themselves. In this situation, I will argue, the fabrication of the truth in the video testimony of the martyr becomes the image par excellence of how within the cultural and historical context of the performance stratum, truth is challenged forth by a combination of human and technological performance.

In the following I will elaborate this point, starting from a closer look at Mroué's account (in *On Three Posters*) of what watching the original rushes of the video testimony did to him and how he wanted to translate this into a performance. His account of the performativity of these video recordings reminds of Barthes' account of photography in his *Camera Lucida*, the book in which Barthes introduces his famous notion of the *punctum* as the seemingly insignificant detail that provides us with a sense of connection to the authenticity of the moment "there and then" when

---

2   Jon McKenzie, *Perform or Else: From Discipline to Performance*, Routledge, London and New York 2001.

the photograph was taken. It is not my intention to present Barthes as an explanation of "how it is" with photography or with the video messages that are the subject of Mroué´s work. Rather, I will argue, Barthes *Camera Lucida* presents a culturally and historically specific account of what photography does. This account is culturally and historically specific in that it is part and parcel of a cultural situation in which media act as the image of a pre-existing reality as a result of which they are capable of causing a temporal hallucination by suggesting the possibility of providing us with a direct connection to the moment there and then in front of the camera. This understanding of the relationship between the media image and reality is both constitutive of Barthes account of photography and reiterated and reconfirmed by it. Such reiteration is also noticeable in Mroué´s account of what the rushes of the video testimony do to him, how they appear as material witnesses of a reality we had not seen before, of the actual reality in front of the camera.

However, as Mroué observes, there is also something peculiar with the video testimony since the temporal hallucination produced by these video images does not only point backward but also forward. The video produces the speaker as the martyr he is not yet at the time of the recording. As a result, the video testimony performs the proof of something that had not happened yet. This potential of video recordings to perform something that was not yet there at the time of the recording would later be the reason that Mroué decided to stop performing *Three Posters* when after 9/11 the audience started to see the video testimonies in a different way. This potential, I will argue, is characteristic for the performance of media technology in the age of the performance stratum. Accounting for this performance of media technology requires a different understanding of how technologies of recording mediate in a reordering of the relationship between past, present and future.

Starting from Mieke Bal´s concept of the navel, I will propose a different reading of this potential, not in terms of an evil genius using the media to frame the performance in an unfavorable way, but as the result of the performativity of media technology, and how this involves precisely the forward directed temporal hallucination that Mroué observes in the video testimony. Like the punctum, the navel describes a seemingly insignificant detail, or a detail that seems to fall outside of what is represented. The navel however does not present the promise of a direct link to the moment of origin but redirects attention to the work going on between what is perceived and the perceiver. Doing so, the navel draws attention to the workings of the lecture machine that is the performance stratum, and how within this cultural condition truth is no longer revealed but challenged forth by the complex interplay of human and technological performance.

Temporal Hallucinations

The video lecture *On Three Posters* opens with a frontal shot showing Rabih Mroué from the waist up and against a white background. He is facing us and seems to be addressing us directly, saying: "Ladies and Gentlemen, good evening. I am happy to be here with you in this room and would like to thank you for are attending this session".[3] With this warm welcome, Mroué mocks *and* highlights the mediated character of his video lecture, and both at the same time. Here with us in this room is where he is not. He is speaking to us from a time that is no more, yet addresses us as if what we see unfolds in the here and now, a here and now of which he is part. This performative gesture of his video lecture thus reiterates the structure of the video messages that were the subject of his performance *Three Posters*.

These testimonies show the resistance fighters talking to the camera like Mroué does, and through this camera addressing their audience as if talking to them in a shared time and space. Time and space, however, is precisely what they do not share with their audiences. Not only because their messages were previously recorded. The disconnection is even more radical. Broadcasting confirms the successful completion of their mission, that is, being broadcasted their messages confirm the persons talking are already dead by the time the video is shown.

The final cut of their testimonies showed their messages as clear and unequivocal statements. What fascinated Mroué about the uncut rushes is how these take us back to the moment in front of the camera, that is, to a kind of non-place between life and death where the martyr-to-be, driven by what Mroué proposes to understand as "unformulated and unformulable desire both to defer death and to withdraw from life",[4] is struggling to record his testimony. Mroué´s description of the stuttering, the hesitations and the little mistakes made by the person in front of the camera the camera, and how these allowed him to connect to the authenticity of the moment "there and then", is similar in many ways to Barthes´ elaborations on punctum as the detail in the photograph that seems to escape coding and intention. Such details, according to Barthes, seem to provide access to the authentic moment then and there in front of the camera.

Barthes wrote his account of photography while being overcome as he puts it "with 'an 'ontological' desire" to know what photography is 'in itself'".[5] He may have been preoccupied with such ontological desire while writing, however, what he writes about is not about what photography is, but about what some photographs do to him. His text is about the performativity of certain photographs. This performativity, furthermore, is not a matter of the qualities of the photographic image, but results from how certain

---

3   Rabih Mroué in *On Three Posters*.
4   Ibidem.
5   Roland Barthes, *Camera Lucida*, trans. Richard Howard, Vintage, London et al. 1993, p. 3.

photographs appeal to his desire for something beyond the image. Actually, Barthes is quite explicit about this. What he is looking for is his mother. Writing shortly after her death, he is looking for a photograph that can provide him with a sense of "yes, there she is". He is looking for the photograph that can bridge the abyss separating her authentic presence "there and then" from him being present here and now. The photograph that does the job for him is the famous Winter Garden photograph showing his mother as a little child, the photo that is for him "the treasury of rays which emanated from my mother as a child, from her hair, her skin, her dress, her gaze, *on that day*".[6]

In Barthes' account, the potential of the photograph to provide this sense of reconnection to the authentic presence in front of the camera is not a matter of the formal qualities of the photographic image. Actually, the performativity of photography has very little to do with what is there to be seen in the image. In this sense one might argue that Barthes' account of photography is not about the photographic image at all. It is about how the medium of photography appeals to our imagination. Important to Barthes' account of how photography appeals to our imagination is how photography presents the promise of a connection to what was there and then in front of the camera.

Importantly, Barthes does not claim that photography actually grants such a direct connection to what was there and then, but only that certain photographs may give us that *impression* of doing so He is writing about a temporal hallucination evoked by certain photographs and he describes this possibility in terms of, on the one hand, something certain photographs do to us and, on the other hand, as the result of what we do to them, what we desire from them, what we are looking for in them. That is, he explains this potential of photography as something happening at the intersection of the performativity of the medium of photography and the performance of perception.

One of the photographs Barthes refers to is a picture showing Lewis Payne, a young man sentenced to death.[7] The photograph shows Payne shortly before his execution, that is, still alive, while we know that by the time we are watching the picture his execution has already taken place, by the time we see the picture he is long dead. Barthes observes: "I read at the same time: 'This will be' and 'this has been'; I observe with horror an anterior future of which death is the stake. By giving me the absolute past of the pose, the photograph tells me death in the future. [...]. Looking at the picture 'I shudder over a catastrophe which has already occurred'".[8] This according to Barthes is the essence of photography. "Whether or not the sub-

---

6 Ibidem, p. 82, italics in the text.
7 Ibidem, p. 95.
8 Ibidem, p.96.

ject is already dead, every photograph is this catastrophe" and "there is always a defeat of time in them: that is dead and that is going to die".[9] Barthes description makes clear that this temporal hallucination caused by the photograph does not result only from what is there to be seen in the image but also from how photography as medium presents the promise of a connection to what Barthes knows, and what he knows to be already dead by the time he is watching the image. He writes: "I exhaust myself realizing that 'this has been.' [...] I passed beyond the unreality of the thing represented, I entered crazily into the spectacle, into the image, taking in my arms what is dead, what is going to die".[10] This is also very poignant in the case of the picture that to him represents the quintessential photograph, the picture of his dead mother. The photograph that convincingly performs this gesture of "Look, there she is" is a photograph that shows his mother not as what she looked like at the time of her death, nor at some other point of her life that Bathes may have remembered, but as she was long before she would even become his mother. It is this picture of his mother as a five year old that after her death most convincingly makes her present to him as he knew her. A temporal hallucination, indeed.

Such a temporal hallucination is also what Mroué's *Three Posters* is about. In the performance, Mroué takes the audience back to the moment in front of the camera, a moment of what he terms "the fabrication of the truth".[11] Behind closed doors, he re-enacts the recording of a video testimony in three takes, while the audience watches him doing so on a video monitor. At some point during the recording, the doors in front of the audience are opened and they are offered a view of what they see in the video recording—they can now see the scene for which the image sets the stage. Then, leaving this scene, Mroué joins the audience in watching three more tapes (the original found footage). With this dramaturgical strategy Mroué invites the audience to look at these from the perspective of their fabrication.

Three Posters does not explain the images that make up the video testimony in terms of what viewers actually see, or how this is or isn't a faithful representation of the reality in front of the camera, or what all of this actually means. Instead, *Three Posters* deploys the strategy of staging to highlight how the image sets the stage for knowledge to appear and how this knowledge involves a claim to truth: the truth about who it is that is speaking to us and why he did what he did. His staging also draws attention to the performativity of this truth—in other words, that this truth is not a matter of a reality of which the video recording is a representation, but instead, that the fabrication of this truth happens *in the image*, as a result of its virtual, phenomenal

9   Ibidem, p. 96.
10 Ibidem, p.107.
11 Mroué in *On Three Posters*. See also his text "The Fabrication of Truth" (2002) and the script for *Three Posters* (2002). [Concept and Text: Elias Khoury and Rabih Mroué. Premiere: Ayloul Festival, September 2000.]

appearance to a beholder.¹² At the moment of seeing, the images will produce the truth about the speaker, a truth that does not even exist yet at the time of their recording—a truth therefore, that, strictly speaking, cannot be recorded. For at the time of recording the person speaking had not yet undertaken his action; it is only after his death, at the moment the video was broadcast on television, that he becomes the martyr he claims to be at the moment of recording. When the testimony was filmed he performed a statement that was not true yet. Which is for Mroué reason to compare the statement to that of an actor saying "I am dead": it is an impossible statement, performing what we might call (after Austin) an infelicitous speech act.

Yet, the testimony is not infelicitous at all if we take into consideration not only what was performed in front of the camera back then but also that what is performed by the combination of the person performing and the performance of technology: as a performance that is extended by the potential opened up by technology to successfully perform a document of what had not yet happened at the time of recording. The performance in front of the camera anticipates this potential. This is a possibility also indicated by Mroué in his video lecture, but not elaborated.

This possibility is my concern here, and how accounting for this possibility requires a different understanding of technologies of recording and how they mediate in a reordering of the relationship between past, present and future. I will do so starting from a photograph that may be called a variation on the photograph that plays such an important role in Barthes account of the temporal hallucination associated with photography; the photograph that for him represents the quintessence of photography, which is the picture of his dead mother. This photograph, in which Barthes finds "the impossible science of the unique human being"[13] is for him the picture par excellence that causes the shudder associated with punctum, providing him with access to a past in which the catastrophe, her death, still has to take place, and allowing him to anticipate what has already happened from a moment after its happening.[14]

Death and the Navel

Many of the photographs Barthes discusses are reproduced with his text. Yet, this most important one, the one of his mother, is emphatically absent. Barthes does not want to reproduce this one because, most likely, we will not see what he sees in this picture, we will not find in it "the truth of the face he loved". The photograph will misperform.

---

12   This paragraph is also part of a more elaborate discussion of the image in the work of Mroué in my text "Performing the Image: Rabih Mroué's Lecture-Performances" in *Rabih Mroué: A BAK Critical Readers in Artists' Practice*, eds Maria Hljavajova and Jill Winder, BAK, basis voor actuele kunst, Utrecht and post editions, Rotterdam 2012, p. 178-199.
13   Ibidem, p. 71.
14   See for a more elaborate account of images in Mroué's work in my text "Performing the Image: Rabih Mroué's Lecture-Performances" mentioned in note 12.

I will show you my picture. Not to give you what Barthes withheld, nor to prove him to be wrong. For, most certainly, this picture will do to you exactly what Barthes feared. It will misperform.

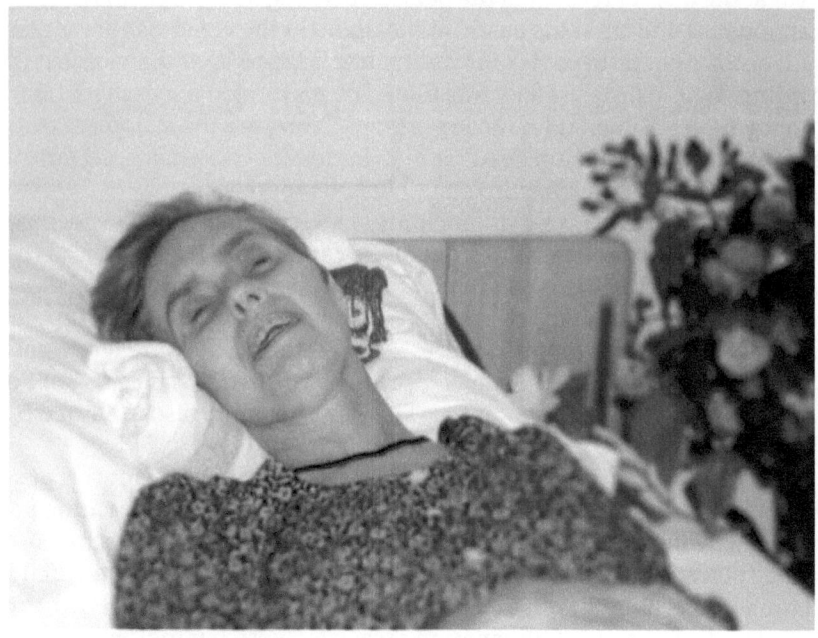

"Liesbeth Bleeker-Wagemakers, April 5 2003"
Photo Maaike Bleeker

Instead of recognizing the truth of her face you may be wondering what it is that you are actually looking at. A woman lying back on a bed. Is she sleeping? Is she peeping at us from under her lashes? She is fully dressed and wearing a necklace. Maybe she is taking a nap. What might make one wonder about what we are actually looking at is the towels supporting her head. Or the single white flower lying next to her instead of being put in the vase. These details may be considered, after Barthes, as examples of punctum. Details that stand out, that may draw our attention. Yet, instead of showing death in the future, here the catastrophe has already happened and if entering the picture allows us to take something into our arms, it is not the dead as still going to die but as already dead.

Why and how this picture for me represents the truth of the face I have loved is an altogether different story. A story indeed that takes us back to the moment in front of the camera, the moment this picture was taken. I am not going to disclose this story to you for this story tells very little about this photograph, and what this photograph does, what it is able to bring forth.

When it comes to understanding my story about how and why this picture represent such truth, the details that, like Barthes' punctum, stick out and may alert us viewers, appear to be of very little help. These details may indeed be read as traces of a situation that was there, in front of the camera. They may alert us viewers to the fact that this woman is not sleeping, nor looking at us from under her lashes. They do so, however, not because they grant us access to the situation that was actually there but because they draw attention to how we read this picture and how we make sense of the situation depicted in it. These details allow for a kind of deconstructive entering of a situation that first may have been taken at face value but then appears to be not quite that what it may have seemed.

Doing so, these details may be considered examples of what Mieke Bal calls the navel of the image. Like Barthes' punctum, the concept of the navel refers to a detail that appears as noise, or an instance of misperformance within what is shown. Bal demonstrates how such moments, instances, elements, may serve as a meaningful pointers, pointing to the work going on between what is perceived and the perceiver. Taken as navel, the details that Barthes identifies as punctum are revealing about what these photographs do to Barthes as well as what Barthes does to the photographs. How his reading is framed by an understanding of photography as a kind of mechanically produced material trace of a moment there and then in front of the camera. A moment that is radically disconnected from the moment of viewing here and now. How the technology of photography makes possible such a disconnection and reconnection, and how it is Barthes perception of what this technology performs that frames his reading of what he sees in these terms. Bal introduces navel as critical concept as part of her critique of Derrida's concept of *dissemination*. Dissemination has proven to be a powerful tool to undermine persistent tendencies to explain what is seen in terms of origins, and for redirecting attention to signs as events with a certain futurity. A potential that Bal would not want to deny or argue against. On the contrary. With her critique she points to the implications of the term dissemination itself: to what this term does or performs, and how its performance is at odds with this intended futurity. She writes:

> Although [Derrida] undermines the phallic view of sign and meaning inscribed in Saussure's semiotic, Derrida is also implicated in it. This is because his dissemination, intended to dissolve the penetrating power of the dualistic sign, sometimes looks like an overwhelming dispersion of semen; coming all over the text, it spreads out so pervasively, so biblically, that it becomes like the stars in heaven or sand at the seashore: a promise to global fatherhood.[15]

15   Mieke Bal, *Looking In: The Art of Viewing*, G & B Arts International, Amsterdam 2001, p. 82.

The navel too points to an origin, however, not in terms of fatherhood, but of motherhood. The navel is a sign of the connection to the mother, yet it is a sign that refers to this connection to origin as always already being cut. The navel is a scar that marks disconnection, being cut loose from origin, and at the same time it is the mark of a new life beginning: a new human life in the case of an actual navel, or the new life of an image cut loose from the situation of its capturing. Notwithstanding the death of the one whose image is captured, the image will live on and will live a new life that does not exist completely independent from its origin and is certainly marked by it, however, what these marks will come to mean, will be at least partly the result of what happens afterwards (its destiny not being in its origin) and will involve a constant renegotiating of the relationship to this origin from which it is cut loose, a renegotiation that takes place from the future. Similarly, in film and video, cut is the disconnection between the here and now, the disconnection that happens at the moment the director says "cut" and the recording stops. The cut does not deny the relationship between the historical moment and its recording, but it is the moment that marks a shift in relationships between them, opening up the potential of renegotiation.

Accounting for such processes of renegotiation is crucial for understanding the circulation of signs and images in global digital culture. The global emergence of technological media and electronic networks, McKenzie observes has caused an epochal shift in the citational network of discourses and turned Derrida´s iterability into a condition of life. Or, as McKenzie puts it: "Highly localized ensembles of words and gestures can now be broken apart, recombined and hyperlinked to different ensembles in ways unlike anything in the past at speeds incredible from all perspectives except those of the future".[16] Accounting for the impact of these processes and how they are part and parcel of the fabrication of truth requires an approach that acknowledges the power of technology not only to capture what was in front of the camera but actually to challenge forth the world.

The Terror of Becoming

Why was the testimony recorded in three takes?, Mroué wonders. This fighter did not fear death. He voluntarily goes out to meet it. "Yet as soon as he steps before the camera to film his testimony, his words betray him, hesitating and stumbling between his lips. His gaze is unable to focus, it wavers and gets lost. These different takes are like those of an actor getting ready to play his role. Why does this fighter try to act?"[17] Mroué seeks the answer in the impossible performance performed in the tapes. These tapes and not his

---

16 Jon McKenzie, *Perform or Else*, p. 22.
17 Rabih Mroué, "The Fabrication of Truth", pp. 114-115.

actual suicide mission, turn the fighter into the martyr he is to become."The martyrdom has taken place before the suicide mission, and therefore, whether this operation has effectively taken place or not no longer makes any real difference".[18]

These tapes challenge forth the fighter as martyr. This becoming martyr is not a matter of his individual intention once there and then in the authentic moment in front of the camera. His successfully becoming martyr has very little to do with the expression of his individual intention, nor with the capturing of this intention in the recordings, but all the more with him being successfully captured as what he is not yet and the circulation of the image, a situation that generations of fighters have well understood.

Technology challenges forth the world, McKenzie observes. He is referring to Heidegger and his understanding of technology as a way of revealing, i.e. of truth. Such truth must not be understood as the correspondence of a representation to reality, but in terms of a bringing forth that at the same time also conceals. For Heidegger technology's mode of revealing is inauthentic. "Instead of channeling the authentic bringing forth of sky and earth, gods and man, modern technology instead challenges forth nature's energies and orders them into reality as 'standing reserves,' as objects on call to subjects who are themselves called forth as challengers".[19] Heidegger acknowledges that the ways in which technology challenges forth the world also impacts how we emerge as subject of knowledge in relation to how the world is challenged forth. He thus acknowledges the performativity of technology while at the same time the performance of his perception, deeming technology's mode of revealing as inauthentic, safeguards a distinction between reality as challenged forth by technology and some more real reality existing independent from this reality.

Precisely the existence of such reality existing independent from our modes of knowing is what has been challenged, not only by technological developments but also by what Lyotard has described as a change in the status of knowledge characteristic of the shift from modernity to postmodernity. Lyotard famously defines the postmodern as "incredulity towards metanarratives", as a situation in which "the narrative function is losing its functors, its great hero, its great dangers, its great voyages, its great goal".[20] The result, McKenzie observes, is delegitimation: "the decline of philosophy and revolutionary politics, the crisis of representation and of the university, and the replacement of universal metalanguages by a plurality of discrete systems".[21] At this moment, performativity replaces traditional goals of

---

18 Rabih Mroué, "The Fabrication of Truth", p. 115.
19 Jon McKenzie, *Perform or Else*, p. 156.
20 Jean-Francois Lyotard, *The Postmodern Condition: A Report on Knowledge*, trans. Geoff Bennington and Brian Massumi, The University of Minnesota Press, Minneapolis 1979, p. xxiv.
21 Jon McKenzie, *Perform or Else*, p. 163.

knowledge, truth and liberation. "The application of this criterion to all of our language games` Lyotard writes, ´necessarily implies a certain level of terror, whether soft or hard: be operational (that is: commensurable) or disappear".²² Or, in the words of McKenzie: *perform - or else*. In this situation, McKenzie observes, the fabrication of truth (to speak with Mroué) is a matter of how truth is challenged forth by the lecture machine that is the performance stratum, that is, by the complex intertwining of discourses and global technologies. Here, the impossible performance of the freedom fighter trembling in the face of the camera that will challenge him forth as martyr, is the example par excellence of the terror observed by Lyotard and McKenzie, the terror to perform – or else.

---

22   Lyotard quoted in Jon McKenzie, *Perform or Else*, p. 163.

Nicolas Salazar Sutil
404, the Performativity of Error: with Insights into Cyber-errorism in *Internacional Errorista* and *Electronic Disturbance Theatre*

Er´ror`ist: One who encourages and propagates error; one who holds to error. (Free Online Dictionary)

Technological communication is bound up with the question of transitivity: to communicate amounts to transferring a unit of communication (say, a message) to someone or something else, via some technological medium. Failure in this transfer can happen for ordinary reasons, as, for instance, in the case of power failure. There are, however, political questions that stem from the technological mediation of human communication, particularly in terms of the inherently error-prone and corrective nature of computer operation systems. In what follows, I will introduce the concept of *errorism* to speak of a type of agency (at once linguistic, technological and political) that holds to, and propagates error through the self-legitimising power of administration. The term is intended as part of a broader discussion on the concept of performativity, which, as I will explain shortly, may be theorised not only in relation to a philosophy of natural language, which focuses on human agency and speech-based performatives, but also a systems approach, which focuses on systems that combine human and non-human agents.

Every operation in human-to-computer interaction, or human-to-human computer-mediated interaction, is subject to protocols defined by the specific technology that is being used (both at the level of software and hardware usage). For example, as I write this essay the Word programme I am using signals by green and red underlining that a mistake has been made (green if the error lies in the sentence construction, and red if it is a spelling mistake). So far, Word has underlined the words "normativisation" and "errorism". For "normativisation", no spelling suggestions are given. As for "errorist", Word suggests that I should go for "terrorist" instead; which, as it will become apparent, is an interesting choice.

I will argue that the internet is a very specific protocol characterised by at least two layers of performative activity: on the one hand, the internet is performative at the level of the technical operations (hardware) and the code languages used to *do* things online (software), and on the other, at the level of the construction of internet-user identities, which I take to be more open and flexible than everyday rule-generated identities. To act out a sense of self via the world-wide-web is thus to obey certain predefined rules of engagement which are faithful firstly to the iterative technical procedures that allow us to operate the technology, and secondly, to certain social protocols that enable users and surfers to re-invoke their own identities online. As I will explain in due course, this occurs in such a way that normative conditions of self-formation are relaxed by the customised and personalised nature of Internet socialisation. In the case of user performativity, internet communication has been theorised as a type of virtual performance of the self,[1] in the sense that millions of individuals who develop e-friendships, use MOOs, IRC, and chat-rooms, or create home pages and blogs, thus constitute notions of performative selfhood, "with the subject being progressively erased, redefined, and re-inscribed as a persona/performer within the proscenium arch of the computer monitor".[2] My initial question is not just how theatrical the performativity of internet communication is, but simply, how performative it is, in other words, how people instrumentalise the internet to *do* things in a given social context.

This essay presents the reader with an Internet-specific theory of performativity in order to discuss, more specifically, what one can *do* with errors- from the linguistic (or code linguistic) to the technological, to the e-political. My claim is that errors constitute unavoidable failures in the process of repetition, which is key to the realisation of a social normativity, insofar as errors need to be corrected, and thus activity can become socially standardised and normalised. By focusing on error as an instance whereby repetition can be troubled, so that the deliberate misuse of code or conduct can generate counter-corrective action that can clog a system, Internet errorism opens up the possibility for political dissidence. In the final section of this essay, I will return to the proposition made by Steve Dixon at the beginning of his book *Digital Performance*, namely, that the performativity of e-identity is akin to a performance of the everyday self, or e-self. I will briefly speak of the Argentine-based group *Internacional Errorista* and Ricardo Dominguez's *Electronic Disturbance Theater* project "Stop the War in Mexico", as instances where the Internet can in fact be mobilised precisely as a theatrical site for counter-performance and political dissidence.

[1] Steve Dixon, *Digital Performance*, The MIT Press, Cambridge, MA 2007.
[2] Ibidem, p. 4.

Theoretical approach: an alternative theory of performativity

The emergence of a philosophy of language approach to performativity theory is gamely credited to J.L. Austin's work on speech acts and his putative distinction between what words *say* (constatives) and what words *do* (performatives). Truth-evaluative sentences, argues Austin, constitute only a small number in a range of utterances. Austin coins the term performativity in order to index utterances that are not measured as truth statements, but which are outcomes of action that can only be deemed felicitous or infelicitous, depending on whether or not they respect certain socially-determined procedures. According to Austin, utterances achieve specific effects on addressees when circumstances are appropriate in certain ways, as when a sanctioned figure can proclaim: "I name this ship the Mr Stalin", and an official christening is thus performed. If the person is not properly sanctioned, however, the action is not a valid performance, in Austin's view, but only a colourable claim, "like a marriage with a monkey".[3]

Although Austin describes his investigations as heralding a "science of language", and whilst citing mathematics, physics and mathematical logic as precedent examples,[4] the fact that a doing with *words* can refer not only to knowledge characteristic of natural language, but to purer formalisations of certain kinds of rationality (say, computer languages), is a function of performativity that Austin acknowledges, but does not address directly. Likewise, Stanley Cavell picks up on the question of linguistic performativity in his essay *Must we Mean what we Say?* to touch upon the idea that if language is functional in consideration to norms of correctness of validity, then language ought to be considered not only in relation to the way we *speak*, but also in relation to formal structures, akin to the rules of a game. As such, using a language like English means "knowing which forms in what contexts are normative for performing the activities we perform by using the language".[5] But because beyond the rules of grammar there is no calculus or algorithmic procedure pointing to how ordinary language is used in social contexts, and because there appears to be nothing that underpins or guarantees the continuation and preservation of a shared world in ordinary language, the analogy with formal languages should not be pushed too far.[6] From its inception, therefore, this line of theorisation has remained entrenched within a theory of ordinary language, that is, within a consideration of what we can do with *words*, and how *words* condition the subject who speaks.

The question of what exactly constitutes a performative utterance results in a controversy taken up as a matter of concern to the philosophy

---

3   John L. Austin, *How to do things with words*, Clarendon Press, Oxford 1962, p. 24.
4   James Loxley, *Performativity*, Routledge, London & New York 2007, p. 26.
5   Stanley Cavell, *Must we mean what we say? A book of essays*, University Press, Cambridge 2002, p. 33.
6   James Loxley, *Performativity*, p. 34

of natural language, most notably, in deconstructionist theory[7] and speech-act theory.[8] The problem of a "total context" in word-based communication prompts Jacques Derrida to ask Austin: could a performative utterance succeed if its formulation did not repeat an iterable statement, if they were not identifiable in some way as citations?[9] Derrida's answer is a firm no, as all language takes on the character of an effraction, according to this author, into the alleged purity of every event of discourse. For Derrida, what makes language communicable is not a subjective intent or a personal interpretation, but an iterable model. A signature must have a repeatable form, being thus able to detach itself from the present and singular intention of its production.[10] Derrida's performativity sets the production of a particular type of *doing* against a self-presence or a conscious intentionality, destabilising the notion of the subject and dislodging the location of agency away from a self-possessed, self-conscious performer, and locating that agency on the credible production of an "authority".

Derrida's approach is famously taken up by Judith Butler, who stresses the performative in relation to questions of political subject-formation, particularly through gender-related normativity or heteronormativity. Butler also sees the iterability of communicable signs as a theory of agency, to the extent that one cannot disavow power as the condition of its own possibility.[11] Thus performativity remains via the work of these two authors inherently about the production of iterable signatures that gain a certain force not only because they are repeated, but because they are agreed to signify by convention, in relation to an origin, and to an authority that presides over the ritual of citation. Derrida's notion of *citation* clearly locates the question of performativity in the iterability of *words*. For these authors, communication is not entirely automated to the point of being a technical or technological performance. Derrida refutes the possibility of a techno-performative function quite explicitly. He writes: "performativity will never be reduced to technical performance. Pure performativity implies the presence of a living being, and of a living being speaking one time only, in its own name, in the first person".[12] But precisely because the question of what performativity might imply in electronic forms of communication remains unattended, these approaches to performativity set us up, at least for this particular debate, on the wrong foot. In their modified version of the concept of perfor-

7   See the following: Paul de Man, *Allegories of Reading. Figural Language in Rousseau, Nietzsche, Rilke and Proust*, New Haven and London: Yale University Press 1979; Jacques Derrida, "Signature, Event, Context", in *Margins of Philosophy*, trans. by Alan Bass. University of Chicago Press, Chicago 1982; J. Hillis Miller, "Performativity as Performance/ Performativity as Speech Act: Derrida's Special theory of performativity" in Ian Balfour, *Late Derrida.*, Duke University Press, Durham, N.C. 2007.
8   John Searle, *Speech Acts: An Essay in the Philosophy of Language*, Cambridge University Press, Cambridge 1969; and "How Performatives work", *Linguistics and Philosophy* 12 (1989), pp. 535-558.
9   Jacques Derrida, "Signature, Event, Context" in *Margins of Philosophy*, p. 326.
10 Ibidem, p. 328
11 Judith Butler, *Gender Trouble* [Third edition], Routledge, London 2006, p. 101.
12 Jacques Derrida, *Without Alibi*, trans. Peggy Kamuf, Stanford University Press, Stanford 2002, p. 74.

mativity, the anthropologists Benjamin Lee and Edward LiPuma write: "the analytical problem is how to extend what has been a speech-act based notion of performativity to other discursively mediated practices".[13] Although the theories of performativity all too briefly surveyed above provide a fruitful set of conceptual frameworks, they remain rooted to speech and to human-to-human forms of communication, which is why a different genealogy of the term is now required.

Talcott Parson's concept of the "performance process"[14] signals an alternative origin of the term- one which runs parallel to the terminology offered by Austin. Parsons' theory opens a social differentiationist approach where socio-economic factors, and by extension technological factors, are given priority. Performance is by Parson's definition a characteristic confined to the category of social objects.[15] According to Parsons, performance refers to a normative force that mobilises the realisation of binding obligations in the interest of effective collective goal attainment.[16] Orientation to the actor's performance may be either ego's or alter's or both, so unlike Derrida's conception, performance here refers to an individual's intention as well as an external authority. The expectation is that the social actor is committed to the achievement of certain goals, and that expectations are oriented to a "success" in achieving them, hence positive sanctions will reward success and negative sanctions will ensue in case of failure to achieve.[17]

Parsons influence on the theorisation of performativity is further evidenced in the work of systems-theorist Niklas Luhmann,[18] Parsons' own student at Harvard, and French theorist Jean-François Lyotard.[19] Drawing on Parsons' definition of the performance process discussed above Luhmann argues that the normativity of laws is replaced in modernity by the performativity of procedures. Performativity assumes a central role in modern systems for it takes precedence over thought itself in the social mind. According to this approach, performativity is set to function in relation to a modern sense of subjectivity or subject-formation defined in and through systems and system-oriented procedures, with the focus no longer being natural language, but social, economic, political, and technological structures that underpin the construction of modern communicational systems. Within this ambit, performance has been theorised in relation to a sex-repressive mode of capitalist production,[20] in relation to market

---

13 Adrian Mackenzie, *Cutting Code: Software and Sociality*, Peter Lang, New York 2006.
14 Talcott Parsons, *The Social System*, Tavistock Publications, London 1952.
15 Ibidem, p. 53.
16 *Talcott Parsons on Institutions and Social Evolution*, ed. Leon H. Mayhew, University of Chicago Press, Chicago 1982, p. 232.
17 Ibidem, p. 64.
18 Nicholas Luhmann, *Legitimation durch Verfahren*, 3 Aufl, Suhrkamp, Frankfurth Am Main 2002 [1993].
19 Jean Francois Lyotard, *The Postmodern Condition*, Manchester University Press, Manchester 1984.
20 Herbert Marcuse, *Eros and Civilisation*, Sphere Books, London 1970.

performativity,[21] and also in relation to the performativity of technological objects,[22] even in the model of technological optimisation produced during the so-called Military-Industrial Academic complex, which has led some scholars to speak of a distinct historical notion of techno-performativity or "techno-performance".[23]

Lyotard joins this genealogy in order to stress specifically the performative character of techno-scientific knowledge. The historical condition described by Lyotard- the postmodern- is conventionalised along with a performative logic, according to which a certain set of success-oriented prescriptions is accepted as knowledge. "There is no denying" says Lyotard "the dominant existence today of technoscience, that is, the massive subordination of cognitive statements to the finality of the best possible performance".[24] Lyotard leaves his mark in any genealogy of performativity theory by providing one of its most cited definitions. Lyotard explains: "performativity is the best possible input/output equation".[25] He adds:

> [Technical devices] follow a principle, and it is the principle of optimal performance: maximising output [...] and minimising input [...] Technology is therefore a game pertaining not to the true, the just, or the beautiful, etc., but to efficiency: a "technical" move is "good" when it does better and/or expends less energy than another.[26]

These approaches to performativity point to a sense in which technological systems function in relation to repeatable and regular sequences of operations, in a context in which speech-acts claim some affinity with the machinic.[27] The defining agency here is not so much the living actor, but actants that can perform as humans and/or machines. A theorisation of what can be done with *code*, particularly in Internet communication, demands an even more specific understanding of performativity. According to Adrian Mackenzie, performativity of technological objects like the Linux operating system hinges on the point that the kernel code succeeds as a performative to the extent that in connecting commodity hardware and convention-governed movements of information, the technological object also makes

---

21   Pierre Bourdieu, *Language and Symbolic Power*, trans. by Gino Raymond and Matthew Adamson, Polity Press, Cambridge 1991; Michael Callon, *The Laws of Markets*, Blackwell Publishers, Oxford 1998; Michael Callon and Fabian Muniesa, "Peripheral Vision Economic Markets as Calculative Collective Devices", *Organization Studies*, 26: 8 (2005), pp. 1229-1250; Donald MacKenzie, Fabian Muniesa, & Lucia Siu, *Do Economists Make Markets? On the Performativity of Economics*, Princeton University Press, Princeton, N.J; Woodstock 2007.
22   Bruno Latour, *Science in Action: how to follow scientists and engineers through society*, Harvard University Press, Cambridge, MA 1987; Adrian Mackenzie, *Cutting Code: Software and Sociality*
23   Jon McKenzie, *Perform or Else. From discipline to performance*, Routledge, London & New York 2001; Donald Mackenzie, *Knowing Machines. Essays on Technical Change*, MIT Press, Cambridge, MA, London 1998.
24   *The Lyotard Reader and Guide*, eds Keith Crome and James Williams, Columbia University Press, New York 2006, p. 128.
25   Jean Lyotard, *Postmodern Condition*, p. 46.
26   Ibidem, p. 44.
27   James Loxley, *Performativity*, p. 91.

a social arrangement for the on-going production of code.²⁸ In addition to hardware performativity, this author speaks of software performativity, according to which software circulates code less in terms of technical performance (i.e. the speed of the machine), and more in terms of code mobility achieved through software circulation.²⁹

Unlike hardware performance Internet performance does not rely entirely on technical factors like connectivity, speed, and modem performance. In addition to these more technical features of Internet performativity, there are those factors involving human and machinic agents in social contexts, which do not entirely do away with Derrida's axioms of the performative: that is, presence, present time, and a sense of subject "I". However, because the Internet enables the constitution of these in a virtual space and time (cyberspace/ cybertime), the performance of e-self is inherently mixed (partly human, and partly not). Internet self is thus constituted as cyber-presence, where e-selves are not entirely devoid of bodies- in fact, I would argue that even internet exchanges have a body language attached to them. Performing a body online, however, is a complex procedure involving the mobilisation of techniques and technologies specific to each form of Internet communication. Thus, bodies relating on Skype are entirely different to bodies relating through cybertext, or indeed through computer-generated avatars. Unfortunately, the question of embodiment lies beyond the scope of this essay, and so I must move. Before doing so, however, it is worth stressing that the sense of a subject "I", as defined earlier by Derrida, does not have to be necessarily singular. Instead, an Internet "I" is subject to the multiplying and distributive factor of the net. In other words, this "I" is no longer one individual located in a physical space, but possibly, simultaneous users, or indeed, not even a (human) user at all.

The "internetisation" of identity refers to profound transformations to language and to self that have occurred in cyber-communication, and which have helped turn the agency of the word and the citational nature of subjectivity at the heart of Derridean and Butlerian performativity into a multi-subjective sense of electronic and computer-coded "Is" that have taken over in online communication. Through the instrumentalisation of Internet technology, the construction of a potential "I", a hyper-self, has become possible beyond the narrow sense of speech-based subject-formation theorised by Derrida and Butler. These new e-personas are communicated not only through the medium of speech or speech-acts, but also in terms of leetspeak (or l33t), an alternative alphabet for the English language used primarily on the Internet which uses various combinations of ASCII characters to replace Latinate letters, and which Jon McKenzie famously used to bring a memo-

---

28   Adrian Mackenzie, *Cutting Code: Software and Sociality*, p. 81.
29   Ibidem, p. 103.

rable text-art end to his book *Perform or Else* (2001).[30] Furthermore, the idea that self is determined by the normativity of language is further problematized by the limitations of natural text in Internet communication, and the dominance of microtext and hypertext. George Landow has further theorised Internet performativity in relation to the problem of reconfiguring the relationship between text as link and the reader as "actively clicking".[31] Finally, there is the question of how computer code itself changes the possibility for a language in technological communication to *do* something, whether through hardware or software performatives.[32]

Within this framework, an electronic performativity approach is appropriate, for instance, to a case study of Facebook identity-fabrication,[33] where the notion of a Facebook persona is often subsumed within a narcissistic, image-obsessive and friend-consumptive sociality that can be normative within this particular technology. Likewise Eric Dishman has discussed the rethinking of technology design through the lens of performative theory in order to argue for a new kind of "performer-designer" role who breaks the traditional paradigm of mimesis and realism, and who can conceive of new internet-specific modalities and discourses on self. Thus, computer designers and programmers can use performance (in its more theatrical acceptation) "to create prototypes of complex, politicised, personalised futures".[34] This theatricalisation of our cyber-persona is further met by Dixon as a problematic fictionalisation: the creation of fictional MUDs and MOOs, and fictional e-friendship relations, relate both to "the fictionality and the performativity of e-life and communication, which also poses serious questions about schizophrenic self-representation and consequent problems of relating to others outside artificial environments".[35] Before we turn to the question of how electronic performativity may be re-conceptualised in relation to the *theatrical* understanding of the term, it is worth re-focusing the question of performativity in relation to non-word based languages used in internet communication.

The Error Code

Internet languages function on the basis of a formalisation and encoding of messages, particularly in the case of computation protocols like Hypertext Transfer Protocol (henceforth HTTP), which is the foundation of data communication in the World Wide Web. It might be helpful to remind my

30   John McKenzie, *Perform or else*.
31   George Landow, *Hypertext: the convergence of contemporary critical theory and technology*, John Hopkins University Press, Baltimore 1992.
32   Adrian Mackenzie, *Cutting Code: Software and Sociality*.
33   Nicole Ellison, Charles Steinfeld and Cliff Lampe, "The Benefits of Facebook 'Friends:' Social Capital and College Students' Use of Online Social Network Sites. Available online at http://jcmc.indiana.edu/vol12/issue4/ellison.html [accessed 12 January 2013].
34   Steve Dixon, *Digital Performance*, p. 175
35   Ibidem, p. 214.

readers that the internet functions as a request-response protocol in communicational exchanges or sessions between clients (e.g. web browers) and servers (e.g applications running on a computer hosting a web site). A client submits an HTTP request message to the server, to which the server returns a response message. To further channel information in the internet HTTP requires protocols of informational transfer or transport protocols. In other words, the movement of information in cyberspace has to be formalised so that once emitted, messages become readable. Thus, a formal HTTP message is both machine-readable (the response contains a status code) and human-readable (the response displays a reason phrase), as in the case of the following unsuccessful response message HTTP/1.1 404 Not Found. A performative agency is thus open to machines and humans alike, insofar as messages are readable (and performable) by both. Now then, although there are a great number of standard and nonstandard HTTP responses, status codes fall into five distinct categories, written as three-digit codes: 1xx (informational or temporary), 2xx (success), 3xx (redirection), 4xx (client error), 5xx (server error). Thus, the first message in each one of these code categories reads:

>   HTTP/1.1 100 Continue
>   HTTP/1.1 200 OK
>   HTTP/1.1 300 Multiple Choices
>   HTTP/1.1 400 Bad Request
>   HTTP/1.1 500 Internal Server Error

The HTTP responses quoted above are all classified in terms of *how* the transaction is performed; they are, as such, classifiable by virtue of their performative function. In other words, HTTP requests and responses are classifiable in terms of what requests *do* to elicit a response. Each one of these categories of response is defined in terms of a distinct performative effect, what one might describe after J.L.Austin as a 'doing with code', which is to generate a temporary status (1xx), to succeed (2xx), to relocate (3xx), or to fail (4xx and 5xx).

HTTP response status codes beginning with digits 4 or 5 indicate cases where the transfer of information between client and server is marred by a misperformance. Thus, the 4xx class of status code is intended for cases in which the *client* seems to have erred (with the server providing an explanation for the error situation and a clarification as to whether this is a temporary or permanent situation). One common error encountered whilst online is the 404 error message, where the requested source cannot be found. But whilst 4xx response codes locate error in the region of the client, so that in a 404 error-message the problem lies apparently in the client's request, a response code beginning with digit 5 indicates cases in which the server is aware that it has encountered an error or is otherwise incapable of performing the request, thus locating the misperformance on the side of the server.

The War on Error

Misuse of language defined George W. Bush's term in office, so much so that the word Bushism does not refer to a political position, but to a slip of the tongue. Like Spoonerism, Bushism is a phenomenon that originates in erroneous use of language, but which, given the performative power of its origination, and given the fact that errors were made by the mass-mediated speaker that was the 43rd US President, they soon become iterable, and thus, normalised. Bushisms, which are now part of American folklore and the subject of a number of published books, are only the superficial signature for a deeper misperformance in this Administration, characterised by blindspots in decision-making, and lack of political vision particularly in international affairs. Bush defended himself in his own terms:

> "They misunderestimated me" [36]

Bushisms triggered all manner of humorous Internet debate, originating a kind of Internet ritual, which spread across the net with viral speed, and which took shape over the course of the noughties through custom-made websites, blogs and debate pages.[37] That words like "misunderestimated" became acceptable turns of phrase in Internet parlance attests to the Internet's capability for more flexible systems of linguistic iterability, in the Derridean sense. Indeed, beyond the restrictions of hardware and software performance, the Internet is a site that can liberate communication through the personalisation of communicational spaces, and the relaxation of communicational rules. The proliferation of error in the internet, with Bushisms providing internet surfers with plenty of ammunition, also attests to the possibility internet communication opens up for the disruption of communicational order, thus allowing failures, misfirings, aberrations, to become celebrated as new original signatures. The Internet provides a more flexible role to the one-who-cites, a subject 'I' that is no longer identified as an author or writer (as in more conventional media like books, newspapers, journals), but a blogger, twitter-user, chatter, yahoo-talker, podcaster, messenger. This proliferation of subject-formative roles online makes available

---

[36] Presidential speech by George W. Bush delivered in Bentonville, Arkansas, 6 November 2000. For further uses of the term 'misunderestimated', see: http://www.dubyaspeak.com/repeatoffender/misunder.

[37] Bushisms are the subject of a number of websites, including *The Complete Bushisms* by Jacob Weisberg, *DubyaSpeak.com*, a website entitled *How To Talk like Bush (and Why you should want to)*, *About.com* (Political Humour), which has plenty of examples of Bushspeak, and *Slate Magazine*, which also has a page on Bushisms. Books devoted to the subject are also aplenty, including Justin A. Frank, *Bush on the Couch: Inside the Mind of the President*; and Mark Crispin Miller's *The Bush Dyslexicon* and Jacob Weisberg's *George W. Bushisms: The Accidental Wit and Wisdom of Our 43rd President*.

a variety of rituals of electronic citation and electronic iterability and repetition, which suggests that Internet performativity is an agency that is mobilised within a less restrictive social authority, leading to the creation of new political and public spaces of representation and self-expression unique to Internet cultures. For this reason, this freely available and (in many cases) non-governmental or privately owned technology is in most cases available for people to navigate at will, within certain technological and financial limits (the cost of internet provision). This general accessibility might in turn explain the freedom of activity that occurs on line, from highly personalised websites, to uncensored content, to hacktivism, cyber-crime, and more generally speaking, a deliberate troubling of political normativity through dissident cyber action. In the case of Bush's Administration, Internet communities nourished a powerful counter-performative sentiment, which led to the so-called "War on Error", launched against the Bush administration online in the early noughties.

Bush's sensational errors extend beyond humorous slips-of-the-tongue, or memorable "bloopers" and "funny moments", which are now widely circulated through popular sites like YouTube.[38] The Bush Administration made key decisions during its term in office from January 2001 to January 2009, which have been recognised, in hindsight, as errors of judgement, particularly in relation to foreign policy. Perhaps the most notable of these was Bush's decision to invade Iraq in 2003. It is precisely the position taken by President Bush and PM Blair to wage a war based on an error of judgement, or at least, a set of justifications that subsequently proved to be incorrect, that US international policy was subsequently labelled a "politics of error". According to Henry Laurens' analysis of regional crisis in the Middle East during the Bush administration, a "politics of error" was at work at the time, which was charactetrised by errors of two types (misconceptions and miscalculations).[39] According to this author, the misperformative nature of the US-led war on terror stems from gross miscalculations, or the estimation and computation of erroneous data based on limited on-the-ground knowledge. Perhaps more worrying are the general misconceptions (that is, errors of understanding or perception) which lead to decisions founded on a misunderstanding of the basic facts pertaining to a given political situation.

One public reaction to the War on Terror that is relevant to this discussion was the so-called "War on Error", which American punk band NOFX proclaimed on 6 May 2003. It is largely due to the release of their album

---

38   For a sample of Youtube's vast reservoir of clips of George W. Bush's "funny moments" and "bloopers", see: http://www.youtube.com/watch?v=Pbt_rizFoxQ, http://www.youtube.com/watch?v=DEbZqvMu2cQ; http://www.youtube.com/watch?v=d2WNKGZqpps [accessed 15 April 2014].

39   See Henry Laurens, "The Politics of Error: the Middle Easton the Threshold of the 21st Century", *Books & Ideas*, 16 October 2007, http://www.booksandideas.net/The-Politics-of-Error.html [accessed 27 December 2011].

"War on Errorism", released on this date, that the term errorist made its way to Internet-speak, and eventually, to urban speech, and to political and artistic movements. The term has subsequently spread not only to take aim at George W. Bush's foreign policy, but also to highlight error and lack of judgement in a number of contemporary political events, including the incarceration of alleged terrorists in Guantanamo and the assassination of Brazilian national Jean Charles de Menezes, who was shot down by London Metropolitan police at Stockwell tube station on 22 July 2005, having been misidentified as a suicide bomber.[40]

Errorism developed over the course of the noughties as an eclectic internet political community, active largely during the height of the War on Terror, which made use of the Internet's freedom of self-expression to develop a characteristic dissident voice, defined by strong anti-War and anti-Bush rhetoric. In addition to pop bands, artistic collaborations, academics, and local networks defining themselves as errorist, the concept expanded to the creation of a new political and net artistic movement in Argentina in 2005 known as *Internacional Errorista* (IE) or Errorist International, led by Federico Zukerfeld and Loreto Garín Guzmán, and the political theatre group *Etcetera*. The movement featured Internet followers from countries across Latin America, Canada and the US. Borrowing notions from Boal's "Theatre of the Oppressed" such as the *spect-actor*, and conventions of popular street theatre, *Etcetera* and IE developed notions of errorist cabaret, "actorcides" and other such theatrics of error, which were performed in a number of "errorist actions" (including protests against Bush's state visit to Argentina as part of the 4th Summit of the Americas, held in Mar del Plata on November 2005). As IE founders explain, errorism was intended to counter the War on Terror, but also, and more generally, to act as a practical philosophy that questions a capitalist ideology of success (perhaps not unlike the performance process in Talcott Parson's terminology), and to provide counter-performative reflection on the creative and self-reflexive possibilities of error.[41]

IE had their manifesto published online in 2005, followed by a number of Internet and real-life political interventions, including an artistic residence at the 11th Istanbul Biennale. *The Errorist Manifesto*[42] describes errorism as a concept and action based political and philosophical movement, which takes aim at linguistic and political liberation through a paradoxical

40   Interview with Federico Zukerfeld and Loreto Garín Guzmán, founders of *Internacional Errorista*, available at: http://vimeo.com/46551356 [accessed 15 April 2014].
41   Ibidem.
42   The *Errorist Manifesto* points to 5 main clauses. Firstly, that error is "reality's principle of order"; that errorism is a philosophically erroneous position, a ritual of negation, a disorganized organization; thirdly, that the field of action of Errorism contains all those practices that aim at the LIBERATION of the human being and language; fourthly, that confusion and surprise - black humor and absurdity are the favorite tools of the "errorists", and finally, that "lapses" and failed acts are an "errorist" delight. For a full version of the *Errorist Manifesto*, visit E-misferica online at: http://hemisphericinstitute.org/journal/2_2/erroristas.html [accessed 15 April 2014].

position celebrating error and also condemning the errors of "Verism", that is, those who commit errors in the belief of a static sense of truth (for instance, Bush's so-called "freedom agenda").

EDT: cyber-errorism and the uses of net-art as political dissidence

Electronic Disturbance Theater (EDT) has functioned as a group of US-based net artists and activists whose aim is political dissidence in the form of electronic theatrical acts. Formed in 1997 by performance artist and academic Ricardo Dominguez and his collaborators Brett Stalbaum, Stefan Wray and Carmin Karasic, EDT developed the concept of Electronic Civil Disobedience (ECD), whose aim is to make use of the internet as a protest theatre and a forum for direct political action. Ricardo Dominguez points out that as a net performer, what interested him the most about ECD is the creation of a matrix that would articulate social issues as well as performative issues with and within the parameters of code.[43] The focus of EDT is not so much the detail of the code language it uses as its communicational tool (Java) – what counts is how the incorporation of a programming language into web browsers affects the ability of the web to be used as a political campaign tool.

Central to EDT's acts of civil disobedience is the development of a software tool known as FloodNet, which is able to autonomate requests to a target website, and in doing so, jam it. On a more general level, EDT's campaign of electronic civil disobedience is constituted by INFOacts, a kind of theatrical hacktivism expressed through and about information. EDT thus performs informational interventions that involve the harnessing of networks, the clogging of websites, and the generation of intense media hype, in order to highlight political crises like the plight of the Zapatista movement in Southern Mexico, or the plight of Mexican bordercrossers. In short, EDT functions as a counter-distribution network of information with about 300 or more autonomous nodes of support, which has enabled marginalised and silenced protest groups like the Zapatistas to speak without having to pass through any dominant media filter.[44]

Dominguez has also promoted the Digital Zapatismo movement as "an open system of sprawling networks", whose aim is to galvanise the invisible and verticalising power of web-based communication to subvert a political and technological establishment, particularly within the context of a neoliberal technocratic political agenda. Digital Zapatismo thus makes use of digital cultures' most basic system of exchange, e-mail, in order "to

---

43   Coco Fusco & Ricardo Dominguez, "Performance Art in a Digital Age: A Conversation with Ricardo Dominguez", *The Hactivist Magazine* 1.0 (2001) http://www.iwar.org.uk/hackers/resources/the-hacktivist/issue-1/vol1.html [accessed 26 December 2011].
44   Ibidem.

disturb the Informatic State".[45] Suspicious of hyper-surveillance filters that seek to regain control of the network, Dominguez has argued for the need to devise inventive methods of Electronic Civil Disobedience: including alternative networks with more access and bandwidth; the development of deep programming (creating Spiders, Bots, and other minor network agents to move against specific URLs without interrupting the Server); and movement to offshore domains to maintain spamming engines for massive e-mail actions.[46]

EDT's first act of Electronic Civil Disobedience against the Mexican Government took place following an attack on the remote village of Acteal in Chiapas on December 1997, during which a paramilitary group shot forty five people dead, most of them women and children. EDT orchestrated their first virtual sit-in in April 1998, during which a repeated reloading of key government websites (including the Mexican president's site and US official sites) managed to block and disrupt normal flows of information. This idea was the jump-off point for the Zapatista Tactical FloodNet, a Java applet developed by EDT members Carmin Karasic and Brett Stalbaum. FloodNet's role was to assist in the execution of virtual sit-ins by automatically reloading the targeted website several times every minute, slowing or halting access to the targeted server. FloodNet also encouraged interaction on the part of individual protesters by allowing users to post statements to the site by sending them to the server log. In this way, net surfers could voice their political concerns on a targeted server via the "personal message" function. Participants who had downloaded the FloodNet program during the *Stop the War in Mexico* performance were asked to input the names repetitively of those that had lost their lives during the Acteal Massacre. In addition to uploading the names of the dead to the Mexican government websites, the software also sent requests to the servers that would compel the server to return an error message each time these URLs would be requested. EDT founder Ricardo Dominguez explains:

> While Floodnet action goes on, EDT not only recalls President Zedillo's web page, but we also call internal searches. For example, we will ask for the names of the dead, or about the question of human rights in Mexico. We ask the server the question, "Does human rights exist on President Zedillo's web site?" And then a 404 file emerges backstage, if you will [...]. We ask President Zedillo's server or the Pentagon's web server "Where is human rights in your server?" The server then responds "Human rights not found on this server". We ask "Where is

45   Ricardo Dominguez, "Digital Zapatismo" http://www.thing.net/~rdom/ecd/DigZap.html [accessed 17 November 2012]. See also Thea Pitman, "Latin American Cyberprotest: Before and after the Zapatistas" in *Latin American Cyberculture and Cyberliterature*, eds Clare L. Taylor and Thea Pitman, Liverpool University Press, Liverpool 2007.
46   Ibidem.

Ana Hernandez?" [one of the victims of the Acteal Massacre] on this server and the server then responds "Ana Hernandez is not found on this server".[47]

Whilst the use of 404 messaging is a well-known gesture among net art communities, EDT re-focused its function towards a political gesture. Thus Dominguez describes his work as "digitally incorrect",[48] insofar as error and inefficiency are deliberately sought after, so that error messaging is meant "to indicate to system administrators the error of their ways".[49] By compelling the targeted sites to respond with a statement declaring an error, a theatrical re-enactment of both the Acteal dead and the acts of human right violation and injustice was produced - was *performed*. By facilitating the emergence of a collective presence in direct digital action, the group espouses a similar political philosophy as that of the Argentine-based *Internacional Errorista*, only the mobilisation of code in the case of EDT calls for a more explicit use of programming languages and error-messaging as a counter-performative tools.

Equally important is the fact that in forcing the server to perform a 404 response: "Justice not found", in the context of a deliberate error, the error message is thus re-enacted in a distinctly theatrical context, that is, in order to stage an absence, and bring back this absence into some kind of theatrical re-embodiment. If there is no justice, then it is up to the theatre as medium to bring back some sense of justice back, at least by representing in cyber space the otherwise unvoiced plight of the dead. Indeed, Dominguez notes that it has always been important to continue the performative gesture and thus retain the notion that EDT is, above all, an electronic theatre group. EDT thus brings to the fore the notion that whilst Internet communication is a distributed and hypermediated form of communication existing in virtual space, it nonetheless actualises a spatiality and dynamic that is, de facto, theatrical. So whereas traditional denial of service attacks use the computers of unknowing individuals as the conduits or vehicles for increased traffic to a given URL, in EDT's virtual sit-ins users are aware that their computers are having an effect on a third party machine or website, which is why members of EDT can maintain the public face of citizens freely expressing themselves as performance artists. The basis of the sit-in is therefore its theatricality and the transparency of the action *qua* theatre, which is why it is so important that the identity of the actual perpetrators is not obscured, but that they openly acknowledge responsibility. So unlike cyberterrorism, which is invisible and which has no audience

---

47 Ibidem.
48 Dominguez, quoted in Evans R. Goldstein, "Politically Incorrect: Ricardo Dominguez's provocations: art or crime?", *The Chronicle*, 3 October 2010, http://chronicle.com/article/Digitally-Incorrect/124649/ [accessed 27 December 2011].
49 Stalbaum, quoted in Evans R. Goldstein, "Digitally Incorrect: Ricardo Dominguez's provocations: crime or art?"

attending by their own free will, EDT's targets are warned in advance and audiences attend willingly, which is why Dominguez can be quoted of saying: "Everything we do is in front of the curtain. In other words, it's staged, it's a performance".[50] Dominguez in fact sees EDT as "agit-prop theatre online", which is why he describes Floodnet performances as following the traditional three-part structure of a play: "Act I is the e-mail call for action to a core actor/audience/network; Act II is the action itself; and Act III is the follow-up discussion".[51]

Conclusion
This essay has presented the concept of error in the light of a very political feature of Internet communication and subject-formation, that is, the Internet's flexibility to create or customise one's own rituals of iterability. So although Internet communication follows restrictions of hardware and software protocols, the social codes mobilised in Internet exchanges are surprisingly free of normative conditioning, given the personalisation and customisation of Internet subjectivities. I have discussed the way in which errors in language impinge upon errors in political thought, and how technological systems reflect political binaries along lines of error-branding and corrective action as well (e.g. Bush's binary equation: democracy v. terrorism, or "good" democratic states v. Axis of Evil). My argument has been that if error is indeed inescapable by way of logic, insofar as communication always functions under certain protocols or rules which can be mistaken, then the creation of performance processes that glorify successful outcomes seems to undermine the possibility for error to bring about change, and new processes of citation. As Mark Nunes states in the introduction to his edited book *Error: Glitch, Noise, and Jam in New Media Cultures* (2010),[52] the ubiquity of error can in effect communicate, albeit, as a communication without a purpose or at cross-purposes to programmatic control. This means that we can bring a concept of creativity to bear on digital and net art, and its "aesthetics of error", by thinking the art of the machine as an art outside the machine's pre-programmed routine; an art outside the errorless algorithm.[53]

My discussion has shifted from a linguistic examination of error, to a discussion of error politics in recent American political administration, to a question of how error can be used net-artistically as a counter-administrative and counter-performative tool, such that error can be deliberately sought after and indeed theatricalised (as in the case of IE and

50   Carmin Karasic, quoted in Evans R. Goldstein, "Digitally Incorrect: Ricardo Dominguez's provocations: crime or art?".
51   Coco Fusco & Ricardo Dominguez, "On-Line Simulations/Real-Life Politics: A Discussion with Ricardo Dominguez on Staging Virtual Theatre", TDR, 47: 2 (2003), pp. 151-162, http://www.jstor.org/pss/1147016 [accessed 28 December 2011].
52   Mark Nunes, *Error: Glitch, Noise, and Jam in New Media Cultures*, Continuum, New York 2010.
53   Ibidem, p. 43.

EDT), to show inconsistencies within an administration (technological and political). In order to tie some lose ends in this discussion I will conclude by saying that although errorism emerges as a distinctly historical idea, specifically as an internet-based opposition movement to the War on Terror (particularly during the mid noughties), it poses interesting and long-lasting questions relating to the performativity of error, and to the possibilities for counter-performative political action. The war on error might not be over just yet.

Part IV
SHIFTING MISPERFORMATIVITY

PART IV
SHIFTING THE
MISPERCEPTION NARRATIVE

Branislav Jakovljević
Continuous and Endless Mistake: (Every House has a) Door on Perpetual War

I

Approximately halfway through *Let us think of these things always. Let us speak of them never*, Selma Banić, Stephen Fiehn, Matthew Goulish, and Mislav Čavajda stand behind a simple table placed at the far end of the performance area [FIG 1.]

In front of each of them is an open laptop. The awkwardly dressed actors fix their eyes on the screens as they perform a series of actions that make no sense to the audience. Unless, of course, the spectators know what is on the monitors. Even then, it is difficult to relate these seemingly random gestures and grimaces to the scene from Dušan Makavejev's *Sweet Movie* (1974):[1] the members of the Vienna-based Action Analytic commune perform SD or Selbdarstellung (literally, Self-Presentation), a group therapy they devised together with the commune founder, Otto Muehl. In his diary, Richard Gardner, a former commune member, describes SD as part of the commune's daily routine. Each evening, commune members would gather and make a circle on the floor until someone decided to get in the middle. The only rules for those participating in SD were that they were not allowed to hurt anyone and, consequently, no objects were permitted "in the mid-

[1] *Sweet Movie* is the first film Makavejev made outside of Yugoslavia. In terms of content and method, it follows up on this previous film, *WR: Mysteries of the Organism* (1971): in both films, using his signature technique of combining compilation and feature film footage, Makavejev investigates vicissitudes of revolutionary ideas in the 20th century. *Sweet Movie* follows Miss World (played by Carole Laure) from North America (where she wins the contest for the prettiest virgin), to Paris (where she "stumbles" into Otto Muehl's commune), and finally to Amsterdam, where the film shifts to its second female protagonist, Captain Anna Planeta.

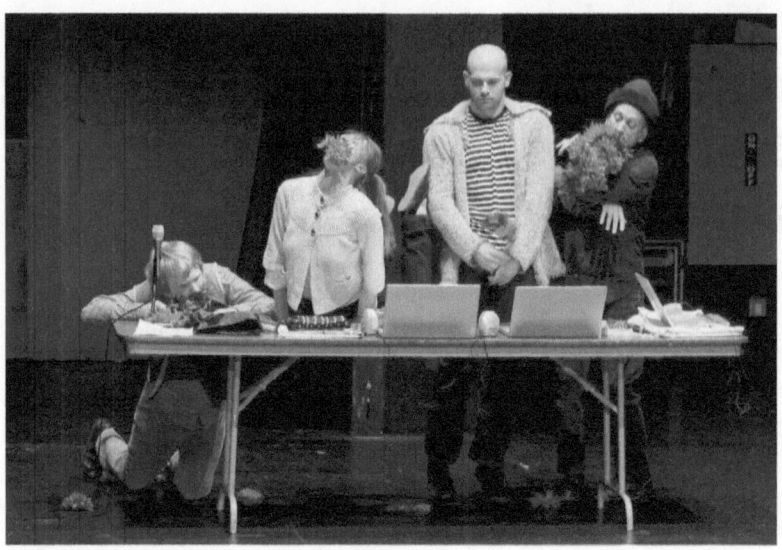

[FIG. 1] *Let us think of these things always. Let us speak of them never*
Photo: John W. Sission, Reproduced by Permission, Courtesy of Every House Has a Door

dle." Relying on their imaginations, SD participants summoned the widest range of objects, images, and experiences. "I saw plane crashes in the middle," writes Gardner:

> I saw nuclear weapons detonated in the middle. I saw bizarre, comical, and horrible sex crimes in the middle [...] It was like seeing the ENTIRE universe run before your eyes like the mother of all films. It was a film you saw, a film you acted in, a film you wrote and edited, and never saw a final version of. [2]

The SD session translated surprisingly well into film. In his essay "On Makavejev On Bergman," the American philosopher Stanley Cavell describes the commune scene as the "film's best remembered feature".[3] He finds especially powerful the juxtaposition of the banquet scene, in which the commune members eat, groan, puke, and engage in food fights, with documentary footage of the exhumation of mass graves in Katyn forest, which Makavejev culled from Nazi propaganda films. While parts of Cavell's essay crop up throughout *Let us think*, his long discussion of the excavation footage, performed masterfully by Matthew Goulish, takes almost the whole fourth (penultimate) section of the piece. Never did film criticism look so

---

2   Richard Gardner, *The Friedrichshof Chronicles*, 10 June 2009, http://artdeadlines.com/rlg/fhc [accessed 15 March 2010].
3   Stanley Cavell, *Themes Out of School: Effects and Causes*, North Point Press, San Francisco 1984, p. 120.

great performed onstage. Nor, I am sure, have many performance artists dared to use writing on cinema as a source material for their work. I want to suggest that by taking up Cavell in their performance, Every House Has a Door engages in debates surrounding theatricality that have been going on in America since the late 1960s, and in doing so, they contemporize this debate in a way that is as adroit as it is subtle.

Every House Has a Door was founded by Goulish and Hixon in 2008 after they disbanded Goat Island, the theater company they started 21 years prior. The new group's first production is a performance essay that engages Cavell's philosophical essay dedicated to Makavejev's film essay. It could be subtitled: "On Cavell on Makavejev on Bergman." This chain is indicated already in the introductory moments of *Let us think*, which closely follow the opening of Cavell's essay. The philosopher takes as his starting point the experiment Makavejev did for a 1978 conference at Harvard, which consisted of splicing together nonverbal scenes from several Bergman films. Every House Has a Door dutifully restages this experiment. Then they reenact Makavejev's actions: following the screening of his "Bergman film that Bergman never made," Makavejev, clad in a cape and a red hat, grinned at the silent audience members for three full minutes. In this lack of audience response Cavell recognizes the absence of "control that film audiences have over the conditions in which they view films".[4] He goes on to say that from this "passiveness" it could follow that "one may have nothing to say in a given moment and that this need be no disgrace".[5] It is precisely this "having nothing to say" that a decade earlier Cavell asserted as one of the basic conditions of theater. In his essay "Avoidance of Love: A Reading of King Lear"—a coda of sorts to his first book, *Must We Mean What We Say?*[6]— Cavell proposes that Cordelia's silence in response to her father's summons to speak, reflects the passivity that is the main condition of theater. In a text published in 1969, as participatory and environmental theater was reaching its apex around the world—from garages in New York's SoHo to beaches in Brazil, from urban communes in Vienna to rural ones in Yugoslavia—Cavell went against the grain of contemporary performance to argue that no act, no gesture can be powerful enough to obliterate the basic condition of theater: "my separateness from what is happening to them; that I am I, and here. It is only in this perception of them as separate from me that I make them present. That I make them *other*, and face them".[7]

This take on the theatricality of the modern subject position represents the unstated starting point of Cavell's lecture on Makavejev and Bergman. While never explicitly mentioned, this idea undergirds his entire

---

4   Ibidem, p. 110.
5   Ibidem, p. 113.
6   Stanley Cavell, *Must We Mean What We Say?*, Cambridge University Press, Cambridge 1969.
7   Ibidem, p. 338.

argument, only to surface in statements such as his assertion that "all our experience" has been converted "into a mode of viewing".[8] In 1969, Cavell did not accuse cutting-edge experimental performance of not being radical enough or effective enough, but precisely the opposite: it was an expression and a symptom of theatricality in an "age in which the organs of news"—or the media as we would call them today—"became distractions from what is happening, presenting everything happening as overwhelmingly present, like events in old theater".[9] This overwhelming presentness is the subject of Bergman's *Persona* (1966), which Cavell sees as a prequel to and an occasion for Makavejev's *Sweet Movie*. In *Persona* an actress is stricken by aphasia in the face of images of atrocities such as the photograph of the boy from the Warsaw Ghetto surrendering to the Nazis, or TV footage of a Buddhist monk's self-immolation in Vietnam. If Cavell's charge about theatricality as radical passivity in the face of an accessible yet unapproachable world was ignored by theater scholars and practitioners of the time, that was far from true for a young art critic who made a similar argument a couple of years earlier on the pages of *Artforum*.

This is not the place to rehearse the debates surrounding Michael Fried's controversial essay "Art and Objecthood" (1967), which Cavell acknowledges as one of the critical sources for his own essay on Lear.[10] Also, it would be beside the point to discuss the performance work of Lin Hixson and Matthew Goulish in terms of Fried's criticism of theatricality, understood as the active involvement of beholders in the work of art. When it comes to questions of space and audience, Goat Island's first instinct was to reject, in one breath, both proscenium and environmental theater. The section "Environment" in *Small Acts of Repair*, a theoretical and critical summation of Goat Island's two decades, is prefaced by Hixson's insistence that the group "doesn't work in a proscenium situation." She goes on to explain that the "audience plays an important part" in their performances, and is quick to clarify: "not directly, in that we do not drag you on the stage or anything".[11] The approach to spectators as witnesses rather than active doers remains unchanged in the work of Every House Has a Door. Sure enough, *Let us think* begins with a direct address to the audience. In an even voice Stephen introduces the performers and then lays out what is coming ahead. It is like a well-composed lecture or a visit to the dentist: relax, we will start slowly, then it will get difficult, and then it will get easier. Selma, Mislav, and Matthew sit on their bar stools, with their gazes cast to the side. They are showing themselves rather than greeting the spectators. Once the

---

8   Stanley Cavell, *Themes Out of School: Effects and Causes*, p. 137.
9   Cavell, *Must We Mean What We Say?*, p. 348.
10   Cavell, *Must We Mean What We Say?*, p. 333.
11   *Small Acts of Repair: Performance, Ecology and Goat Island*, eds Matthew Goulish and Stephen Bottoms, Routledge, New York 2007, p. 29.

action begins, this situation of being put on display is repeated over and over again.

Here, as in many of Goat Island's performances, the stage is "neither proscenium based nor conventionally 'in the round'".[12] The performance is in the *middle*. However, it does not offer itself as an instance of uncontrollable authenticity, but as a scrupulously organized structure of actions. Instead of seeking to induce trance in its audience, it asks for their attention. Bryan Saner, one of the members of Goat Island, wrote: "our performances are crafted to allow meditative, mind-wandering space".[13] As Carol Baker put it so aptly, as audience members, "we become invested in the investment of the players—their commitment to their actions sparks our own".[14] And it is precisely this chain of "investment" that came to occupy the primary focus of Fried's art historical work. Whereas in his art criticism of the 1960s he considered literalness and in-between-ness the primary properties of theatricality, in his art historical work of the 1970s and beyond, he assigns that place to absorption. In a nutshell, Fried's argument in his art historical trilogy (*Absorption and Theatricality* [1980], *Courbet's Realism* [1990], *Monet's Modernism* [1996]) is that, while in pre-modern religious painting the image directly addressed the viewer-devotee, by the mid-eighteenth century, a new alignment of representation turned the image inward, away from the beholder. Devotion is now replaced by the absorption of the viewer. Importantly, Fried argues that this new order of representation in painting is not sufficiently addressed by art criticism of the period, and that it requires an equal attention to the debates surrounding theater to be fully understood. That being the case, Fried makes a methodological point in the initial volume of the trilogy on drawing not only on Denis Diderot, the leading art and drama critic of the period, but also on his immediate predecessors. Had he taken into account Diderot's contemporaries and followers, Fried would have had no choice but to consider Jean-François Marmontel's ideas about theatrical illusion, which challenged Diderot's adherence to Cartesian nature of the subject facing the painting.

Two points are of special importance for this discussion.

First: Starting from Diderot's encyclopedia definition of "to absorb" and continuing chiefly by relying on his art criticism, Fried identifies absorption with a state or a condition that is marked by a certain automatism of the subject, her engrossment in an activity, the result of which is her obliviousness to the beholder. That is especially striking in compositions involving groups of figures. The pictorial organization of these paintings boils down to a choreography of gazes. Here, the composition becomes a "single collec-

---

12 Ibidem, p. 35.
13 Ibidem, p. 61.
14 Ibidem, p. 50.

tive act of heightened attention".[15] Fried emphasizes that in these works the "various figures are differentiated psychologically and emotionally from one another".[16] Had he not stopped his art historical project at around the 1860s, and had he lived up to his methodological demand for the inclusion of theater into the study of art, Fried would have discovered the same techniques of staging in the theater at the turn of the twentieth century. Whereas this principle of composition originated in the theater of Diderot and Lessing, it reached its most advanced form in Stanislavski's stage work. And had he pursued the development of this principle of composition even further, Fried would have found that absorption as a compositional principle not only precedes but also outlives genre painting, and as such is not, as a device, limited to realistic representation. The choreography of gazes is established as much through contrast between figures as it is through their concert. Fried leaves behind this contrast all too easily. We find it, for example, used to a supreme effect and to non-absorptive and anti-theatrical purpose in the theater of Stanislavski's best student, Vsevolod Meyerhold.[17] Meyerhold's best student, Sergei Eisenstein, abstracted this principle from theater and used it as one of the basic premises of his dialectical montage. In his lectures on expressive movement from the 1930s, he elevates the principle of contrast, which he identifies with "recoil movement" (stepping back in order to launch forward), to an "organic law" of composition: "If a recoil movement is needed for hitting a nail on the head, then for a 'blow' on the psyche of the spectator, when you have to 'thrust' one or another expressive scenic element into it, your action must resort to the very same recoil principle".[18] The principle of montage as the "blow on the psyche" is apparent in the juxtaposition of acted and documentary film footage that Eisenstein's best student, Dušan Makavejev, brought to perfection in his films *Innocence Unprotected* (1968), *WR: Mysteries of the Organism* (1971) and *Sweet Movie*.[19]

The second point concerns anti-theatricality, and it also leads to Makavejev, but via a different route. The aim of the first point is not to say that Fried fails to indicate the limits of absorption. Already in his doctoral

---

15   Michael Fried, *Absorption and Theatricality: Painting and Beholder in the Age of Diderot*, University of California Press, Berkeley, Los Angeles, London 1980, p. 55.
16   Ibidem, p. 55.
17   Consider the scene "Reading the Letter" from Meyerhold's 1926 production of Nikolai Gogol's *The Inspector General*. The photograph was reproduced in Konstantin Rudnitsky, *Meyerhold, the Director*, trans. George Petrov, Ardis, Ann Arbor 1981, p. 411.
18   *Eisenstein in Meyerhold, Eisenstein, and Biomechanics: Actor Training in Revolutionary Russia*, eds Alma Law and Mel Gordon, McFarland, Jefferson, N.C. 1996, p. 193.
19   Eisenstein is the third and last generation in the extraordinary series of teachers and students that took stage art from the 19th to the 20th century, from monarchic to soviet Russia, and from theater to film. Makavejev marks the shift from direct to elective genealogy, so characteristic of 20th-century avant-garde movements. In this kind of relationship, the absence of immediate contact only enhances the closeness of the student to his selected predecessors. In retrospect, the opening statement of Makavejev's article "Ajzenštajn – crveno, zlatno, crno" [Eisenstein: red, golden, black] published as the introduction to the Serbian translation of Eisenstein's film essays, reads as the first sentence of an autobiography written in third person: "Those who knew him personally report that he was a very joyous man" (Dušan Makavejev, "Ajzenštajn – crveno, zlatno, crno", in Sergej Ajzenštajn, *Montaža atrakcija: eseji o filmu*, Nolit, Beograd 1964, p. 9).

dissertation "Manet's Sources: Aspects of His art, 1895-1865," Fried acknowledges the historicity of theatricality based on absorption.[20] According to him, the primacy of theater in the representation of action in French painting reaches its peak at the turn of the nineteenth century. He argues that the first great rebellion against this dictatorship of theatricality in painting was led by Theodore Géricault, the author of the iconic painting of French Romanticism, *Raft of the Medusa* (1819).

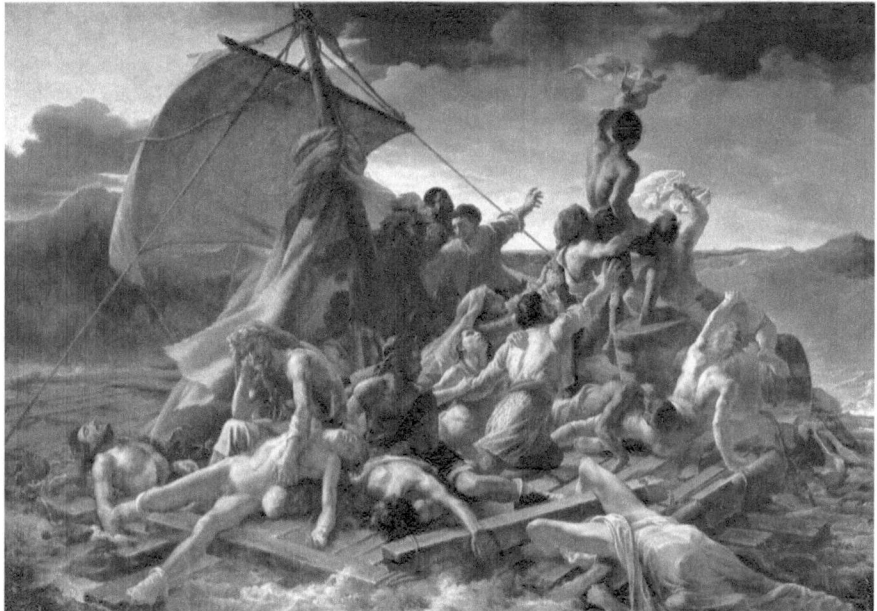

Theodore Géricault, *Raft of the Medusa* (1819)
© RMN-Grand Palais / Art Resource, NY

Fried's discussion of Géricault merits extensive citation:

> [He] seems to have found the theatricalization of action personally intolerable—to have experienced it as a loss of the world, understood as that set of conditions, that *ground*, upon which self-sufficient action is alone possible, and the self in its essential unity of inner meaning and outward expression is alone realizable other than as a theatrical performance.[21]

---

20 It was published as a sole article in the March 1969 issue of *Artforum*. Fried used it as the starting point for the concluding volume of his art historical "trilogy" *Manet's Modernism, or, The Face of Painting in the 1860s*, University of Chicago Press, Chicago and London 1996.
21 Michael Fried, "Thomas Couture and the Theatricalization of Action in 19th Century French Painting", *Artforum*, 8: 10 (June 1970), p. 43.

This writing predates *Absorption and Theatricality*, and it is intriguing why Fried decided to ignore the following insights in his consideration of threats to theatricality within Greuze's paintings, especially as they relate to his depiction of children, which are often associated with animals (a dog, a bird):

> Géricault's extensive reliance on animals, especially horses, in his paintings and lithographs must be seen partly in this context. He appears to have found in the representation of horses, either alone or in conjunction with human riders, a means of representing actions and expressions that literally exceed human capabilities, but which by virtue of their essential nature—their animality—escape being seen as theatrical [...]. In fact, the representation of animals whether active or in repose seems to have provided Géricault with the only refuge from the theatrical that he had: as if the relation of animals to the world—the terms on which they may be said to *have* a world—are such as to preclude the theatricalization of that relation or those terms no matter what. [22]

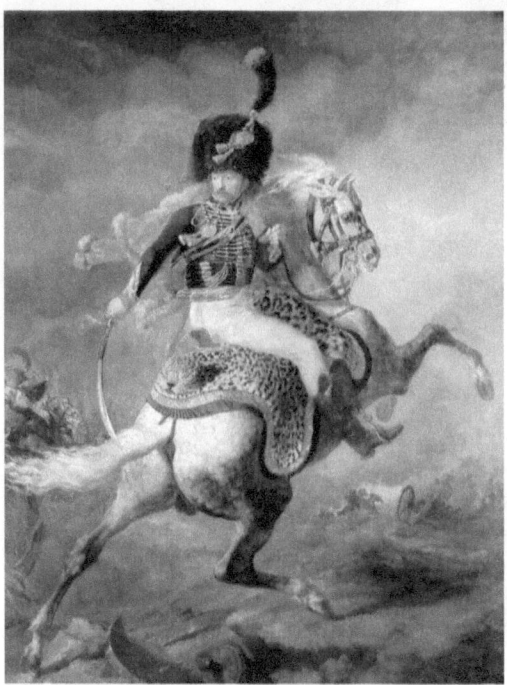

Theodore Géricault: *Officer of the Imperial Guard* (1814)
© RMN-Grand Palais / Art Resource, NY

---

22   Ibidem, p. 43, italics in the original.

And it is precisely bestiality as a means of overcoming theatricality that is at the center of Géricault's most powerful work:

> In [Géricault's] art animality becomes an ideal of humanness—a modality of possessing, or *being in*, both body and world—which ultimately turns out to lie beyond our reach. (The unattainability and consequent bestializing of that ideal is part of the tragic content of the *Raft of the Medusa* and the magnificent but sexually berserk paintings of severed heads and limbs that immediately preceded it). [23]

How is it possible that Cavell, the other member of the tag team of theatricality from the late sixties—who in his essay from *Must We Mean What We Say?* writes about the similar desublimation of King Lear and his "abdication" to the state of a child—does not recognize that experiments such as Otto Muehl's commune stand at the far end of the Romantics' dreams of overcoming the theatrical norm? While at one point in his essay he invokes Medusa from ancient Greek mythology, why does he fail to acknowledge that in Makavejev's *Sweet Movie*, the boat *Survival*, that site of the obscene seduction of children, with its Medusa-like head of Marx at the stern, belongs to the same atrocious fleet as *Raft of the Medusa*?[24]

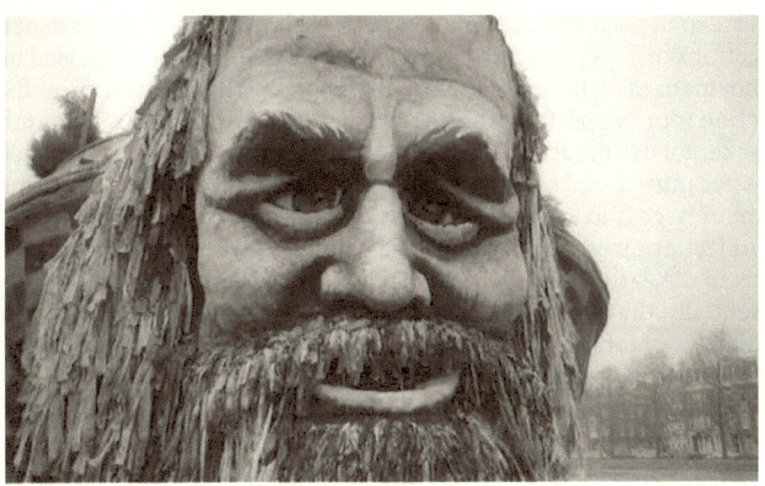

Dušan Makavejev, *Sweet Movie* (1974)
Reproduced by Permission of Dušan Makavejev

23 Ibidem, italics in the original.
24 This scene is one of the most controversial in the movie. Here, the character Anna Planeta (played by Anna Prucnal), symbolizing the soviet revolution and providing the counterpart to American Miss World, performs a striptease in front of a group of pre-pubescent boys. Cavell writes that this scene of a mature woman seductively undressing inches from the faces of young boys "forms one of the most difficult passages, from the perspective of ordinary sensibility, of this difficult film" (Stanley Cavell, "On Makavejev On Bergman" in *Themes Out of School: Effects and Causes*, p. 312).

II

By now, I hope it is clear that what is at stake in the debates about theatricality that started in the late 1960s is the nature of artistic illusion, and further, the conceptualization of the self-contained and seemingly ideologically neutral techniques of representation of action. It is not surprising that, far from being confined to theater, debates around theatricality involved painting, sculpture, film, and performance; nor is it surprising that they started in the United States when they did, in the midst of Vietnam War, and continued there, off and on, for the next 40 years. Taking all of this into account, the source films that Hixson and Goulish chose for this project is significant, as both Makavejev's *Sweet Movie* and Bergman's *Persona* deal with atrocities and their representation in the media. Originally recorded on film stock and screened in movie theaters, these films are now received through digital media, on LCD screens. I want to suggest that Every House Has a Door's endeavor ultimately results in the disentanglement of theatricality, both in terms of intermediality and geography. The ambition behind this is not, as Fried would say, in overcoming theatricality, or, as his mentor Clement Greenberg would argue, in establishing medium specificity, but in initiating a reflection on the ethical potential of performance in its immediate historical moment.

Over the past decade, advances in digital technology reinvigorated the use of video in performance. What is curious, however, is that these new applications of data projectors and oversized video screens often lead to redeployment of techniques already discovered with the insertion of film projection into live performance. What in the 1930s and 1960s amounted to experimental use of recorded moving images in live onstage action, in the 2000s became the norm. Almost as a rule, this involves actors performing in front of large film screens. Whereas in experimental theater of the 1960s film projections were usually used as a background for live performance, already in the early 1970s video radically reversed this relation. This reversal is, essentially, the question of the apparatus. Jean-Luc Baudry argues that the cinematographic apparatus, conceived as a process of the recording and projection of moving images, is an extension of the visual representation established by European easel painting that "elaborates a total vision which corresponds to the idealist conception of the fullness and homogeneity of 'being'".[25] He argues that, in order to maintain the effects of fullness and homogeneity, film has to deny its own constitutive fragmentations: from cuts between shots, to the physical and temporal processes that take place between camera, editing table, and projection room.[26] If the apparatus of film projection conceals and represses the fragmentation and difference

---

25 Jean-Louis Baudry, "Ideological Effects of the Basic Cinematographic Apparatus" in *Cinematographic Apparatus: Selected Writings*, ed. Theresa Hak Kyung Cha, Tanam Press, New York 1980, p. 28.
26 Ibidem, p. 29.

that are inherent in the process of filmmaking by establishing an illusion of continuity on the film screen, then experimental works that combine projection and live performance reestablish this originary difference, albeit on a completely different level. Whether it is the case of an action performed in front of the projection of a blank film reel, as in Nam June Paik's *Zen for Film* (1964),[27] or the projection of found footage that is synchronized with live action, as in ONCE group's *Unmarked Interchange* (1965), performance doesn't alter the basic situation of the apparatus for reception of the movie image: the beam of light coming from an outside source and falling on the screen.[28] Whereas most contemporary uses of digital images in theater resort to the old practices of inserting live performers into a projected background, thus naturalizing the digital environment and occluding the apparatus, Every House Has a Door reverses this relation. They accomplish this reversal by simply changing the screen's magnitude.

As Mislav sings, Matthew props an open laptop in front of his face and Selma holds a microphone close to his mouth. The screen is turned away from us, so we look at Mislav looking at the screen as he staggers across the stage. Matthew positions the laptop as if he is operating a movie camera: trying to get the right angle, keeping the actor's face in front of it. While resembling a film shoot, this scene effectively reverses its process: instead of camera capturing the live performer, the performer takes down the movements from the screen in front of him. These movements belong to Ivica Vidović, and the scene is from the final moments of Makevejev's *WR: Mysteries of the Organism*. Vidović, playing the Russian ice skater Vadimir Ilyich who had just decapitated the Yugoslav girl Milena, is lip-synching the ballade "Villon's Prayer" by Russian poet and chansonneur Bulat Okudzava. Vidović's—and Matthew's—prayer is addressed to a horse, who in performance is impersonated first by Stephen and then by Selma. Unlike Géricault's beast, this pale horse does not resist theatricality, but is instead fully incorporated into it. The tragic content of Makavejev's great movies, *WR: Mysteries of the Organism* and *Sweet Movie*, is in the realization that consciousness, not bestiality, underpins the most unspeakable acts. [FIG. 2]

Although memorable, the "banquet scene" from *Sweet Movie* in which the members of the Muehl commune use food in variety of ways, including simulated self-castration, does not last very long. Staged, or rather "taken down" from laptop screens, in *Let us think of these things always. Let us speak of them never* this scene becomes excruciatingly long. The banquet becomes a gaping mouth that swallows and spits out individual actions, scenes, dances, and songs. As the table is gradually pushed towards the back of the stage,

27   Or, for that matter, of a blank projection without performance taking place immediately in front of the screen but instead throughout the auditorium, as in Claes Oldenbourg's *Moveyhouse* (1965).
28   For a very useful survey of the uses of film in experimental theater of the 1960s, see the special issue "Film and Theater", *TDR: The Drama Review*, 11:1 (T33) (Fall 1966).

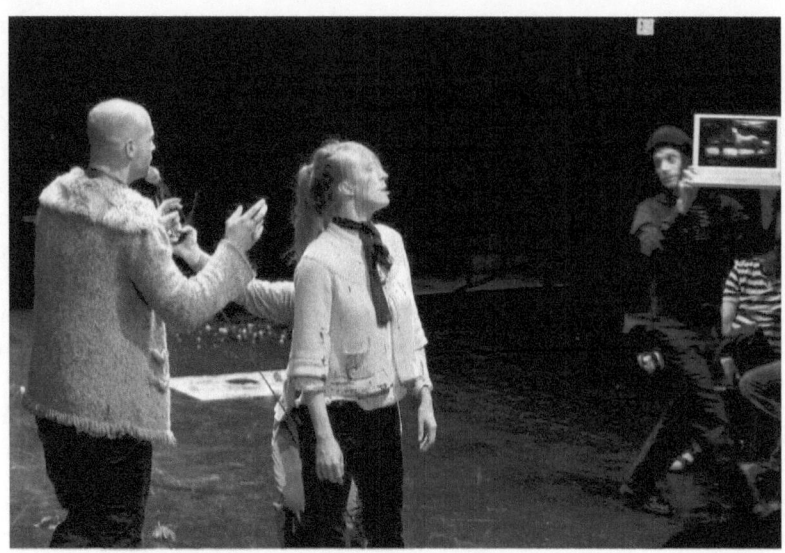

[FIG. 2] *Let us think of these things always. Let us speak of them never*
Photo: John W. Sission, Reproduced by Permission, Courtesy of Every House Has a Door

the banquet turns into a general ambiance that engulfs the entire performance. Matthew, Mislav, Selma, and Stephen perform standing behind the table, an open laptop in front of each of them. This is not a film shoot. There are no microphones, and the static laptops lined up on the table resemble footlights, not cameras. It is a theatrical replication of a performance captured on film. The players copy, as closely as possible, the gestures, grimaces, and actions of the participants in the banquet scene that unfolds on screens in front of them. It is not that they drag spectators into the action: instead, *they bring spectatorship onstage*. Absorbed in the images that unfold on their screens, they handle bouquets of kitschy artificial flowers instead of the food and kitchen utensils featured in the film. The fake flowers and real apples, electronic and otherwise, epitomize the unsustainable internal division of *spectators who are actors at the same time*. This inner split precisely delineates the limit of absorption, and with it, of theatricality as conceived by Diderot and, by extension, by Fried and Cavell.

This limit has been observed and described by the earlier mentioned Jean-François Marmontel. In his writings on tragedy, this playwright, novelist, contributor to the *Encyclopedia*, and onetime protégé of Diderot argues that theater is a "mixture of the real and the unreal, and that such a mixture, concocted by art, constituted the quintessence of dramatic illusion".[29] Much

---

29   Michael Cardy, *The Literary Doctrines of Jean-François Marmontel*, The Voltaire Foundation, Oxford 1982, p. 112.

like Eistenstein and Makavejev,[30] Marmontel saw in front of a stage or a canvas not a perceiving eye or a disembodied mind of a Cartesian subject, but a human being endowed with senses other than sight and experiences that go beyond the "continuous presentness" that unfolds in front of her. In Marmontel's theater, the mechanics of illusion—and that of the subject—are much more complex than in Diderot's. According to Marmontel, the viewer cannot be abstracted from the situation in which the beholding takes place. A stage (or a canvas or a page) works to undermine the very illusion that it makes possible. In his article "Illusion" for the *Encyclopedia*'s supplement, Marmontel called this state a "demi-illusion": a *"continuous and endless mistake mixed with a self-reflection that belies the error"*.[31] In their reading of Marmontel, John Bender and Michael Marrinan distinguish three indivisible aspects of this notion of artistic illusion: "the subtle play of illusion with a self-conscious awareness of its operations", "the pleasure that arises from this self-awareness", and "the danger presented by complete illusion to destroy this dialectic".[32] It is only the inability of the spectator to fully partake in illusion—in other words, the mistake that produces demi-illusion—that guards the subject from her complete absorption in, and annihilation by, the unreality of the spectacle.

The banquet scene in *Let us think* is the staging of demi-illusion in all of its odd and outlandish richness. In front of us is a group of spectators who act. Engrossed in the images before them, they are oblivious to their immediate surroundings. They are here and not here. Their behavior is odd, as if they are in the wrong movie. The oddness of this performance has nothing to do with its "script". In other words, it does not come from the orgy captured on film juxtaposed with the documentary footage of Nazis exhuming mass graves in Eastern Europe. The long banquet scene itself is juxtaposed with the long monologue composed from sections of Cavell's essay "On Makavejev on Bergman", which Matthew Goulish reads onstage. This reading takes place alongside a sign of the complete evacuation of the eidetic content of the piece: as Matthew sits next to the table immersed in the text he holds in his hands, Mislav, Selma, and Stephen clear the stage and cover the table with white cloth.

> The conscience of *Sweet Movie* is most hideously captured in a sequence of literal excavation—the Nazi documentary footage of German troops exhuming bodies from mass graves in the Katyn Forest. Let us call Makavejev's methods of construction "the film of excavation." /1/ By this I mean my sense of his work's digging to unearth

---

30   And, following the principle of elective genealogy, we should add here Lin Hixson and Matthew Goulish.
31   John Berman and Michael Marrinan, *The Culture of the Diagram*, Stanford University Press, Stanford, 2010, p. 109, italics added.
32   Ibidem, p. 121

buried layers of the psyche but also my sense that these constructions have the feeling of reconstruction—as of something lost or broken. A lifelong participant in a society of declared socialist aspirations, Makavejev is asking: Was my revolution capable even of this? Has it cannibalized everything that has touched it? Is it true that the Red Army committed a mass murder of the Polish officer corps? The film shows a card which contains Anthony Eden's response to this news: "Let us think of these things always. Let us speak of them never." /2/ For Makavejev, that conspiracy of silence, call it mass hypocrisy, is a prescription for self-administered mass death. Mere film alone cannot prove who caused and buried the corpses in the Katyn Forest, but this film directly refuses the conspiracy of silence about it.[33]

Intensity of this scene depends entirely on the ability of discourse to evoke an image in the mind. As I watched, it reminded me that, throughout the performance, no images from any of the films used as sources were ever fully and explicitly shown. In itself, withholding of images proves to be an effective assault on the theatricality about which Cavell was warning. But also beyond that, emptying the stage not only of images, but also of objects and actors, enhances the ethical density of onstage events that now fully coincide with discourse. There is no easy way out as the eye lazily lingers on a stage cleared of any illusionism. This is Cavell's essay that Cavell never wrote and it deals with the excavation not of past atrocities but of ongoing ones. In 2011, as we approach the 10th anniversary of the "war on terror," the "conspiracy of silence" and "mass hypocrisy" no longer apply to Nazi Germany or the Soviet Union or the Socialist Federative Republic of Yugoslavia. This performance is not about atrocities in the Second World War, or in Vietnam, or those more recent in the region of the former Yugoslavia. It goes there and comes back. In the most literal sense, it brings the war back home. The banquet scene, that strange dance to the score of invisible images, epitomizes the choreography of everyday life in America during the first decade of the wars in Iraq and Afghanistan. More than anyone else, the beholders absorbed in images, who are actors, at the same time resemble players immersed in the virtual environment of video games. Sales revenues indicate that first-person shooter games such as "Call of Duty: Modern Warfare 2" and "Medal of Honor 2010" became the primary medium for the representation of the ongoing wars to US consumers of images.[34] These kinds of games

---

33   Matthew Goulish and Lin Hixson, *Let us think of these things always. Let us speak of them never*, Unpublished script, 2010.
34   In his 2010 article published in *The New York Times Magazine*, Chris Suellentrop argues that "video games that evoke our current conflicts" have become "the most popular fictional depictions of America's current wars." He supports this claim by citing the profits generated by *Call of Duty: Modern Warfare 2* which easily left behind films such as *The Hurt Locker* and approached (and perhaps even exceeded) the blockbusters such as *Avatar* (Chris Suellentrop, "War Games", *The New York Times Magazine*, 8 September 2010, http://www.nytimes.com/2010/09/12/magazine/12military-t.html?_r=1&scp=2&sq=chris%20suellentrop&st=cse [accessed 2 March 2011]).

are inherently dependent on the immersion of the spectator in the field of representation.

Needless to say, the notion of absorption enters game design theory through an understanding of immersion seen as a form of a *"suspension of disbelief,* a state in which the player's mind forgets that it is being subjected to entertainment and instead accepts what it perceives as reality".[35] Arguing against such "immersive fallacy" Katie Salen and Eric Zimmerman suggest that the illusion of immersion is not created by game's virtual environment, but by an "engagement that occurs through the play itself".[36] In other words, the experience of immersion is not created by an illusion of reality but through an illusion of agency. Considered in the light of their ideological effects, new technologies continue and expand the cinematic apparatus by not only establishing an illusion of continuity on the film screen, but by expanding it to include the viewer. And furthermore, this illusion is not limited to the situation of reception (cinema, video console), but strives to penetrate and structure all everyday experiences. In other words, the apparatus is no longer something that encloses the (viewing) subject, but instead becomes involved in the most direct and literal way in the reshaping of that subjectivity. That is to say, "democratization" and "individualization" of viewing technologies established their ideological function. The gap of Marmontelian continuous and endless yet emancipatory mistake is closing. *Let us think of these things always. Let us speak of them never* is one of the extremely rare, hence ever more valuable attempts at a systematic widening of this gap.

While in the case of Vietnam the arena of representation and resistance to the war was constituted by, as Cavell claims, "the organs of the news" which presented "everything happening as overwhelmingly present", in Afghanistan and Iraq the representation of the war changed and became at the same time more distant and more overwhelmingly present. If at the end of their first decade the new wars are still very much undecided out there in the field, at home they were clearly successful from day one. Evidence of this decisive victory is reflected in the absence of any significant responses to the wars in American arts. This inability and unwillingness of contemporary US theater to address the wars is in large part due to the new theatricality that comes out of and at the same time feeds into the new wars. What Every House Has a Door's excavation reveals is precisely this new theatricality that is at the very foundation of the new technologies of the everyday.

The finale of the performance, which immediately follows the "excavation scene," establishes an unambiguous connection to this theatricality of the vast offstage space. The rehearsal lights are on, and Selma comes to

---

35 François Dominic Laramée, *Game Design Perspectives*, Charles River Media, Higham, MA 2002, p. 61.
36 Katie Salen and Eric Zimmerman, *Rules of Play: Game Design Fundamentals*, MIT Press, Cambridge 2004, p. 451.

the middle. Stephen invites her to participate in a simple onstage experiment: he will run out of theater and call her name, then come back to check if she has heard him, and repeat this same action until she can no longer hear him. The purpose of this operation, he says, is to determine "where the theater ends". She agrees and Stephen and Mislav run out, holler, come back, check if they were heard, and then run out again. As they come and go, they take the theater with them, presumably to the lobby and then to the street. What they bring back, however, is a negative imprint of theatricality of the everyday. The audience members, seated on U-shaped bleachers that surround the stage on three sides, look at each other, wriggle in their seats and smile uncomfortably. This discomfort comes from the absence of anything to look at and get immersed in. No actors, but also no screens, no sounds, no cell phones, no earphones. In its final gesture, the performance manages for a brief moment to suspend the apparatus. It asks me to read the title, *Let us think of these things always. Lets talk about them never* in the same way in which the actors/beholders reenact the banquet scene: in its original setting and at the same time radically removed. It is now clear that all along the sheer fact that they can not enter and fully inhabit that which they impersonate is what has kept this performance at a distance from me.

This introduction of the "immersive experience" into the field of visibility adds another layer to the meaning of performance. Contrary to what many video game theorists claim, the emphasis here is not on the new quality of immersion but on the excavation of an obscure meaning of experience. In *This New yet Unapproachable America* Cavell suggests that the semantic meaning of "experience" "goes through ideas of peril, trail, birth, way or journey, approach, all of which are development of the root *per*.[37] This opens the way to an idiosyncratic reading of performance as not only that which disintegrates in the very moment of its emergence, but also as that in which pleasure is inseparable from peril, and whose appeal is in its unapproachability.

---

37 Stanley Cavell, *This New yet Unapproachable America*, Living Batch Press, Albuquerque 1989, p. 101.

Laurie Beth Clark
& Michael Peterson
MisTopian Performance

Introduction

Lately, we find ourselves wanting from performance the same things we want from cooking and entertaining. Or from hanging out with friends at a great bar, like one we found in the old town in Rovinj, Croatia called *Limbo*, a tiny place outside which patrons sit on the steps up and down the street, murmuring softly into the night. Or, for that matter, from a well-known restaurant we stopped at in Zurich on the way to Croatia: *Blinde Kuh* (blind cow), where diners are literally in the dark. In these cases, scenography, hospitality and, yes, an economic exchange, are configured to promote a kind of public yet intimate contemplation.

We're often frustrated at parties by the lost opportunity of a room full of intellectuals gossiping and making small talk. When we can entertain, we do have a bias toward dinner guests who can maintain a "real" conversation. So we became attracted to conferences as a performance venue because they're an opportunity to "entertain" within a frame that in theory encourages serious intellectual play. At conferences, however, it's often the local context that is lost. Conferences can be insular – conversations in bubbles. And so we've started looking for ways to intervene in these dynamics: reframing dinner just enough to encourage the production of knowledge, pushing the "captive audience" of conference crowds into an expanded context.

On a personal dimension, in recent years we've realized how much our creative energy has been (satisfyingly) spent on various kinds of entertaining, from simple meals with friends to elaborate theme parties. We wanted that expenditure to "count" more; we want to count it ourselves as creative work, and to understand why we had not previously, to re-frame it and in our own way pursue the classic course of playing with the boundary between art and life.

During our first 20 years together, we made both elaborate dinner parties and humble barbecues, hosted crowds of 100 and improvised breakfast for visiting friends, developed elaborately themed parties and celebrated food from our garden and simple ingredients like homemade pickles and miso. We never treated these aesthetic endeavors as part of our professional work as practicing artists.

On our twentieth anniversary, we decided to formalize a connection between our professional lives and our personal hospitality. Under the company name Spatula&Barcode, we have committed ourselves for the *next* twenty years to make at least one performance annually that draws on the aesthetics we had previously reserved for domestic "entertaining".[1]

The first of these took place in Zagreb in 2009. It happened at the end of a year-long round-the-world trip and so the event, called *Misadventure*, focused on travel and presence. After a year back from our travel, we turned our focus to home and absence. At the second Misperformance gathering in Rijeka, documented by this volume, we offered a performance in one of the "shift" slots combined with one of the dinner gatherings. We wanted to assemble artistic, culinary, academic, and social ingredients and put them both in and out of place, put them into a shifted scene, explore how travel and privilege intertwine with the longing for those you wish were here. As the title suggested, *Mise en Place / Mise en Scene / Wish You Were Here* involved three main elements: the gathering of participants and ingredients, the placing of those elements into the "scene" of downtown Rijeka, and the (missed) connections among participants both present and absent. The three main parts of this essay outline our approach and process in making this type of performance and elaborate theoretically on some of what we learn from making it. This includes some of our satisfactions with these experiences, but also some less than celebratory notes on the notion of misperformance so recently valorized. When things truly go awry, misperformance can seem less like appealing happenstance and more like actual error.

We drew inspiration for *Mise en Place / Mise en Scene / Wish You Were Here* from established formations of space, time, food, entertainment, and sociality. In different ways, they represent a collectivity attempting to reflect on and even redress asymmetries of knowledge, cultural capital, and even material privilege. Like a *picnic*, whose now obsolete definition was "a fash-

---

[1] Spatula&Barcode has been busier than we expected, producing more than a dozen works by the end of 2013, including numerous works for conferences and organizations and commissions for the Wisconsin Triennial at the Madison Museum of Contemporary Art and for SARAS, an international environmental science group based in Uruguay.

ionable social event at which each guest contributed a share of the food" (OED), we hoped it would feel cool to be there. We think a good conference already feels a bit like a *Chautauqua*, the democratically-inclined summertime educational gatherings that take their name from their origin near Lake Chautauqua, New York, in the late 19th century. Finally, preparing this project felt a lot like hosting an arduously slow-cooked *barbecue*, which in American practice means a relaxed, celebratory feast, *preceded by long, meticulous preparation* (a kind of folk *mise en place*).

As we made arrangements for this performance, worrying on the one hand what the guests would bring to it, and worrying, on the other, about how much we were spending on the event, we found something helpful in thinking of it as a *potluck potlatch*. A "potluck," in contemporary American food vocabulary, is a dinner to which everyone brings something, with no organization of what; a pot luck can sometimes be a meal that is predominantly one kind of food or another, rather than a controlled balance. A "potlatch" is a term anthropologists use to describe social practices by some northwest Native American cultures whereby status is gathered and maintained through the sharing and even destruction of wealth, especially of food.

In these early pieces, then, we begin from a collision of genres – art genres, academic genres, genres of social interaction – in pursuit of performance experiences that bring together aesthetic, analytic, and social pleasures and challenges.

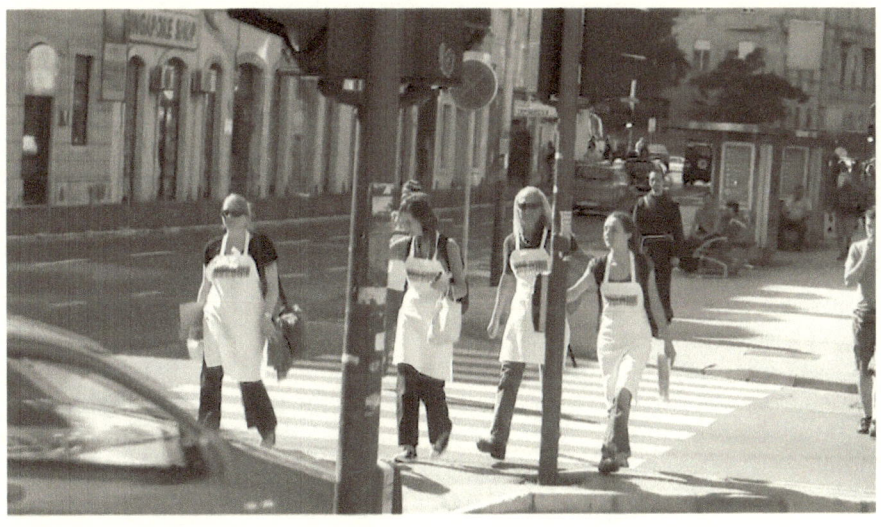

Photo: Spatula&Barcode

Mistopias

What kind of place does performance need to be in order for hybrid amalgamations of theorizing and sociality to succeed? What needs to be *put into place* in order to facilitate them? Half seriously, we suggest a neologism: we are in pursuit of a *mistopian* performance.

Mistopia is a permutation of heterotopia. Heterotopias promise spaces outside the flow of life to dramatize or critique "reality." Mistopias are interventions *within* the flow of life, embracing but also interrupting the quotidian. Mistopias are not necessarily comfortable: you don't know what matrix you are in, you may be disoriented.

Foucault's discussion of the mirror as both utopia and heterotopia is a particularly useful point of reference here:

> I believe that between utopias and these quite other sites, these heterotopias, there might be a sort of mixed, joint experience, which would be the mirror. The mirror is, after all, a utopia, since it is a placeless place. In the mirror, I see myself there where I am not, in an unreal, virtual space that opens up behind the surface [...] But [...] the mirror functions as a heterotopia in this respect: it makes this place that I occupy at the moment when I look at myself in the glass at once absolutely real, connected with all the space that surrounds it, and absolutely unreal, since in order to be perceived it has to pass through this virtual point which is over there.[2]

Mistopias as we imagine them offer this mixed experience with the ratio inverted: while the mirror creates an immense not-there world in an object with a small physical existence, the mistopia imbues every element of the real world with a potential to shift, to slip, or even to disappear.

Mis- is not Dys-. A mistopia is not a place where everything is wrong or upside-down. Clearly it's not utopia, either, but it certainly doesn't imply absolute failure or a malign atmosphere. Mis- is also not Dis-. We're not talking about distance or estrangement in the classical Brechtian sense. In mistopic performance, estrangement comes about as a matter of course, but it is not the point, and certainly not the fetish of the performance, as in the Epic theatre commonly understood. In mistopia, estrangement, strangely enough, comes naturally.

There is a dystopia of travel, with which many tourists are familiar, and which travelers sometimes jokingly compare to the truly hellish displacements that are endured by the violently displaced, the political and economic refugees, and those illegally imprisoned or kidnapped to be rendered to torture. And there is a utopia of travel, which most of us have not really

---

[2] Michel Foucault, "Of Other Spaces", trans. Jay Miskowiec, *Diacritics*, 16: 1 (1 April 1986), pp. 22-27.

experienced, but which we can imagine and describe. More often, for privileged tourists, there is the *mistopia* of travel, when all is strange but almost all seems possible. While this is a pleasurable state, it is also discomfiting, and travelers reject or ameliorate that in diverse ways. In US airports there is the remarkable sight of grown adults carrying full-sized feather pillows from home, like toddlers clutching a teddy bear. For some, continuing one's exercise routine while on the road is a way of orienting to the new place. Tourists put themselves out of place and then often go about performing a *mise en place* in relation to their new location.

Our current work together draws on our attempts over a period of three years to creatively confront asymmetries of time and place in our joint research (in 19 different countries) and in presentations and performance works on tourism at multiple conferences. Our suspicion is that while the inherent asymmetries of these encounters are often unjust, asymmetry itself offers the leverage (temporarily) to re-order and re-arrange them. If it happens, that re-arrangement occurs in mistopic space. We use the term "asymmetry" here not to obscure the inequalities involved in such encounters, but to emphasize that they are a part of lives *differently shaped* in a multitude of ways.

We conceived of the mistopia in part in response to the Rijeka conference's three-day celebration of MisPerformance – of the ways in which one's willingness to embrace missteps and even mistakes is a critical ingredient of creativity. We were also influenced by the conference organizers' emphasis on the idea of shifts and "shifting". Mistopias offer shifted experience, shifted frames.

However, we try not to be starry-eyed[3] about the social good represented by the kinds of gatherings that inspire us. While they can feed and nourish all guests equally, they are also often constituted by exclusion, and often function as a display of privilege more than a redistribution of it. And while the components of education, of shared creative play, or the collective production of knowledge may be under-recognized elements of the aforementioned food ways, all ritualized gatherings can of course function to consolidate existing asymmetries of power, knowledge and wealth, rather than to transform social relations toward justice. The church suppers of Michael's childhood formed "community," but also played an important role in maintaining a deeply unjust social order. Even in this global recession the conspicuous consumption of the various oligarchies around the world seem to suggest that unapologetic waste is the order of the day. While reminded of the ugly potential of consumption and even "community," we also took comfort in remembering George's Bataille's interest in the whole realm of "non-

---

3   The venue for the final part of our piece in Rijeka was Konoba Nebuloza; nebuloza means "starry" or "nebula" but can imply fuzzy-headed or drunk.

productive expenditure" as an excess of capitalism. The point of performance might be necessity, or critique – or there might not be any point at all.

While we are addicted to travel, as we demonstrated in our Zagreb performance the previous year, we are also compulsive home-makers, which seems to be our response to the pleasures and challenges of mistopian space. We travel, and then nest. And after putting our few (yet too many) things in place, we often try to cook. Sometimes this just means shopping and then laying out a picnic, but often we are able to satisfy some of our longing for real cooking. On our way to Rijeka, on a little two-burner stove in Rovinj, we made pasta with a sauce of squid, leftover *bronzino*, chanterelles, tomatoes, red peppers and Istrian sausage. A year before, in Buenos Aires, we stayed two months and gave four parties.

But beyond the literal importance of exercising creative control over our nourishment, we also cook conceptually, and one of the privileges of travel is to perform this action constantly: to select, arrange, contemplate and remember experience. We are greedy for these procedures. These are often mistopian encounters, pursuing our impulse to consume intensely, to come to know a place by walking and tasting, through its map and its cuisine, to interrupt host/guest asymmetries, to entertain. To put it all into place, not for fixity, but to see what happens next.

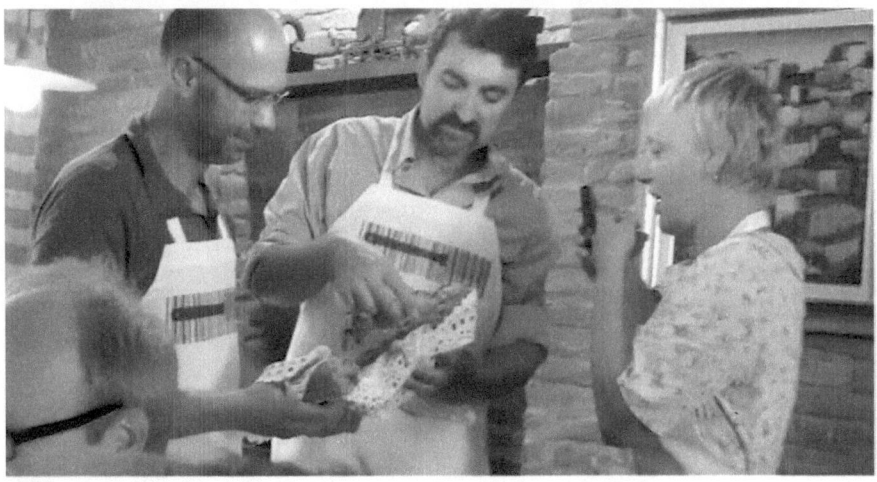

Photo: Spatula&Barcode

Mise en Place

Mis en place is a cooking term meaning to prepare and arrange all the ingredients of a dish before beginning to cook. To clarify: the meaning of *mise en place* is to put into place everything that is needed for the doing. For many cooks, this means lots of little bowls, each holding a single ingredient, already chopped, grated or measured. But one's *mise* is not necessarily a bounded, precisely delimited matrix: salt and fish sauce are simply at hand. Or take the *mise* for risotto, which should include a pot of simmering broth that exceeds what the rice might take (also a ladle and a bottle of wine). *Mise en place* means never having to say "I forgot". *Mise* means you're ready, in a state of consciousness and energy, poised just before the fat hits the pan.

It's worth noting that *mise* developed with the rise of restaurants, and is a product of a kind of industrialization of cooking. In food writer Peter Wells's terms, *mise en place*

> comes from restaurant kitchens, where a brigade of helpers spends the day getting everything ready for the dinner rush. It comes from a French phrase meaning "make the new guy do it". In my mind, it stands as an unattainable ideal, a receding mirage, a dream of an organized and contented kitchen life that everyone is enjoying except me.[4]

But a proper *mise en place* does not remove uncertainty from the kitchen. No amount of little bowls or piles of cut vegetables can fore-ordain what is to come. The *mise* rather represents the necessary and sufficient conditions for a range of outcomes, many desired, some not so much. Without *mise*, there is chaos. With *mise en place*, chaos may still come, but for a moment there is order.

Mises: All the conference packets are arranged on the table, name tags in alphabetical order, student volunteers smiling at the ready. The inquisitor displays the instruments of torture as the first step in terrorizing the victim. The absinthe and sugar, the ice and the match.

The rubric of *mise en place* was for us a way to indulge our impulse to carry props across the world. In our bags we carried costumes, not just for us but for all the conference attendees. We carried 50 porcelain Chinese spoons and 100 Chinese food take-away containers that Richard Gough left behind at our house five years ago when he was making an installment of his ongoing *Last Supper* performances. We also carried souvenirs (including 50 bottles of Wisconsin maple syrup), totemic objects representing our special guests, half a dozen cameras, again as many hard drives, and so on. Normally we leave home with too many gifts and fill the space they make in our luggage with too many souvenirs. This time, we had the neat trick of off-loading properties and loading up on the "ingredients" for the performance that we asked each conference participant to carry from home.

---

4   Pete Wells, "Food - Prep Work", *The New York Times*, 14 September 2010, section Magazine http://www.nytimes.com/2010/09/19/magazine/19food-t-000.html [accessed 24 April 2014].

We had written in advance to all the conference-goers inviting them to join us for dinner and asking each to help build the *mise en place* of the performance by bringing a food item or utensil that invoked a sense of "home" (however defined). This request yielded the following food ingredients: a Cherry Ripe bar and a jar of Vegemite (from Australia), orange marmalade, honey, wholemeal flour, and tinned Corned Beef (from the UK), chanterelles and cloud berries (brought from Finland but representing Sweden), olive oil, red pepper, garlic and basil (from Italy), a home-baked Serbo-Croatian bread and a bottle of the sweet Croatian soft drink called pašareta; and the following utensils: a measuring cup (with both metric and Imperial markings), a rolling pin, a potato masher, a knife sharpener and some toothpicks; as well as the following conceptual ingredients: guilt and innocence.

Our international collaborators (see below) also contributed ingredients. We asked them to suggest to us items that would invoke their presence should the Internet fail us (which in three cases it did). For Eduardo, we brought *dulce de leche*, a uniquely Argentine caramel. We chose *masa de arepas* for peripatetic Marlon because he told us he never travels without this Venezuelan flour. Joseph wanted us to bring yams because his plan was to be eating a yam porridge for the concurrent meal. Franki and Ravi both requested rice, Franki the curried rice that would be part of his dinner and Ravi the red pigmented rice that is used ceremonially in India. Thembinkosi suggested two books that were currently influencing his thinking (Foucault's *The Care of the Self* and Kierkegaard's *Works of Love*), while Kaylene asked us to bring "hell money" which she would actually direct participants to use during the performance. For the team eating dim sum in China, we arranged to get the only two kinds of dumplings available at Rijeka's single Chinese Restaurant.

With all these ingredients on hand, we intended to have a collaborative "cooking" event, where devising conceptual recipes would stand in for the physical chopping and merging of ingredients that might have gone on in a real kitchen. We would have devised recipes, collaboratively, together with our international partners, conceptual amalgamations that merged stories with foodstuffs, theories with kitchen implements.

We experienced clarity quite quickly about gathering the "ingredients" and moving participants through the locale, but struggled a bit more with the question of how to think about the performance genre of the concluding event. We thought of the meal as an intellectual *paella*, a party meal where the hosts provide the rice and the guests add meats and fishes from their own regions. We also wanted to invoke the "stone soup," in which the hosts convince you that things will taste great if you just add that little something of your own.

But one of the elements of our mistopia in Rijeka was that the event we hosted was perhaps too heavily matrixed into the pre-existing food service scheme. In other words, instead of having a kitchen and dining space under our own control, we were trying to prepare and serve our "courses" in a restaurant environment, Konoba *Nebuloza*, that had already been defined for attendees by two prior dinners there. And we were trying to devise collaborative performance with dinner guests who had had no "down time" in three days, who rightfully wanted to talk to one another about all the interesting issues that had been presented in dozens of hours of seminar meetings. Given those circumstances, we found participants remarkably good-natured and willing to play along. In some ways this made the event exactly mistopian – the boundaries between real dining (as hosted by the *Nebuloza* staff) and conceptual dining (as hosted by Spatula&Barcode) were hard to delineate.

Yet some extremely memorable recipes were concocted and enacted. Reana Senjković and Lada Čale Feldman devised a recipe for an action that was performed by Branislav Jakovljević and Marin Blažević in which a traditional bread (that Reana had baked) was "struggled" over and broken (between a Serb and a Croatian) and then served to guests who had to choose which half of the same bread they would receive. Equally resonant but much less pleasurable was the loss of Freddie Rokem's ingredients: fresh chantarelle mushrooms and a liter of cloudberries, evocations of his Swedish childhood which he hand-carried from Finland. These had been taken into custody by the restaurant owner two days earlier with directions for how they should be prepared for the guests. When, late in the meal, we realized that these were not being served, and in fact were no longer in the kitchen, the loss we experienced as diners (for the anticipated tastes Freddie had so vividly described) and the tension between Freddie and Igor (the res-

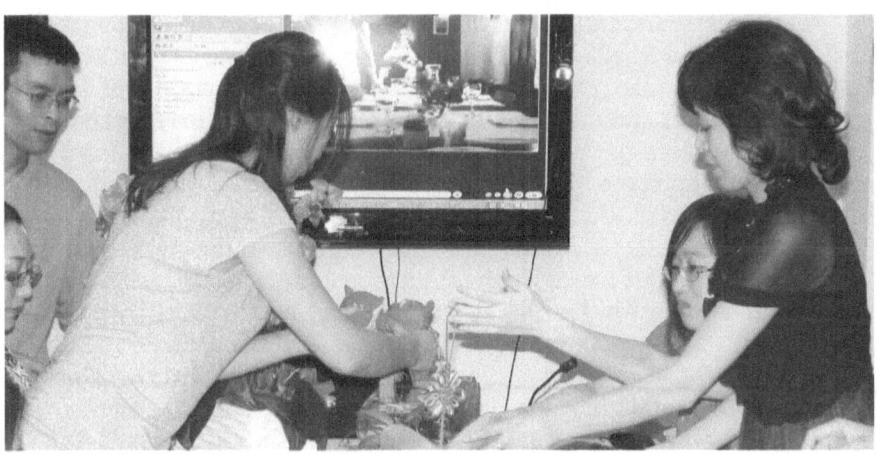

Photo: Spatula&Barcode

taurant owner, who had "mis" understood the instructions and taken the ingredients home to his family), made for an experience that was more painful than interesting. In contrast to Reana and Lada's effective, ironic staging of the remnants of the former Yugoslavia, this "non-productive" (even counter-productive) loss could not be recuperated as a "signifying" event.

Mise en Scene

Mise en scene means to put into the scene. It refers to everything that contributes to the intelligibility of the event, not just the principal actors who are delivering lines, but also those that appear in the background. The phrase *mise en scene* draws attention to the role of props, costumes, scenography, in determining meaning. In our case, we were interested in moving participants out of the lecture hall and theatres and into the *scene* of the city, and in intervening in the scene of the city by adding small enigmatic performances, highlighting our idiosyncratic relationship to the scene of Rijeka.

You know those little maps you accumulate when you travel? Not the ones from the tourist office, full of advertising from places you would never go – by virtue of the fact that they would advertise on a map distributed by the tourist office. No, we mean the maps that people draw for you (if you are lucky) to explain how to find some place. They are never to scale and are usually full of idiosyncratic landmarks. They're sketched on pages torn out of books, or on the back of something else. They are among our favorite souvenirs, because they record your (attempted) route but are marked by the hand of their maker. From the point of view of spatial precision, this vernacular cartography is often full of mistakes. From the point of view of travel, it produces maps of mistopias.

Vernacular cartography was our first labor on site in Rijeka; we created a map of "Our Rijeka." This map both ameliorated and exaggerated the "information asymmetry" of travel, providing helpful directions but also obscure references and mis-directions. We redrew the city to reflect bits of history ("this bridge on Mrtvi Kanal used to be the border crossing from the restaurant and hotel [i.e., Croatia] into Italy"), idiosyncratic experiences ("Molekula, our hosts and sponsors. If you didn't see a performance in the beautiful space there, too bad for you – one of the last of the great smoke-filled performance art shrines"), the childhood haunts of our hosts ("Bar Capitano, [conference organizer] Marin [Blažević] used to play hooky to drink here"), the services we sought out as travelers ("Mr. Grinch, a funky cafe and bar with rock music at night. Lots of advice for tourists here"), the places we walked and ran ("The closest beach is about 2 km that way, in Pećine. Michael swam there on his way back from running in Trsat"). Our map showed 33 sites, half a dozen of which figured in our actual performance itinerary.

We were lucky to be able to persuade Nina Benović to work with us as a singer and musical dramaturg for the performance. We first met Nina, an actor, singer, dancer and member of the internationally known *klapa* group HKUD Željezničar in 2009 when she worked as the "fixer" and stage manager for our first Spatula&Barcode production in Zagreb. Towards the end of that performance, which dissolved as intended into a free-form party, Nina surprised us by bringing a group of her friends to sing the *a capella* music that they tour. The intense sound reverberating in the vaulted ceiling of the Kino Europa's upstairs lobby was deeply moving; for *Mise en Scene* we wanted to pass along that kind of surprising gift to our "guests" in Rijeka. We thought of this moment as a kind of *pâte fermenté*, a baking technique in which a bit of the dough for one loaf of bread is carried forward as a starter for the new one.

Nina recruited Jelena Horvat, Kristina Rašeta, Ivana Lalić, Marko Robinić (all members of HKUD Željezničar) to be singers and guides for the performance. The idea of these folks as guides was a bit mistopic, since none of them were from or knew Rijeka. All traveled from Zagreb for the performance.

Participants (roughly thirty) met their guides at the last panel session of the conference, where they recieved S&B aprons and were divided into small groups with shuffled itineraries. Each group would make the same types of stops but spread through the city. We arranged a series of memorable moments, small in scale. We sought to bring participants in small individually guided groups to five locations in Rijeka of personal significance (to us and/or to our site hosts) and to give a memorable experience of the city *scene*. Groups encountered a character named Igor Žganci Grabancijaš Nebuloza (played by Michael, in a chef's hat covered by a mask of the absent Richard Gough), who served each person a delicious local fig while singing snatches of a Los Fabulosos Cadillacs song that had featured in our previous piece. Concious of the length of the conference day and of our project, we then bought everyone an espresso at the legendary coffee house / rock club Palach. We arranged to keep a vendor open at the otherwise closed market place to give flower bouquets to each group. And each guide contrived a simple but surprising tableau, their groups stopping in front of a place of architectural interest (a church, in front of the harbor, an old theatre, etc) to sing for them a quiet solo folk song.

In this shifted, mistopic mindset, we looked to *procedure* as the source of security and comfort. Not technical exactitude of the sort that both attracts and repels Michael from the alchemy of baking, but the *order* implied by the *recipe* as both a product of and a process for devising. Like a Fluxus score or a *comedia dell'arte* scenario, the recipe asks for actions which are in turn open to interpretation. While we wanted to avoid any religious connotation for this event, we are both drawn to the Passover *seder*, both for its clarity and order and for its imperative to improvisation, debate and play. The very word "seder" means order. The seder is a meal defined by procedures: recite, wash, eat a green vegetable, hide a cracker, tell a story, wash, eat a cracker, eat a bitter herb, eat a sandwich, eat dinner, find the hidden cracker, say thank for the meal, recognize one's own good fortune, conclude with rowdy singing. Within that order, other moments are also defined including drinking four glasses of wine and opening the door to welcome the spirit of strangers into one's home.

Misplacing artists into the street can be a risky business but the walking tours came off without a hitch. Participants reported being pleasurably surprised by the small treats and the singing skills of their guides. This is not always the case with mistopian performance. Often the removal of a clear matrix for the performance leads to painful and sometimes calamitous misunderstandings, as was the case when Janez Janša was taken into custody by the police for inviting audience members to cut up a flag. It maybe that all the flag cutters understood their actions as taking place within the *heterotopic* space of the art museum, but the state authorities' failure to accept this distinction opened the door to real and genuinely undesirable legal and financial consequences for the artist and the presenting organization.

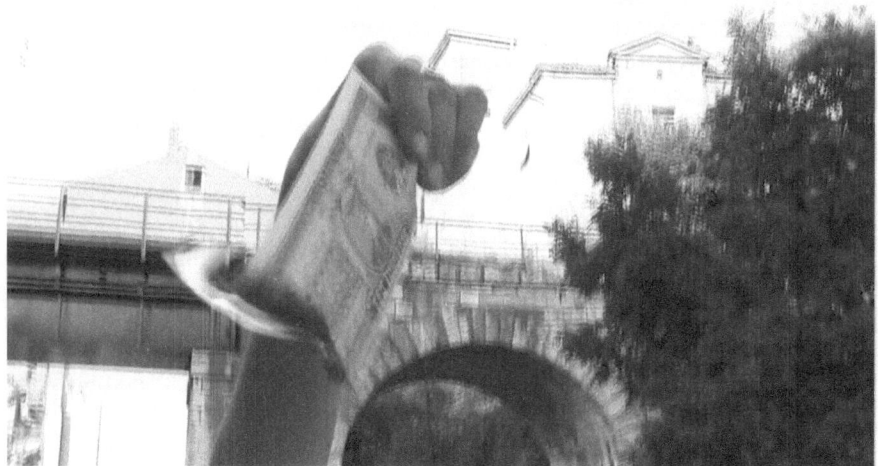

Photo: Spatula&Barcode

Wish You Were Here

"Wish you were here" is a stock phrase, a clichéd sentiment from souvenir postcards. It draws attention to the absence of the recipient from the privileged location of the traveler. The rubric of "mis" that these two Croatian conferences and this volume celebrate encouraged us to pay attention to what and who was missing from this scene.

While the gathering in Rijeka included scholars from both Western and Eastern Europe, North America, and Australia, we noticed the absence of colleagues from Asia, Africa, and South America; we responded by inviting as dinner guests colleagues from countries and continents not represented. Kaylene Tam in Singapore, Franki Raden in Jakarta, Eduardo Santiere in Buenos Aires, Marlon Barrios Solano in Quito, Joseph Adande in Porto-Novo, Thembinkosi Goniwe in Johannesburg, Ravi Khote in a village outside Mumbai, and May Hu in Beijing were all scheduled to dine with us via Skype.

Our goal was to have concurrent meals in seven distinct time zones. For Marlon, who was just arriving in Ecuador the night before, it would be breakfast time during the performance. In Benin, Joseph would sit down to lunch in another Hemisphere but in the same time zone. Franki, in Indonesia, would be breaking his Ramadan fast for the day, and his first course would be dessert. In China, May Hu would be eating takeout dumplings with eight of her friends in one of their office conference rooms just after their work day ended. And for Kaylene in Singapore, it was nearing bedtime.

Preparing for this dinner using Internet telephony made us aware indeed of the "failed chronotypes" invoked by the organizers. Technologies such as Internet video-conferencing draw attention to how much absence a tele-presence can invoke, to the pang of distance made apparently shorter, to the deep incompleteness of connecting, and to the asynchronicity of synchronous communication. In devising this event, we hoped that temporal asymmetries would stand in for other cultural and geographic displacements.

In the end our dinner made both more and fewer connections than we anticipated. Franki was joined by his apprentice Zaki Andiga. May's table in Beijing also included Emily Meng, Lucy Feiyang, Xiangquan Zheng, Tiancheng Li, Hua Han, Fei Yan, Sha Sha, and Xiaoxia Guo. But three of our eight scheduled connections failed entirely. Marlon's residency was not able to provide a internet connection at all, and our repeated efforts to contact Joseph did not succeed although he and his "web master" spent four hours waiting at his computer on campus at the Université d'Abomey-Calavi, and we never were able to connect with Thembinkosi. Of those that connected, the quality varied. Kaylene Tam's directions from Singapore for burning money for the dead, enacted by Selma Banich and Nicki Polykarpou in Croatia, turned emotional and poignant. Marco (one of our singer guides) turned out to have conversational fluidity in almost all the native languages of our international guests and flitted from table to table making small talk in Chinese, Spanish and Indonesian. But the restaurant was crowded, the participants – garrulous, unwinding after several intense days, and as the event went on in some cases increasingly inebriated – were in not necessarily in the mood for struggling with the barely audible Skype connections or for bringing new acquaintances into the ongoing conversations of the conference.

As we review the video tapes of *Wish You Were Here*, one of the least fraught aspects of the dinner seems to have been the haunting musical performances of the members of HKUD Željezničar. While other elements of the dining experience were out of (our) control, these musical disruptions produced the strangely pleasurable, not-fully-recuperable-through-exegesis, moments that are the best that mistopian performance can offer. We had hoped, through the service of small unfamiliar bites to be eaten with out of context utensils (chopsticks, straws, etc.) to produce a parallel culinary mistopia, but the owner and staff at Konoba Nebuloza did not understand or decided not to participate in our vision; after the first course the meal devolved into long waits for large volumes of already familiar dishes.

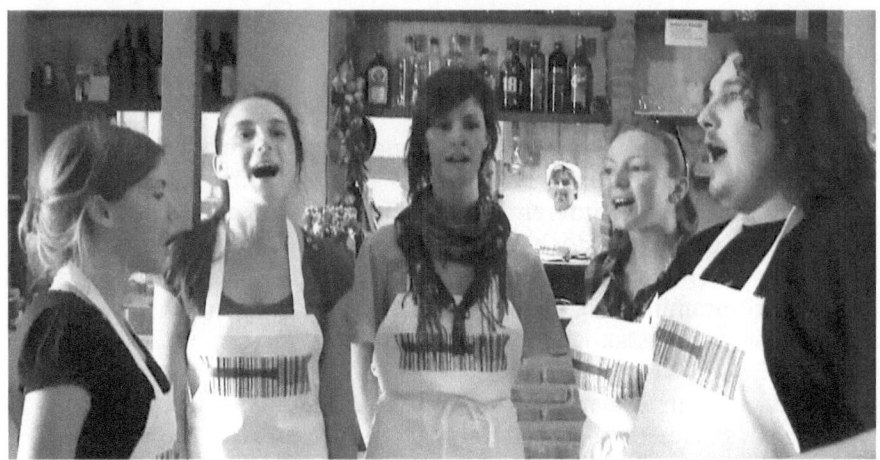

Photo: Spatula&Barcode

Misperformance and Asymmetry

We know that in cooking, as in performance, mistakes only sometimes lead to disaster. Sometimes the failure of a technology signifies – and sometimes it just fails. While we never hope for a soufflé to fall, we often court the discomforts of unfamiliar cuisines and the surprises of "new gastronomy". While we are drawn to the care-free attitude suggested by the celebration of misperformance, we find ourselves thinking that some misses are, in fact, losses. Frankly, the image of Joseph and his "web master" waiting for four hours on campus at Université d'Abomey-Calavi breaks our hearts.[5] We're

---

5 We were therefore elated to feature Joseph as the guest of honor the following year, via a perfect web connection, for a small project called "On Order" which was based on our interest in the seder procedure.

still longing for chantarelles and cloudberries and we're still struggling to devise a Rijeka Misperformance cookbook based on the ingredients. But we are also gladly carried forward the "old dough" (*pâte fermentée*) of vernacular cartography, to revive it as the starter for our next planned event, in Utrecht, called *Bicycle Map Spoon*.[6]

Though we continue to be interested in the opportunities offered by the category of conference performance, which we recognize as an opportunity to make work for small captive audiences of international intellectuals displaced from their home space, we have come to appreciate some of its vulnerablilities and limitations. Perhaps the least of these problems is the heightened professional risk of offering one's least structured work for the scrutiny of one's most exacting colleagues. So far, this is balanced by the rewards of making work for a semi-specific, semi-known audience.

More troubling is that the "in group" quality of conference performance tends toward not only the insularity from spatial context (that we had sought to redress through vernacular cartography in *Mise en Scene...*) but also a social insularity that keeps locals on the outside of conference proceedings. We became aware of this dynamic early on during our stay in Rijeka when, in advance of the arrival of other PSi conferees, we attended several events events of the Zoom Festival and found ourselves surrounded by a group of people who clearly knew one another and who formed a social network that sustained a thriving scene of alternative music and experimental cafés. Some of this we sought to highlight though the cartographic *mise en scene* project. The lack of overlap between the two constituencies was most apparent in the afterparty. This *mis*connect may be attributed to the inevitable "asymmetries of travel", the first of which is that you, the traveler, are away from home, while usually at least some of those others around you are not.

However, to note the asymmetries that abound in tourism (and tourism studies) is to discover not just that the various performances involved sometimes or often "miss", but that those very interactions are structurally mis-shapen – that is, asymmetrical. Obvious examples include the asymmetries in financial and social capital reflected in the stereotypical tourist encounter. In tourism which moves from the rich "West" to the "developing" world, however, *information asymmetry* also becomes a crucial counter-balance to unequal privilege. In this case the locals' exploitation of their knowledge of the objects of tourism can be seen as a "weapon of the weak",[7] while tourist guidebooks and other organizations of tourist knowledges function like economic espionage or even counter-insurgency. In touristic and scholarly encounters, asymmetries result from people out of

---

6   *Bicycle Map Spoon* developed many of the themes discussed here, organizing groups of participants for self-directed cycle tours of Utrecht, focusing on a mix of touristic and more marginal and counter-cultural sites.
7   James C. Scott, *Weapons of the weak: everyday forms of peasant resistance*, Yale University Press, 1985.

place, from time out of sync, and from allegiances that are ultimately misalliances. The misinformed tourist, no less than the "naive" local, may appear to be mis-informed when more appropriately their relation can be said to be mis-performed *in an expression of their asymmetry.*

In crafting performance experiences in environments that are not our "home," asymmetry is a central resource. But shaping asymmetric encounters – mistopian spaces – means accepting the full range of potential misperformances. We remain skeptically interested in mistopia, but we resist as much as possible the impulse to redefine it *post facto* as "success." What is interesting about mistopia as the space of asymmetric encounter is that the situation is by definition not subject to our approval.

IN ADDITION TO FOLKS MENTIONED IN THE ESSAY, THANKS ALSO TO:
Ric Allsop, Una Bauer, Maaike Bleeker, Ramsey Burt, Marin Blažević, Preeti Chopra, Petra Corva, Club Sušačani, Hrvoje Dimbek, Henry Drewel, Drugo more, Marica Dujmić, Peter Eckersall, Rachel Fensham, Matthew Fink, Siniša Fuak, Igor Jagić, Dale Kaminski, Igor Knežević, Tomislav Longinović, Jon McKenzie, Dorla Mayer, Davor Mišković, Marisa Maksimović, Sophie Nield, Dajana Prizmić, Alan Read, Nick Ridout, Heike Roms, Douglas Rosenberg, Annalisa Sacchi, Ed Scheer, Sara Schneckloth, P.A. Skantze, Alan Vukelić, Jasna Velejanlić, Hongtao Zhou, Jasna Žmak, Nancy Zucker.

Ric Allsopp
Walking Backwards

We enter the future walking backwards.
—Paul Valéry[1]

This paper suggests some ways in which the action and metaphor of walking (and looking) backwards might help us to think about performance as a temporary zone or project space. As a form of mis-performance, walking backwards – an action "contra naturam" and often associated with resistance, ridicule, reversal – disrupts and shifts our expectations and refocuses our modes and habits of attention.[2] The imaginal spaces generated through walking or looking backwards as strategies or tactics for situating performance suggest new, provisional forms of interaction and participation, temporary zones that in turn might lead to innovative forms and processes of working together. The view of art work and performance taken here – as I will discuss later – is unashamedly utopian in Walter Benjamin's sense,[3] and locates utopia in the heart of the present moment as an imminent potential

---

1   In the French original – "Nous entrons dans l'avenir á reculons" - Paul Valery, "Variété 3" in *Oeuvres* Vol.1, Gallimard (Bibliothéque de la Pléiade), Paris 1957.
2   I would like to thank Ed Scheer for reminding me of the rich comic vein of "funny walks" – in particular Max Wall, Spike Milligan, George Carl, Billy Dainty and John Cleese – which might well take this paper in another direction as it were. The following is from *The Guardian* in 2003 – the year after Spike Milligan died. "It is the place Spike Milligan labeled 'the world's only above-ground cemetery', but from today the New South Wales town of Woy Woy is celebrating the comedian in a week-long festival. A settlement of 10,000 people two hours' drive north of Sydney, Woy Woy has had a troubled history as the butt of Milligan's jokes since his parents moved there in the 1950s. [...] In keeping with Milligan's spirit, not everything has gone swimmingly for Spikefest since its inauguration last month. Plans to commemorate the 1956 Goon Show song, *I'm Walking Backwards for Christmas*, had to be kept modest because of fears the council would face lawsuits if anyone injured themselves while walking backwards: the 300 walkers in today's opening parade will be wearing their clothes backwards, but walking forwards." (David Fickling, "Town lampooned by Spike Milligan bends over backwards to laud him", *The Guardian*, 4 October 2003, http://www.theguardian.com/world/2003/oct/04/australia.davidfickling [accessed 25 April 2014]).
3   "For in [the future] every second was the narrow gate, through which the Messiah could enter." (Walter Benjamin, "Theses on the Philosophy of History" in *Illuminations*, ed. Hannah Arendt, Pimlico, London 1999 [1940], p. 253-64).

of history imagined as discontinuous, fractured and intense. Art can be thought of as the continual setting up of potential conditions within which the unpredictable might take place.

I would like to refer briefly to some examples of walking backwards as a deliberate tactic of mis-performance – i.e. an action or image that disrupts and breaks with the *status quo* of the present. Unpredictability within a set of performance conditions is perhaps like looking for the Perseids, the annual meteor-shower in mid-August. There is the possibility of a bright trail, a flash in the corner of the eye, a shower of celestial fireworks radiating from a know position. The general conditions are there: planet Earth passes through the tail of the Swift-Tuttle comet, but the specific local conditions of cloud cover, direction, light pollution, may prevent us from seeing anything at all. The constellation of Perseus – the radiant point from which the Perseid meteor shower appears to be coming – provides a mythological instance of walking backwards as a tactic, in which Perseus in his quest to slay the Medusa, walks backwards to avoid the Medusa's direct gaze that turns one to stone, using his shield as a mirror. The backward look, as a form of interdiction and its subsequent violation, is familiar in the myths of Orpheus and Eurydice, and of Lot's wife.[4]

In folklore, walking backwards as a reversal of normative behaviour, that is, a progressive moving forward with all the positive implications our western culture has invested in it, is associated both with fortune (the fulfilment of wishes, the ability to see the future) and with misfortune or evil intent (the bringing of bad luck). The folklore tradition, however, is not about setting up conditions from which the unpredictable might emerge, but the opposite – setting up conditions which allow predictions to be made. The 800-year old yew-tree in the churchyard at Stoke Gabriel on the River Dart near where I live in South Devon, England has a traditional rhyme that claims to provide a way in which wishes can be fulfilled:

Walk ye backward round about me/ Seven times round for all to see/ Stumble not and then for certain/ One true wish will come to thee.

Similarly, the making of a "dumb-cake" – a cake made from flour, eggs and water and placed by the fire at mid-night on Christmas Eve or St. Agnes' Eve as a form of love divination – provides a vision or dream of a future spouse. The recipe must be prepared in silence (hence "dumb-cake") and (at least in one variant) requires the maker to walk backwards to bed after making it. There are of course many possible examples and trajectories of reverse movement, and retrograde walking in mythology, folklore, the circus world

---

4   Both Orpheus and Lot's wife break interdictions against looking back; the former, losing his wife, "clutched at nothing but receding air" – see Ovid *Metamorphoses* Bk.10: 1-85; the latter "looked back from behind him, and she became a pillar of salt" – see *Genesis* 19: 17-29.

of reversal and "upside-down" experience, and not least in contemporary arts and performance.

To return to the shifts in attention that the unpredictable might generate: it is probably worth taking a little time here to unpack the relationship between forms of attention and what I am calling "temporary zones" or "project spaces".

In his work on attention, spectacle and modern culture *Suspensions of Perception*, Jonathan Crary argues that the late nineteenth century saw the "emergence of attention as a model of how a subject maintains a coherent and practical sense of the world, a model that is not primarily optical or even veridical" – that is, does not coincide with reality. He notes that "[w]hat is important to institutional power [...] is simply that perception function in a way that insures a subject is productive, manageable, and predictable, and is able to be socially integrated and adaptive".[5] Crary relates this to the "collapse of classical models of vision and of the stable, punctual subject these models presupposed". The emphasis here shifts from thinking of performance as a unifying and integrative form of temporary shelter. Instead transitory architectures of power created by specific and particular performance forms are increasingly distributed in terms of their duration, location and access. The temporary zone of the traditional theatre space is a spatial construct that demands and produces a certain type of attention, at least in its physical manifestations. This can be viewed as a limitation of theatre; a limitation which incapacitates both theatre and its participants. Such limitation of capacity is also linked to the question of participation in performance that, as Kai van Eikels has noted, is not simply to be identified with participating in an event.[6]

This underlying uneasiness about theatre and the performance event as a space of unification, of community, as a space of shared (as oppose to individual) attention, is not only a recent concern. It finds its origins in part in the modernist tradition as well as in the historical avant-garde. Writing in the margins of his 1910 manuscript *The Notebooks of Malte Laurids Brigge* the poet Rainer Maria Rilke identifies precisely the problem of unified attention and echoes (or rather confirms) the beginning of a new economy of attention when he notes:

> Let us be honest about it: we do not have a theatre, any more than we have a God. That would require true community, whereas each individual one of us has his own ideas and anxieties, and allows others to see as much of them as suits his purposes. We are forever watering

---

[5] Jonathan Crary, *Suspensions of Perception: Attention, Spectacle, and Modern Culture*, MIT Press, Cambridge, Mass 2001, p. 4.
[6] See Kai Van Eikels, "What Parts of Us Can Do With Parts of Each Other (and When): Some parts of this text", *Performance Research*, 16:3 (2011), pp. 2-6.

down our understanding, stretching it to go round, instead of wailing at the wall of our common distress, behind which that which passeth understanding would have time to gather its forces.[7]

The shift of attention from performance space to what can be called "project space", from the event as a means of attempting to produce a focused attention to other forms of participation and engagement with the work or labour of art, is a means whereby other alternate constructions of the common can be attempted. The common is not necessarily a located, temporal event but an involvement in the making of temporary zones or project spaces in which forms of living together, of negotiation, critique and transformation might be tried out. I am not here referring to the production of "virtual" spaces for interaction (such as Second Life), but to the development of project spaces in and through which other engagements with performance can be carried out and which utilise and enable public access in alternate ways. The use of "virtual" here probably resonates more with Susanne Langer's notion of virtual space as "intangible image" than with digitally generated worlds, which of course produce their own virtual spaces in Langer's terms. Janez Janša's *Pupilia* is a good example of "walking backwards" in the sense I am trying to establish.[8]

These temporary zones which propose a different focusing of attentions through time, as opposed to a unified space of attention, are perhaps the equivalent, in a digital rather than analogue environment, of Rauschenberg's surfaces and combines, flatbeds and transfer works which, as Johanna Drucker observed, "montage the heterogeneity of [Rauschenberg's] experience into a space irreducible to any unity of value or meaning";[9] in other words a temporary zone which resists a singular concentrated attention (the focus and unification of a civic public reflecting itself as value) and becomes a dispersed space or project space – the product of a distributed and dispersed/ disseminated attention. No longer the ideal civic public of the theatre – but a multiple participatory audience proposing and realising multiple forms of access and participation in shifting and transforming project spaces.

To return to my theme of walking backwards and my own attempts to define what constitutes a space of appearance – the space that frames that moment in the art work when something unpredictable happens in excess of the conditions in which it takes place. A relationship between two par-

7   Rainer Maria Rilke, *The Notebooks of Malte Laurids Brigge*, trans. Michael Hulse, Penguin Books, London 2009 [1910], p. 150.
8   See Janez Janša's reconstruction of Dušan Jovanović's original *Papa Pupilia* (1968), *Papa Pupilia and the Pupilceks* (2007), http://www.maska.si/index.php?id=154&id=154&tx_ttnews[tt_news]=89&cHash=20cf0178b96288bbd54c1b24484c86da&L=1 [accessed 8 May 2014].
9   Johanna Drucker, *Theorising Modernism: Visual Art and the Critical Tradition*, Columbia University Press, New York 1996, p. 56.

ticular images of walking backwards formed the starting point of this paper. The first was during a performance of Bruno Beltrao's choreography *H3* at La Raffinerie in Brussels in 2008;[10] and the second a line in a news report of the arrest outside the Pentagon of the Catholic peace activist Liz McAllister in 2001.[11]

Virtuoso backwards running might be a more accurate description of a large sequence of Beltrao's *H3* in which, to quote the critic Jeroen Peeters:

> Most prominent are the various moments in which the dancers are running backward rapidly, one by one, in duets after being thrown into the arena by four colleagues, or everyone together. Once more the dancers embrace absence, this time including the endless space behind their backs, symbolizing their own blind spots.[12]

The technical skill and speed with which the dancers execute their large circular backwards movement is without doubt something in excess of the expected conditions of physical performance. Peeters notion of the "blindspot" – the absence that is the endless space behind their backs – links metaphorically with the blind-spot of the second image – the erasure of the expressive means – writing, speech, movement – that give us the means to protest and to be heard and seen: the freedoms of speech and of assembly.

Liz McAllister – a committed peace-activist maintaining since 1974 a witness against the violence and power of the US military-industrial complex – was "arrested while holding a blank sign, having tape over her mouth and walking backwards". What is significant here is the resistant use of non-violent symbolic actions which, through simple reversal, contradict expectations, and appear to conform with orderly behaviour – the holding of a blank sign, the restriction of speech, walking away from confrontation – whilst symbolically resisting both restrictions of free speech and free assembly, and providing in the blind-spot a telling image of the perceived and actual violence that the State supports. This links back to Jonathan Crary's analysis of attention that "[w]hat is important to institutional power [...] is simply that perception function in a way that insures a subject is productive, manageable, and predictable, and is able to be socially integrated and adaptive".[13]

It is the unpredictability of art that resists the uniformity and conformity of institutional power and the deadening effects, in Benjamin's terms, of

---

10   See KunstenFestivaldesArts Edition 08, http://archive.kfda.be/2008/en/home [accessed 8 May 2014].
11   Liz McAllister, "Honouring the Prophets on Retreat – Transforming the Earth" in *The Common Good*, 21 (Spring 2001), http://www.catholicworker.org.nz/cg/CG21-Honouring.htm [accessed 24 April 2014].
12   Jeroen Peeters, "Running backward in advance of oneself: Bruno Beltrão and Grupo de Rua" in *Corpus* (21 May 2008), http://www.corpusweb.net/running-backward-in-advance-of-oneself-6.html [accessed 24 April 2014].
13   Jonathan Crary, *Suspensions of Perception: Attention, Spectacle, and Modern Culture*, MIT Press, Cambridge, Mass. 2001, p. 4.

historical continuity. In his recent book *The Angel of History* the philosopher Stéphane Moses notes that Benjamin contrasts the "false continuity postulated by historicism with the reality of discontinuity manifest in the always unpredictable appearance of new works of art"[14] and that "[i]n contrast to the Marxist idea of the 'end of history', based on a quantitative and cumulative vision of historical time, what is drawn here is the idea, borrowed from Jewish messianism, of a utopia appearing in the very heart of the present, of a hope lived in the mode of today".[15] The French artist Christian Boltanski has described this sense of "hope lived in the mode of today" as "small memories" – an attention to the seemingly irrelevant details of the everyday.

What then is seen as "art" is unpredictable and at the same time its revelation is at the level of the everyday; not a grand epiphany but a slight shift in attention of the order, for example, of Duchamp's "readymade" *Sculpture for Travelling* (1918); the overheard instruction "Walk backwards, the sky won't fall if you walk backwards" that provides the structure for Stefan & Franiszka Themerson's film *The Adventure of a Good Citizen* (1937); the experiential architecture of Bruce Nauman's *Corridor Installation* (1971); Francis Alÿs' list of negations in *As Long as I am Walking* (1992); Liz McAllister's acts of civil disobedience (2001) or Bruno Beltrao's backwards running in *H3* (2008). These slight shifts of attention – the space of appearance that is opened up in the epiphanic or utopian moment that the temporary zones or project spaces of art can bring about – are forms of interruption, interference or delay. The trope of walking backwards that we find in the previous list of examples (and it cognate "looking backwards" that we find in the mythic and biblical images of Perseus, Orpheus and Eurydice and Lot's Wife) provides an array of striking images of interruption, interference, delay and discontinuity.

I would like to take as an example Marcel Duchamp's *Sculpture for Travelling* (1918) Duchamp's work provides a clear originary example of the interjection of delay and interference into the notion of the art work as progressive, moving towards a meaningful end. In its original version the "readymade" (now lost) consisted of different colored rubber strips cut from bathing caps. Duchamp cemented these pieces together at random intersections and tied the whole construction up with strings attached to the corners of his studio in New York. In 1966, Duchamp called it a type of "voyage sculpture".[16] In fact, it was literally intended for travelling and could be recreated "out of his suitcase at every stop on his trip from New York to Buenos Aires in 1918".[17]

---

14 Stéphane Moses, *The Angel of History: Rosensweig, Benjamin, Scholem*, trans. Barbara Harshav, Stanford University Press, Stanford 2009, p. 109-10.
15 Ibidem, p. 108.
16 Pierre Cabanne, *Dialogues with Marcel Duchamp*, trans. Ron Padgett, Thames & Hudson, London 1971, p. 59.
17 Dawn Ades, *Marcel Duchamp*, Thames & Hudson, London 1999, p. 159.

Duchamp described this Readymade in the following manner in a 1966 interview:

> Naturally, they took up a whole room. Generally, they were pieces of rubber shower caps, which I cut up and glued together and which had no special shape. At the end of each piece there were strings that one attached to the four corners of the room. Then, when one came in the room, one couldn't walk around, because of the strings! The length of the strings could be varied; the form was *ad libitum*. That's what interested me. This game lasted three or four years, but the rubber rotted, and it disappeared.[18]

The idea of interference in movement or "delay" that is implicated in the work is formulated in the working notes in the *Green Box*, itself an image of a "work" without a defined sequential order. Duchamp articulates what he call a "delay in glass" in negative terms: "A delay in glass does not mean a picture on glass". The notion of "delay" also speaks to a type of futurity – the postponement of the yet-to-come, the stilling of movement, to slowing or refraction of our attentions and perceptions. Duchamp understood delay as being "merely a way of succeeding in no longer thinking that the thing in question is a picture".[19] And of course by analogy such "delay" or shift of attention enables us to no longer think that the work in question can only be encountered within the framework of theatre or performance. It opens the possibility of encountering the work in other terms, using other criteria – terms that engage us in the present moment of production rather than passive consumption of the work. Duchamp's central question: "Can one make works which are not works of art?" implies the set up of a future, a set of open possibilities for the boundaries of arts.[20]

To conclude I would like to draw further on Walter Benjamin's thinking around the materiality of history, and the function of art as a means of actualising spaces of appearance – a "utopia in the heart of the present."

The Jewish philosopher Franz Rosenzweig, a contemporary of Benjamin, defined in 1921 two modalities of the present, contrasting "today which is only a footbridge to tomorrow" to "the other today which is a springboard to eternity". Stéphane Moses notes that for Rosenzweig:

---

18   Pierre Cabanne, *Dialogues with Marcel Duchamp*, pp. 59-60.
19   Marcel Duchamp, Georg Heard Hamilton & Richard Hamilton (1976 [1960]) *The Bride Stripped Bare By Her Bachelors, Even* – a typographic version by Richard Hamilton, trans. G.H. Hamilton, Edition Hansjörg Mayer, Stuttgart, London, Reykjavik 1976 [1960].
20   For an earlier discussion of shifts in attention and the production of futurity in performance see Ric Allsopp, "Still Moving: 21st Century Poetics" in *Uncalled: Dance and Performance of the Future*, eds Sigrid Gareis and Krassimira Kruschkova, Berlin: Theatre der Zeit/ Recherchen 68, Berlin 2009, pp. 68-78, 247-255.

> The *present-footbridge* is the one that, on the linear axis of time, links the past moment to the moment to come. [...] This is the present conceived by historical Reason: an ideal point both separating and connecting two other points on an undifferentiated line that can be extended indefinitely, or else an infinitesimal unit of time on a vector oriented toward an ideal end where the unlimited sequence of causes and effects can be linked together. [...]
>
> In contrast to the present-footbridge, the *present-springboard* is a single moment of time when time is perceived in all its wealth and diversity. In the qualitative experience of time, as seen by subjectivity, every moment is unique; the present minute is not comparable to the one that precedes it or to the one that follows it. This is why moments cannot be summed up; time will then no longer appear as a river that flows towards its estuary but as a discontinuous sequence of states of quality and intensity that are each unique. The image of the horizontal will be contrasted here with that of the vertical: certain privileged moments will give the impression of suddenly breaking the litany of the days, or the anticipated chain of events, and opening a breach in time, through which the brand-new can break through.[21]

This second modality – the *present-springboard* – links closely to Benjamin's idea of "now-time" in which he frames the utopian moment:

> The primary movement of historical consciousness involves, not as its consequence, but as its fulfilment, the utopian tension towards the future, or more precisely, the anticipation of utopia in the heart of the present. In reality, the thwarted hopes of past generations are but the soil on which we build our own dreams. In Benjamin, utopia is the function of memory. "The seer", reads a note to *The Arcades Project*, "turns his back on the future: it is through the twilight of the past, slowly vanishing before him into the night of time, that he glimpses her face"[22]

To return to Stéphane Moses' analysis:

> "While the idea of continuity crushes and levels everything in its path", wrote Benjamin, "the idea of discontinuity is the foundation of authentic tradition". It is not from the endless flow of instants that the new can reappear, but from stopping time, a break, beyond which

---

[21] Stéphane Moses, *The Angel of History: Rosensweig, Benjamin, Scholem*, p. 60-61.
[22] Ibidem, p. 121.

life begins again in a form that constantly eludes all prediction. Hence the essential relationship that, in Benjamin, binds tradition and Redemption; it is the break of time, that is, meaning, that reappears. "The Messiah interrupts history," he wrote, "the Messiah does not appear at the end of evolution".[23]

We tend to shift constantly between Rosenzweig's two modalities of the present – the *present-footbridge* and the *present-springboard*. The utopian moment that forms within a 'space of appearance' as a potential of performance, is something that can and might actualise at any given moment, and in doing so shift our attention and our means of interacting and, by extension, our possibilities for living together. It is not the forms of interruption, delay and discontinuity in themselves that give rise to a space of appearance, but the shifts of attention that they provoke. The use of such images provides a metaphor that allows us to imagine ways of living, participating and interacting that are based on discontinuity; that we can and do walk backwards into the future.

23 Ibidem, p. 61.

P.A. Skantze
Shift Epistemologies: Gap Knowledge

"Shift yourselves" the British say, which means get a move on, engage your body, alter your position. To shift is not to rupture or sunder but to adjust, TO BECOME BY MOTION AWARE of what was just out of range of vision, of hearing, of sensing. As we shift, the contours of the landscape offer new patterns; just tilt your head a bit down and to the left and suddenly the hill is at an intriguing angle to what looked like solid ground. Since curating *Shifting Shift* and working subsequently with Matthew Fink on artists' pages for *Performance Research* about shifting, I have become more and more convinced that the notion of the shift created by the organizers of PSi15 gave embodiment, gave shape (changing, shifting shape) to a form of thinking, of making, of thinking in making and making in thinking already alive in the practice as research work underway for many performance artists/scholars and theatre makers. Not unlike the uncanny, historical shifts (the word in the English translation) Foucault brought into theoretical relief, reliefs, in *The Order of Things* until he saw how and showed his readers how between the grid of cultural assumptions and the possibility of something new came a small space, a gap, a space of possibility where previously there had been only seamless lines in ordered blocks. The gap invites movement, running one's eye back and forth over what at first appeared a fixed grid, trying to see the new shapes forming out of the newly perceived curve in the boundaries, hearing some bit of sound that had before been pulsing underneath the recognizable chord.

Shift: Gap Knowledge

A productive gap happens for me with the word epistemology. Recently and rather wonderfully I heard the philosopher Gayatri Spivak emphatically (if that is not an oxymoron Spivak and emphatic) pronounce the word as EPI – stem – Ology. Whenever I read or heard the word, it made a gap, the sound or sight of the word triggers something that slides through my mind with no referents to catch up to it or better to catch it up on as its slides, to hook a bit of the word to something conjurable. Like a hook or the "tug at the end of one's line" that is creative thinking as Virginia Woolf describes it. Like a willow tree or a goose or a hat. Epistemology has always been a bit like one of those clubhouse words you had to know to pass into the parlour of thinking, to be served by a sombre waiter who poured your philosophical whiskey and lit your scientific cigar.

Oxford English Dictionary places the word in a secure grid of definition: "The theory or science of the method or grounds of knowledge". But wait a bit, what about that "or" – isn't that a shift? Are methods and grounds really equal partners in the thinking trade? One moves, the other doesn't, or at least one makes by motion and the other only moves if there is a seismic shift. With the OED one of the discovery pleasures comes at the foot of the entry where we see the word making its way through aural history:

> 1856 FERRIER *Inst. Metaph.* 48 This section of the science is properly termed the Epistemology... It answers the general question, "What is Knowing and the Known?" or more shortly, "What is Knowledge?"

The general question – what is knowing? The particular answer – how do we find out? Recently I wrote to Justin Hunt, a young scholar and teacher finishing his PhD at Roehampton: "All the knowing/knewing reminds me that as I read your work, listened to the papers, I more and more come to think about how people I am working with - nay love - are exploring the epistemology of practice, defining forms of knowing and enacting those forms (and really this is simultaneous and the discoveries go both ways) as I thought of when Fabrizio [Manco, performance/sound artists also doing a PhD] suggested an 'enabling awareness' as a form of knowing."

Natalie Seremetakis creates in her explorations an audible memory of taste and hear: "the object invested with sensory memory speaks; it provokes re-call as a missing, detached yet antiphonic element of the perceiver. The artefact laden with perceptual recall is a temporal conduit... the artefact as the bearer of sensory multiplicity is a catchment zone of perception, a lens through which the senses can be explored from their other side... between the body and its non-identical doubles, the senses exist in transit... The memory of the senses speaks to a reception theory of material culture."

If the senses exist in transit, then they aid in making it possible to linger in the gaps, because of course traditional academic knowledge [and event the once innovative now too pressed for time academic knowledge] get nervous in the presence of the unexplained, which is not the same as the unexplored. In factual economy, gaps in knowledge are a bad thing and signal lack or laziness. But if gaps instead signify, if they call us towards not just what we do not know, but towards making sense, in Seremetakis' zone of perception, then we become what Foucault, who for me represents the exemplar, calls theorists of possibility. We use other tools, slipperiness as Rebecca Schneider has suggested or incongruously bodily modes of finding out, or shifting to become by motion aware. The gap instigates a reminder that habit settles as fast as a cat in the sun, halfway into a closed curve of familiar fur, content, immovable. So, for example, we are told incessantly we are a society dependent on the image, and everyone begins to lick their fur and expect a visual image to account for all. But gap knowledge suggests a yes, but. Yes, we are, but why are my ears still twitching?

Shift: When Giorgio Agamben Calls the Gap a Show

Okay, so Agamben does not really call the gap a show, but I might try to persuade him that the way he articulates the term "paradigm" ends up making in the showing a gap or a gap in the showing where the paradigm was. Returning or perhaps I might say shifting again towards Foucault's *The Order of Things* Agamben muses on a common criticism of Foucault that he must have known/should have known Thomas Kuhn's work on paradigm in order to write his own philosophy. Agamben spends some time turning paradigm as a thinking tool around and around. He suggests the definition of a paradigm is "the common possessions of the members of a certain scientific community" in motion, namely, he continues, "the set of techniques, models and values to which the group members more of less adheres". I remember feeling like a moving van had come in the night to deliver this unwieldy thing Thomas Kuhn demarcated as paradigm which should have suited me down to the ground since it usually went out on its critical walks with its companion word "shift" as in paradigm shift. But I never could get past the static bulk of the word, as delineated thing, as a model, some form carefully constructed, stable, and inevitable.

Here Agamben when he demonstrates, at least in my interpretation, paradigm, the one that is in motion, the set of techniques to show, more or less:

> "Paradigms obey not the logic of the metaphorical transfer of meaning but the analogical logic of the example [...] more akin to allegory than to metaphor, the paradigm is a singular case that is isolated from its context only insofar as, by exhibiting its own singularity it makes

intelligible a new ensemble [...] to give an example is a complex act which supposes that the term functioning as a paradigm is deactivated from its normal use [to become by motion aware, to shift to see], not in order to be moved into another context but, on the contrary, to present the canon – the rule – of that use, which *cannot be shown in any other way*".[1]

Shift yourselves, shift ourselves, into a mode of disappearance we can get behind, a definition of paradigm as a mode of disappearance for use – the necessity of something that, deactivated from its normal use not simply for the kinkiness of using it differently or, as Agamben says more decorously, not in order to be moved into another context, but to present the canon or rule, yes, but also to become by motion aware and to demonstrate by letting go because it cannot be SHOWN in any other way.

Here we are at the crux of shifts, at the shift epistemology of gap knowledge, here we are becoming aware by motion of two glories of the human condition – and not just these two – that are by definition in motion, gifts and performances. Two acts vital to our moment in time – and not just these two – interventions pedagogical and aesthetic depend on being able to show while letting go of the value of what you have used to make something come to light. It's so lovely, I think, that allegory, that analogy, that metaphor I just employed in the process of showing to become by motion aware – but if I get distracted by its fineness, begin to think, oh let's just hold onto that until everyone has appreciated its beauty and the craft of its making, nay its maker, I forget and grab onto it, I stop and I hoard, I no longer show, I tell; it gets a category and a name, shift studies, spectator studies... So this motion and the show that depends upon the offering and fading away of what has made it possible to show is for me the essence of the epistemology of shifts.

Shift: A Performance of Appositive Strategy
On the grammatical gap – the appositive:

First, it's not so easy. I march over to the bookcase, certain of my purpose and confident of help, and remove the Dictionary. No appositive... apposite... apposition as in "placing of a word in syntactic parallelism of another, especially an addition of a noun."

PAUSE

Distracted by the rich strangeness of syntactic (arranging together) parallelism (keeping equidistantly apart). I do this too, but not with nouns usually adjectives, one following the other in order to deepen or pervert or extend

---

[1] Giorgio Agamben, *The Signature of All Things: On Method*, Zone Books, New York, 2009, p. 18

the meaning, accumulate them in a style that has always marked me as more oral than scripty, texty, papery, writery.

PAUSE

Return. So one way to consider the strategy of the appositive is to consider its architectural structure. You know it by its boundary markers, two commas holding back, in their modest way, the logical force of the noun marching towards its verb undeterred until patiently paused by that small curve, that powerful piedi or foot that holds the door of the sentence ajar a little bit longer.

My partner, Mr. Word Corrector as he is known in the household, an appellation borrowed from Sancho Panza who uses it for his Don Quixotic as I use it for mine. Mr. Word Corrector HAS found a definition for appositive in Webster's Seventh New Collegiate Dictionary which reads: "of, relating to or standing in grammatical apposition." But this unsatisfying simplicity issues from a mistake of parts, appositive as adjective, not the noun.

PAUSE

Distraction: 2nd definition of the noun apposition: "an act or instance of apposing specifically the deposition (lay down, place, let fall) of successive layers upon those already present (as in prison cell walls)." The prisonhouse of language indeed.

Appose, striking one.

"to place in juxtaposition or proximity" – (Hum then sing) Oh no, it's just the nearness of you.

The Dictionary delivers its wares: a huge block of bricks wrapped in plastic (nouns), tubs of mortar (verbs), boards for roughing out (prepositions), finishing material (adjectives). Crawling about I see a little note after the definition of appose that says "more at pose" – hmm I think, a secret cache of construction materials I can raid from the building site under cover of darkness.

More at pose.

And then I find the first definition of pose is to rest, to pause.

PAUSE

To think of construction materials is to clarify my earlier claim for the centrality of the curvaceous comma – she, and I confess essentialism here, like the Pantheon overturning the straight-edged status quo, she the comma is in service to the demi-godess of sentence ecstasies.

But Mr. Word Corrector interrupts the certainty of my grammatical gaze to say, M Dashes, no?

PAUSE

Damn. M Dashes yes. Well it's an interesting combination, an androgynous joining of the appositive that waits to intervene in the temporal process of the sentence and those little border guards, flinging themselves into position like a barrier or perhaps more accurately cordoning off the interruption – you can skip this bit if you want to say m dashes, just read around us, no fraternizing between the interrupters and the interrupted. Between the siren song of pausing or augmenting its natural amplification. GIRLS KEEP OUT.

I always feel m dashes signal an apologetic stance – I had to say it this way but I'd best dress it in an outfit that makes it clear it could be beside the point.

PAUSE

Beside the point, which is to say in proximity… so I return to the preferred companion, the comma, she who slides the eye toward the pause in the temporal march of the sentence. Come this way, the interruption is worth the detour, you can continue on your way after this curve, you can follow the road. I promise there is another comma waiting to guide you.

PAUSE

But this is too casual, the invitation implied a meandering when in fact the pursuit of this … pursuit argues in its curving and sliding way, that the pause creates the space for the intuition to develop the idea. Something like this:

Here I begin to posit an idea, the sentence develops COMMA Can you reader or you listener, for whom the comma is a pause and an aural shifting in my voice, please add this bit of thinking or can I remind you of a cautionary consideration, or you really need this piece of information to continue but it needs to be set in proximity not laid out tongue in groove COMMA We sweep on but we do so changed, changed by the temporal and spatial demands of augmentation, of taking care to think all the way through the complexities of what we are making, taking care to acknowledge what we might be excluding and why.

PAUSE

When I teach I hear myself asking "does that make sense?" a pedagogic tic, but I think what I mean to say is "Did your senses make that?". In the air between us while I was turning an idea this way and that, did your senses, your intuition finish the work mine had begun? Some writers and theorists make my heart beat faster, they make me run ahead of them in excitement, sensing something coming round the next bend and yet knowing that the bend itself makes what's coming revelatory – skip the bend, skip the revelation.

PAUSE

Fred Moten, he who makes my heart go pitter patter, my mind go whoop de do, suggested recently that time and the manipulation of it is at the heart of power today. He suggested what we need are "temporal insurgencies" to take our time, to take time back.

PAUSE POLITICALLY

A comma is an invitation to the insurgent or perhaps a coercive component of combat. Think how interruption undoes the capitalist logic:
I want my MTV.
I want, but not before peace in our time, my MTV.
Or another more painfully recent instance. The speech on the Emergency Budget made at the dawn of the new Conservative Lib Dem Government in the UK:[2]
This emergency Budget deals decisively with our country's record debts.
This emergency Budget deals decisively, if you are willing to concede that murky threats of percentages to be cut from public services is a form of decisiveness, with our country's record debts.
It pays for the past.
It pays, by disenfranchising the present generation whose stake is only in the future, for the past.
And it plans for the future.
And it, with an eye on the oracle of the Great Soothsayer FTSE, plans for the future.
It supports a strong enterprise-led recovery.
It supports, because it hopes it will not have to do anything but wait for business and the banks to regroup, a strong enterprise-led recovery.
And it protects the most vulnerable in our society. Yes it is tough; but it is also fair.

PAUSE

Let me be plain, I don't suggest political action is enhanced by snide asides. To augment is to take the sentence seriously. These appositive corrections

---

[2] See http://www.theguardian.com/uk/2010/jun/22/emergency-budget-full-speech-text [accessed 8 May 2014].

to Osbourne's "just the facts mam" delivery have to do with a pause, in this pause we must act, the responsibility is ours to balance the complex with the supposedly simple – temporal insurgency – slowing George down. But the appositive is a different tempo than the dismissal, the voice has a different tone to that of the easy commentary with no call to change or improve, those BBC/ITV/SKYMurdoch commas that signal: now watch how much smarter I am than him. Those are not siren songs of promise, but the very debilitating narcissism Richard Sennet diagnosed in our public life years ago in the *The Fall of Public Man*.

PAUSE

My commitment to appostiveness has caused me trouble in scholarly circles, in scholarly writing. An editor from Routledge reads the text of what was a successful workshop/seminar on sound, Shakespeare and durational performance and writes of how she was itching to edit those complex sentences. When did complex become an insult?

PAUSE

The convention of scholarly writing builds its house on evidence, on clarity, on analysis. Analysis, a breaking down, a dividing in order to conquer, a skill praised for its rigour. Sprung from the head of all those Dads – Freud, Adorno, Kant – I learned to equate the fully dissected with the convincing, a convincing argument because it left its object of scrutiny immobile, quasi morto as the Italians would say, still, mapped out, finished.

PAUSE

I go back to the dictionary – there again among the construction materials scattered about the site I see a gem: convince, "to FIRMLY persuade." Ah hah! I knew it, the relations between argument and analysis, the academic love of the firm or that particularly British form of praise rigour with a U as in U are firmly persuading me and this exchange has nothing of the erotic in it – we are all rationalists here, our sentences go in a straight line from beginning to climax, procreating but never promiscuously.

PAUSE

Angela Carter wields a mean comma, but the appositive was loved by Henry James. Training is sexist but inclination can free us up to wield both, the pleasure of a short sharp shock amidst the temporal insurgencies of the determinedly complex.

PAUSE

To draw out a vision of urgent and methodically meandering scholarly discourse is to stress the "inter" of interdisciplinary, to take this day on writing and architecture at its word. But the editor she of the itching fingers to undo complexity reminds me that not only our words cast across a page need training as insurgents, but our ears, our eyes when we read, our bodies when we take in, as readers/receivers we must attend complex sentence boot camp.

PAUSE

Imagine yourself reading. The sentence begins… your follow, you begin to take in the meaning, your are freed with a comma. Now here's the tricky part, it's not simply heavy lifting, but a kind of balancing, a talent for shifting, to keep what has come before in mind, shift your attention to take in this curve of thought, pivot to see how already what you have been holding now combines and changes with what has been added, then go on with both, let something go, let a third or fourth component sliding out of your memory adjust or calibrate the meaning.

PAUSE

Okay so it's like dancing. All good and complex things are. Remember that phrase, dancing is like sex standing up? Mind dancing, it's just like thinking standing up.

> STAND UP
> CLOSE YOUR EYES
> MAKE AN APPOSTIVE MOVE
> NOW GET STRAIGHT TO THE POINT
> GOOD.

SHIFT: CODA, GAP DANCING

I have always been attracted to epistemological practice of longing; just hearing the word produces the sensation. Susan Stewart long ago pulled me willingly along the longing gap, a gap I choose to experience as productive rather than debilitating. And thought works like this too according to Foucault and Agamben, albeit a thinking perhaps more early modern than post: "Yet semiology and hermeneutics do not perfectly coincide by means of resemblance; between them there remains a gap, where knowledge is produced."[3] Having written this Agamben quotes Foucault:

---

3   Giorgio Agamben, *The Signature of All Things*, p. 59.

"...because the similitudes that form the graphics of the world were one 'cog' out of alignment with those that form its discourse, knowledge and the infinite labour it involves find here the space that is proper to them: it is their task to weave their way across this distance, pursuing an endless zigzag course from resemblance to what resembles it".[4]

So let me end with an Ode on the term Fred Moten uses to shift, Oscillate. Here are the synonyms for the word from Roget's Thesaurus 1879 new and revised edition:

1st set at Change: Fluctuate, vary, waver, flounder, flicker, flitter, flit, flutter, shift, shuffle, shake, totter, tremble, vacillate, wamble, turn and turn about, ring the changes, sway, shift, shift to and fro, change and change about, vibrate, oscillate between two extremes, alternate, have as many phases as the moon.

2nd set at Motion: Libate, alternate, undulate, wave, rock, swing, pulsate, beat, wag, waggle, nod, bob, courtesy, curtsy, tick, play wamble, wabble, dangle, swag, fluctuate, dance, curvet, reel, quake, quiver, quaver, shake, flicker, wriggle, roll, toss, pitch, flounder, stagger, totter, move, bob up and down and etc., pass and repass, ebb and flow, come and go, vacillate, brandish, shake and flourish.

[4] Foucault quoted in Giorgio Agamben, *The Signature of All Things*, p. 59.

CONTRIBUTORS

RIC ALLSOPP is Head of Dance and Professor of Contemporary Performance at Falmouth University. He is a co-founder and joint editor of Performance Research, a quarterly international journal of contemporary performance (London & New York: Routledge, Taylor & Francis). He was an integral part of Dartington College of Arts and taught at the renowned SNDO in Amsterdam in the 1990s. He helped develop the Inter-University Centre for Dance (HZT) at the University of the Arts, Berlin and lectured in Choreography at ArtEZ, Netherlands.

CAROL BECKER is Professor of the Arts and Dean of Columbia University School of the Arts. She is a member of the World Economic Forum Global Agenda Council on The Role of Art in Society. She has authored numerous articles and several books including: *The Invisible Drama: Women and the Anxiety of Change* (with many foreign editions); *Zones of Contention: Essays on Art, Institutions, Gender, and Anxiety*; *Surpassing the Spectacle: Global Transformations and the Changing Politics of Art*, *The Subversive Imagination: Artists, Society, and Social Responsibility*, and the most recently *Thinking in Place: Art, Action, and Cultural Production*.

MARIN BLAŽEVIĆ is Associate Professor of Dramaturgy, Theatre and Performance studies at the Academy of Drama Arts, and Opera Dramaturgy at the Music Academy, University of Zagreb. With Matthew Goulish he co-edited a double English issues of Performing Arts Journal Frakcija (Fraction): *Reflections on the Process / Performance: A Reading Companion to Goat Island's 'When will the September roses bloom?'* (2004/2005). With Lada Čale Feldman he co-edited *Actor as/and Author* thematic issue for *Frakcija* (2001), and *MIS-performance* for Performance Research (including DVD *On PSi#15 Shifts*, co-edited with Una Bauer). Marin's most recent edited book was a collection of essays on Slovenian performance-theatre company Via Negativa titled *No*. Authored books: *Razgovori o novom kazalištu* (*Conversations on the New Theatre*, 2007) and *Izboren poraz* (*A Defeat Won*, 2012), on the theory of new theatre and its peculiar history in Croatia. Marin was conference director of PSi#15 in Zagreb on the theme *MISperformance* (2009). He is curator and director of dramaturgy for PSi's dispersed international conference project in 2015: *Fluid States: Performances of unKnowing*.

MAAIKE BLEEKER is Professor and Chair of Theatre Studies at Utrecht University. She studied Art History, Theatre Studies, and Philosophy at the University of Amsterdam, and obtained her PhD from the Amsterdam School for Cultural Analysis in 2002. She has worked as a dramaturge for various theater directors, choreographers, and visual artists, ran her own theater company (Het Oranjehotel), and was an Artist in Residence at the Amsterdam School for the Arts (2006–2007). She published in international journals such as Theatre Research International, Performance Research, Maska, Women & Performance and Arcadia, as well as in numerous edited volumes. She edited several books including *Anatomy Live: Performance and the Operating Theatre* (Amsterdam University Press 2008). Her book *Visuality in the Theatre: The Locus of Looking* was published by Palgrave. Bleeker is president of Performance Studies international.

MORANA ČALE is Professor at the Department of Italian Studies at the University of Zagreb, where she teaches courses on Dante, the Italian Renaissance literature and the Italian 20th century theater. She has published six books of comparative studies in Croatia and various papers on Italian (Dante, Petrarch, Croce, Manganelli, Eco, Pirandello, D'Annunzio, Morante, Saba, Tommaseo) and Croatian authors (Marinković, Krleža, Begović, Vojnović), as well as on literary theory and criticism, in Croatia, Italy, Poland, Czech Republic, Hungary, Germany, Austria, Great Britain, France and Slovenia. She co-edited three volumes of proceedings of international conferences. She has also translated several books from Italian and French (Manganelli, Eco, Pirandello, Verne, Saba, Guicciardini, Goldoni, Buzzati, Ammaniti, Compagnon, Calvino, Barthes). In 1993 she was granted the annual award for foreign Italianists by Zagreb Italian Institute of Culture.

LADA ČALE FELDMAN is Professor at the Department for Comparative Literature on the Faculty of Humanities and Social Sciences, University in Zagreb, where she teaches drama, theatre and performance studies. Her publications include *Brešanov teatar* (Ivo Brešan's theatre, 1989), *Teatar u teatru u hrvatskom teatru* (Play-within-the-Play in the Croatian Theatre, 1997), *Euridikini osvrti* (Eurydice's turns, 2001, "Petar Brečić" Award, 2005), *Femina ludens* (2001), *U kanonu* (In the canon, with M. Čale, 2008), *U san nije vjerovati* (Dreams are not to be trusted (2012) and *Uvod u feminističku književnu kritiku* (Introduction to feminist literary criticism, with A. Tomljenović, 2012). She also co-edited *Fear, Death and Resistance, an Ethnography of War* (with I. Prica and R. Senjkovic, 1993) and *Etnografija domaćeg socijalizma* (An ethnography of indigenous socialism, with I. Prica, 2006).

ARSELI DOKUMACI completed her PhD in performance studies at Aberystwyth University and is currently an FQRSC-funded (Fonds Québécois de Recherche sur la Société et la Culture) postdoctoral fellow at McGill University, Social Studies of Medicine Department. She is also working as a research associate at Concordia University's Mobile Media Lab for the Canadian Consortium on Performance and Politics in the Americas (CCPPA). In her doctoral project, supervised by Professor Mike Pearson, Arseli explored experiences of invisible disabilities, in particular pain and mobility-related impairments, through the creation of a two-hour ethnographic documentary on everyday life task performances. Materials from this research have appeared in *Disability in Judaism, Christianity and Islam* (2011) and Performance Research (2013). In her current postdoctoral project, Arseli is investigating the uses of performance as a concept and a measurement tool in biomedicine and contemporary health care. At the same time, she is working with Professor Kim Sawchuk on a CCPPA-funded project for building an archive on performance and disability in the Americas. Arseli is the current chair of Emerging Scholars Committee at Performance Studies international.

BRANISLAV JAKOVLJEVIĆ is an Associate Professor at the Department of Theater and Performance Studies, Stanford University. He specializes in avant-garde and experimental theater, performance theory, critical theory, and performance and politics. His works have been published in the United States (Theatre Journal, TDR, PAJ, Art Journal, Theater) and in Europe (Serbia, United Kingdom, Spain, Sweden, Croatia, Poland, and Belgium). His book *Daniil Kharms: Writing and the Event* was published by Northwestern University Press in 2009. He recently completed his second book manuscript, *Beyond the Performance Principle: Self-Management and a Political Economy of the Live, Yugoslavia 1945-1991*. In 2013 he chaired the 19th annual Performance Studies international conference "Now Then: Performance and Temporality" at Stanford University.

JOE KELLEHER is Professor of Theatre and Performance and Head of Department for Drama, Theatre and Performance at Roehampton University London. He is co-author with Claudia and Romeo Castellucci, Chiara Giudi, and Nicholas Ridout of *The Theatre of Societas Raffaello Sanzio* (Routledge 2007), co-editor with Ridout of *Theatres in Contemporary Europe* (Routledge 2006), and author of *Theatre & Politics* (Palgrave Macmillan 2009). His articles have appeared in journals such as Performance Research, Maska, Frakcija, and Theater. His essays have been published in various edited collections including, most recently, International Politics and Performance, ed. Jenny Edkins and Adrian Kear (Routledge 2014), and *Intimacy Across Visceral and Digital Performance*, ed. Maria Chatzichristodoulou and Rachel Zerihan (Palgrave Macmillan 2012). He is currently completing a book titled The Illuminated Theatre: Studies on the Suffering of Images for Routledge (2015).

JON MCKENZIE is Professor of English at the University of Wisconsin-Madison, where he teaches courses in performance theory and new media. He is also Director of DesignLab, a digital composition center whose mission is to democratize digitality. An affiliate of the Digital Studies program, he likewise coordinates the Digital Humanities Initiative, a network of faculty, librarians, and technologists dedicated to enhancing the cyber infrastructure of artists and humanists. Jon is the author of *Perform or Else: From Discipline to Performance* (Routledge 2001) and such articles as "Global Feeling: (Almost) All You Need is Love," "Abu Ghraib and the Society of the Spectacle of the Scaffold," and "Towards a Sociopoetics of Interface Design: etoy, Etoys, and TOYWAR." His work has been translated into a half-dozen languages, and with Heike Roms and C.J. W-L. Lee, he is co-editor of *Contesting Performance: Global Sites of Research* (Palgrave 2011). Jon has produced a number of experimental video essays, including *The Revelations of Dr. Kx4l3ndj3r* (2012) and *This Vile Display* (2006), and he gives workshops on performative scholarship and emerging scholarly genres. In fall 2013, HOBO Art Foundation and New Theatre in Warsaw co-produced *Katastronauci*, based on *Perform or Else*. Jon's homepage is labster8.net.

SOPHIE NIELD teaches theatre and film at Royal Holloway College, University of London. She has published widely on questions of space, representation and theatricality in political life and the law, and on the performance of borders of various kinds: the international border, the experience of the border-crosser, and the problem of the corpse in representation. Her current project focuses on the theatricality of spectacular politics and spaces of resistance.

ANNALISA SACCHI is post-doctoral scholar and Visiting Lecturer in Contemporary Theatre in Europe at Harvard University, where she already held the Lauro De Bosis Lectureship in the History of Italian Civilization in 2012/13. Her doctoral research, conducted in Italy and France (Università di Bologna and Université Paris III) analysed the modes of production of director's theatre in modernism and the contemporary period. In particular, she worked with the Italian Theatre Group Socìetas Raffaello Sanzio. She has published several articles on this subject, three books (*Itinera, trajectoires de la forme Tragedia Edogonidia*, with Enrico Pitozzi, ActesSud, Arles, 2008; *Il posto del re. Estetiche del teatro di regia nel Modernismo e nel contemporaneo*, Bulzoni, Roma, 2012; and *Gli Shakespeare della Socìetas Raffaello Sanzio*, forthcoming in 2014, ETS, Pisa) and a special double issue (edited with Aleksandra Jovićević) of the journal *Biblioteca Teatrale*. She was the editor of independent magazine *Art'O_cultura e politica delle arti sceniche* (2005-2012) and has been the cultural correspondent from NYC of the communist newspaper *Il manifesto*. As an independent curator she has worked for international theatre festivals (Santarcangelo dei teatri, Biennale di Venezia, Under the Radar Festival among the others). In 2013 her Italian translation of Freddie Rokem's *Philosophers and Thespians. Thinking performance* was published by Mimesis.

NICOLAS SALAZAR SUTIL works as a Lecturer in Dance and Digital Arts at the University of Surrey. He is a performance theorist and practitioner, whose work focuses on interdisciplinary research combining symbolic languages (computer code, mathematics) and movement studies. Salazar Sutil holds a PhD in cultural studies from Goldsmiths College, having completed a thesis on mathematical thinking in avant-garde theatre and performance in 2010. He trained as an actor in the Malgrem-Laban system of character analysis at the Drama Centre London, and at the Universidad de Chile. He has worked as a visiting lecturer and director at Brunel University and at the University of Essex (East 15), and he has been a researcher fellow in various projects related to sci-art collaboration and technology development at the London School of Economics, Goldsmiths College, and University of Surrey. He is the artistic director of C8 Project, a dance-theatre company that works on mathematical models in digital performance. He is also the cofounder of an electronic research collaborative called MoVe (Movement Visualisation in e-cultures), with Professor Rachel Fensham.

EDWARD SCHEER is Professor at the School of the Arts and Media UNSW, Australia and is the author of *Scenario*, a study of new work from the iCinema Project (UNSW Press and ZKM, 2011) and *Multimedia Performance* (Palgrave 2012) with Rosie Klich. Scheer's study of Mike Parr's performance art, *The Infinity Machine* (Schwartz City Press, 2010) investigates the role of duration in performance art. Scheer was President of Performance Studies international from 2007-2011. He is joint chief investigator on the ARC funded projects, *Towards an Experimental Humanities* and *New media Dramaturgy*.

P.A. SKANTZE is a director, writer and spectator of theatre and performance based in London and Italy. She works internationally with her performance company Four Second Decay. Her performance projects include *All that Fell* an experiment in physical radio, *Audible Montage or Eurydice's Footsteps*, and *Stacks*. Author of *Stillness in Motion in the Seventeenth-Century Theatre* (Routledge 2003) and *Itinerant Spectator/Itinerant Spectacle* (Punctum 2013) Skantze also writes on sound and the sonic arts, practice as research as a method of considering 17th-century theatre, questions of reception and representation of race and of gender. P.A. Skantze is currently Reader in Performance Practices in the Department of Drama, Theatre and Performance at Roehampton University.

SPATULA & BARCODE is the collaborative artmaking group founded by Laurie Beth Clark and Michael Peterson, who both teach at the University of Wisconsin. Spatula&Barcode makes social art projects with a focus on community, hospitality, discussion, food, and souvenirs. Since 2009, they have created more than twenty projects from intimate to large scale in Brasil, Canada, Croatia, Germany, Morocco, the Netherlands, the United States, and Uruguay. More information about Spatula&Barcode can be found at spatulaandbarcode.net.

ANA VUJANOVIĆ (Berlin/Hamburg – Belgrade) is a freelance cultural worker – researcher, writer, lecturer, dramaturge, curator – in the fields of contemporary performing arts and culture. Holds Ph.D. in Theatre Studies from the Faculty of Dramatic Arts, Belgrade. She is a cofounder and a member of the editorial collective of TkH (Walking Theory), the Belgrade-based theoretical-artistic platform, and chief editor of *TkH journal for performing arts theory*. Her particular commitment has been to empower the independent scenes in Belgrade and former Yugoslavia (Druga scena, Clubture regija, and others). She has lectured and given workshops at various universities and independent educational programs throughout Europe. She engages in artworks in the fields of performance, theatre, dance, and video/film, as dramaturge, co-author, performer and artistic collaborator. She publishes regularly in journals and collections (*TkH, Maska, Frakcija, Teatron, Performance Research, TDR* and others) and is the author of four books, most recently *Public Sphere by Performance* with Bojana Cvejić (Berlin: b_books, 2012). She is currently international visiting professor at the Dpt. for Human Movement/Performance Studies, University of Hamburg. In recent years her research interest has been focused on the intersections between performance and politics in neoliberal capitalist societies. http://www.anavujanovic.info/

Marin Blažević
and Lada Čale Feldman

**MISperformance:
essays in shifting perspectives**

PUBLISHED BY
Maska, Institute for Publishing,
Production and Education,
Metelkova 6, 1000 Ljubljana,
Slovenia
www.maska.si

IN PARTNERSHIP WITH
Performance Studies international
www.psi-web.org

Drugo more (The Other Sea),
Korzo 28, 51000 Rijeka, Croatia
www.drugo-more.hr

Doctoral program in literature,
performing arts, film and culture
- Faculty of Humanities and Social
Sciences, University of Zagreb,
Filozofski fakultet, Ivana Lučića 3,
10000 Zagreb

Introduction, selection and
editorial matter © Marin Blažević
and Lada Čale Feldman 2014

Individual chapters
© contributors 2014

FOR THE PUBLISHER:
Janez Janša

DESIGN AND LAYOUT:
Ajdin Bašić

PROOFREADING:
Una Bauer

PRINTED AND DISTRIBUTED
by Lulu.com

www.lulu.com

..maska   PSi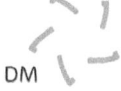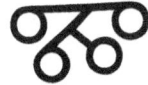

BOOKS BY MASKA

TRANSformacije Series

PRISOTNOST, PREDSTAVLJANJE, TEATRALNOST, zbornik

Blaž Lukan
DRAMATURŠKE FIGURE

Bojana Kunst
NEMOGOČE TELO

TELO, UJETO V DROBOVJE RAČUNALNIKA, zbornik

ZADNJA FUTURISTIČNA PREDSTAVA, zbornik

TEORIJE SODOBNEGA PLESA, zbornik

Jana Pavlič, Boris Pintar
KASTRACIJSKI STROJI

STELARC, zbornik

Amelia Jones
BODY ART. UPRIZARJANJE SUBJEKTA

ZERO VISIBILITY, zbornik

Alexei Monroe
PLURALNI MONOLIT. LAIBACH IN NSK

Hans-Thies Lehmann
POSTDRAMSKO GLEDALIŠČE

THE FUTURE OF COMPUTER ARTS, zbornik

Tomaž Toporišič
MED ZAPELJEVANJEM IN SUMNIČAVOSTJO

Bojana Kunst
NEVARNE POVEZAVE

Katrien Jacobs
LIBI_DOC: JOURNEYS IN THE PERFORMANCE OF SEX ART

Katrien Jacobs
LIBI_DOC. SLOVENIJA: MISTIFICIRAJ TELO, POVZDIGNI DUHA

READY 2 CHANGE, zbornik

DEMOKINO - VIRTUAL BIOPOLITICAL AGORA, zbornik

SODOBNE SCENSKE UMETNOSTI, zbornik

Inke Arns
AVANTGARDA V VZVRATNEM OGLEDALU

Nicolas Bourriaud
RELACIJSKA ESTETIKA. POSTPRODUKCIJA

Jacques Attali
HRUP

Beti Žerovc
KURATOR IN SODOBNA UMETNOST: POGOVORI

Aldo Milohnić
TEORIJE SODOBNEGA GLEDALIŠČA IN PERFORMANSA

PRIŠLI SO PUPILČKI, zbornik

Jacques Rancière
EMANCIPIRANI GLEDALEC

Zdenka Badovinac
AVTENTIČNI INTERES

NE, VIA NEGATIVA 2002-2008, zbornik

Gerald Raunig
UMETNOST IN REVOLUCIJA

Jonathan Burrows
KOREOGRAFOV PRIROČNIK

SVOBODNE ROKE. ANTOLOGIJA TEORETSKE MISLI O SLOVENSKEM GLEDALIŠČU (1899-1979)

HIBRIDNI PROSTORI UMETNOSTI, zbornik

Bojana Kunst
UMETNIK NA DELU

Claire Bishop
UMETNI PEKLI

Mediakcije Series

Serge Halimi
NOVI PSI ČUVAJI

Naomi Klein
NO LOGO

Sandra Bašić Hrvatin, Lenart J. Kučić
MONOPOLI. DRUŽABNA IGRA TRGOVANJA Z MEDIJI

Olivier Razac
EKRAN IN ŽIVALSKI VRT

Ariel Dorfman, Armand Mattelart
KAKO BRATI JAKA RACMANA. IMPERIALISTIČNA IDEOLOGIJA V DISNEYJEVIH STRIPIH

McKenzie Wark
HEKERSKI MANIFEST

Mike Davis
BUDOV VOZ. KRATKA ZGODOVINA AVTOMOBILA BOMBE

Uroš Hočevar
ESTETIKA REPORTAŽNE FOTOGRAFIJE

Marc Augé
NEKRAJI

Alexander R. Galloway
TEORIJA VIDEO IGER

Maurizio Lazzarato
PROIZVAJANJE ZADOLŽENEGA ČLOVEKA

Franco Berardi - Bifo
DUŠA NA DELU

Special editions

FAMA

POSTDRAMATIC FISHING

MEMORY_PRIVACY_SPECTATORSHIP

COLLECT-IF

ON FORM/YET TO COME

WATCH IT!

Janez Janša
LIFE [IN PROGRESS]

RECONSTRUCTION, VOICE, IDENTITY

V IMENU LJUDSTVA!

ZID OBJOKOVANJA / THE WAILING WALL

DINAMIKA SPREMEMB V SLOVENSKEM GLEDALIŠČU 20. STOLETJA, zbornik

NO ONE SHOULD HAVE SEEN THIS

PRAZNOVANJE MOŽNOSTI TRANSFORMACIJE

SVET KOZMONAVTOV, BALERIN IN SVEČENIC

Janez Janša
LIFE II [IN PROGRESS]

www.ingramcontent.com/pod-product-compliance
Lightning Source LLC
Chambersburg PA
CBHW020634220526
45464CB00001B/147